Laos

Claire Boobbyer

Credits

Footprint credits
Editor: Jo Williams
Production and layout: Emma Bryers
Maps: Kevin Feeney

Managing Director: Andy Riddle
Commercial Director: Patrick Dawson
Publisher: Alan Murphy
Publishing Managers: Felicity Laughton,
Jo Williams, Nicola Gibbs
Marketing and Partnerships Director:
Liz Harper
Marketing Executive: Liz Eyles
Trade Product Manager: Diane McEntee
Account Managers: Paul Bew, Tania Ross
Advertising: Renu Sibal, Elizabeth Taylor
Trade Product Co-ordinator: Kirsty Holmes

Photography credits
Front cover: Luang Prabang,
Masterlu/Dreamstime.com
Back cover: Kuang Si Falls, Ikunl/Shutterstock

Printed in Great Britain by CPI Antony Rowe,
Chippenham, Wiltshire

FSC
www.fsc.org
MIX
Paper from
responsible sources
FSC® C013604

Publishing information
Footprint *Focus Laos*
1st edition
© Footprint Handbooks Ltd
October 2012

ISBN: 978 1 908206 88 6
CIP DATA: A catalogue record for this book
is available from the British Library

® Footprint Handbooks and the Footprint
mark are a registered trademark of
Footprint Handbooks Ltd

Published by Footprint
6 Riverside Court
Lower Bristol Road
Bath BA2 3DZ, UK
T +44 (0)1225 469141
F +44 (0)1225 469461
footprinttravelguides.com

Distributed in the USA by Globe Pequot
Press, Guilford, Connecticut

The content of Footprint *Focus Laos* has
been taken directly from Footprint's
Southeast Asia Handbook which was
researched and written by Claire Boobbyer,
Andrew Spooner and Paul Dixon.

Contents

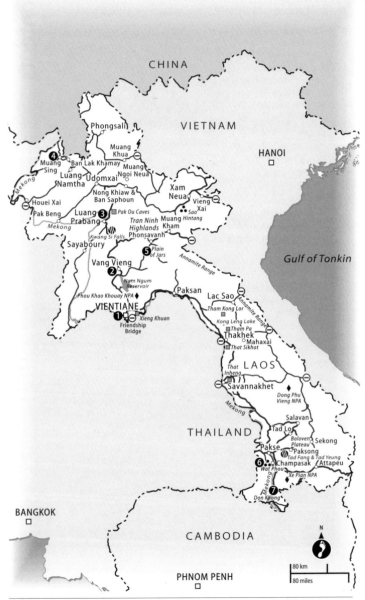

Laos is fast becoming the darling of Southeast Asia, satisfying all the romantic images of perfumed frangipani trees, saffron-robed monks, rusty old bicycles and golden temples, all set among a rich tapestry of tropical river islands, ethnic minority villages, cascading waterfalls and vivid green rice paddies, and bound together by the mighty Mekong River, the country's lifeline. The vernacular architecture, which other countries have swept away in a maelstrom of redevelopment, survives in Laos. Simple wooden village homes, colonial-era brick-and-stucco shophouses and gently mouldering monasteries mark Laos out as different. Traditional customs are also firmly intact: incense wafts out of streetside wats, monks collect alms at daybreak and the clickety-clack of looms weaving richly coloured silk can be heard in most villages.

As compelling as these sights and sounds are, the lasting impression for most visitors is of the people and their overwhelming friendliness. Many believe the best thing about Laos is the constant chime of *sabaidee* ringing out from school-children, monks and other passers by, extending an invitation to join their meal. This is a land that endures the terrible legacy of being the most bombed country per capita in the world, yet its people transform bomb casings into flower pots and bomb craters into fish ponds. Regardless of their history and their poverty, people here radiate a sunny, happy disposition.

Life is simple in Laos but the people share with their former French colonists an infectious joie de vivre that ensures that good food and great company are the pinnacle of enjoyment. If you're seeking a relaxed lifestyle and a warm welcome, you've come to the right place.

Planning your trip

Getting to Laos

Air
The easiest and cheapest way to access Laos is via Bangkok, to which most major airlines have direct flights from Europe, North America and Australasia. Laos is only accessible from within Asia.

Road, rail and river
Laos is a land-locked country and foreign visitors travelling overland between neighbouring countries are restricted to a handful of key crossing points. For much of its length, the Lao–Thai border is defined by the Mekong, with bridges and ferries to link the two countries. In 2009 a new railway line opened over the Mekong at the Friendship Bridge linking Nong Khai and Thanalang, just outside Vientiane. Though only a couple of miles long this signalled Laos' entry into the railway age and is the nation's first public train service. To the east, the Annamite mountain range forms a spine separating Laos from Vietnam, with a few cross-border buses running from Vientiane to Savannakhet. There is only one official border crossing between Laos and Cambodia in the south and between Laos and China in the north. Foreigners are not permitted to cross between Laos and Myanmar (Burma).

Transport in Laos

Air
Lao Airlines runs domestic flights from Vientiane to Phonsavannh (Xieng Khouang), Houei Xai, Oudomxai and Pakse. Foreigners must pay in US dollars for all Lao Airlines flights. There are three types of plane: French-built *ATR-72s*, and Chinese-built *Y-7s* and *Y-12s*. The latter two are a risk. The most reliable, comfortable and newest machines – the *ATR-72s* – operate on the most popular routes (Vientiane–Bangkok, Vientiane–Luang Prabang, Vientiane–Pakse). Within Laos there is also a smaller, newer carrier, **Lao Air** (www.lao-air.com), which run flights to Xam Neua and Phongsali.

Boat
It is possible to take riverboats up and down the Mekong and its main tributaries. Boats stop at Luang Prabang, Pak Beng, Houei Xai, around Don Deth, Don Khong, and other smaller towns and villages. Apart from the main route, Houei Xai to Luang Prabang, there are often no scheduled services and departures may be limited during the dry season. Take food and drink and expect somewhat crowded conditions aboard. The most common riverboats are the *hua houa leim*, with no decks, the hold being enclosed by side panels and a flat roof (note that metal boats get very hot). Speedboats also chart some routes, but are very dangerous and never enjoyable. Prices vary according to size of boat and length of journey.

Road
The roads are not good, but they are improving. Many have been repaired or upgraded in recent years, making journeys faster and infinitely more comfortable. Quite a few bus, truck,

Don't miss...

tuk-tuk, songthaew and taxi drivers understand basic English, French or Thai, although some (especially tuk-tuk drivers) aren't above forgetting the lowest price you thought you'd successfully negotiated before hopping aboard – it is best to take this sort of thing in good humour. Even so, in order to travel to a particular destination, it is a great advantage to have the name written out in Lao. Many people will not know road names, but they will know where all the sights of interest are – wats, markets, monuments, waterfalls, etc.

Bus/truck It is now possible to travel to most areas of the country by bus, truck or songthaew (converted pickup truck) in the dry season, although road travel in the rainy season can be tricky if not impossible. VIP buses are very comfortable night buses, usually allowing a good sleep – but watch out for the karaoke. In the south of Laos a night bus plies the route from Pakse to Vientiane; book a double bed if you don't want to end up sleeping next to a stranger. Robberies have been reported on night buses so keep your valuables secure.

On certain long routes, such as Vientiane/Luang Prabang to Xam Neua, big Langjian (Chinese) trucks are sometimes used. These trucks have been colourfully converted into buses with divided wooden seats and glassless windows. In more remote places (Xam Neua to Vieng Xai, for instance), ancient jeeps are common.

In the south of the country, Japanese-donated buses are used although you may see the occasional shiny Volvo bus. Breakdowns, though not frequent, aren't uncommon. For some connections you may need to wait a day. During the rainy season (June to December) expect journey times to be longer than those quoted; some roads may be closed altogether.

Car hire This costs anything from US$40-100 per day, depending on the vehicle, with first 150 km free, then US$10 every 100 km thereafter. The price includes a driver. For insurance purposes you will probably need an international driver's permit. Insurance is generally included with car hire but it's best to check the fine print. A general rule of thumb: if you are involved in a car crash, you, the foreigner, will be liable for costs as you have more money.

Motorbike and bicycle hire There are an increasing number of motorcycles available from guesthouses and other shops in major towns. 110cc bikes go for around US$4-10 a day, while 250cc Hondas are around US$20 per day. Bicycles are available in many towns and are a cheap way to see the sights. Many guesthouses rent bikes for US$1-2 per day.

Tuk-tuk The majority of motorized three-wheelers known as 'jumbos' or tuk-tuks are large motorbike taxis with two bench seats in the back. You'll find them in most cities and

Price codes

Where to stay

$$$$	over US$100	**$$$**	US$46-100
$$	US$21-45	**$**	US$20 and under

Price codes refer to the cost of a standard double/twin room in high season.

Restaurants

$$$	over US$12	**$$**	US$6-12	**$** under US$6

Price codes refer to the cost of a two-course meal, not including drinks.

metropolitan areas; expect to pay around 10,000-15,000 kip for a short ride. They can also be hired by the hour or the day to reach destinations out of town.

In city centres make sure you have the correct money for your tuk-tuk as they are often conveniently short of change. Also opt to flag down a moving tuk-tuk rather than selecting one of the more expensive ones that shark around tourist destinations.

Where to stay in Laos

Rooms in Laos are rarely luxurious and standards vary enormously. You can end up paying double what you would pay in Bangkok for similar facilities and service. However, the hotel industry is expanding rapidly. There is a reasonable choice of hotels of different standards and prices in Vientiane, Luang Prabang and Pakse and an expanding number of budget options in many towns on the fast-developing tourist trail. First-class hotels exist in Vientiane and Luang Prabang. The majority of guesthouses and hotels have fans and attached bathrooms, although more and more are providing air conditioning where there is a stable electricity supply, while others are installing their own generators to cater for the needs of the growing tourist trade. Smaller provincial towns, having previously had only a handful of hotels and guesthouses – some of them quaint French colonial villas – are now home to a growing number of rival concerns as tourism takes off. In rural villages, people's homes are enthusiastically transformed into bed and breakfasts on demand. While Vientiane may still have little budget accommodation, many towns in the north, such as Vang Vieng, Muang Ngoi, Muang Sing and Luang Namtha, have a large choice of very cheap, and in some cases very good accommodation, including dorm beds. In the southern provinces, upmarket and boutique accommodation has popped up in Pakse and Don Khong. There are several excellent ecolodges in the country, most notably the Boat Landing at Luang Namtha and the Kingfisher Ecolodge at Ban Kiet Ngong in the south. Many tour companies offer homestays in ethnic minority villages and camping as part of a package tour.

Food and drink in Laos

Lao food is similar to that of Thailand, although the Chinese influence is slightly less noticeable. Lao dishes are distinguished by the use of aromatic herbs and spices such as lemongrass, chillies, ginger and tamarind. The best place to try Lao food is often from roadside stalls or in the markets. The staple Lao foods are *kao niao* (glutinous rice), which is eaten with your hands, and fermented fish or *pa dek* (distinguishable by its distinctive smell), often laced with liberal spoons of *nam pa*, fish sauce. Being a landlocked country, most of the fish is fresh from the Mekong. One of the delicacies that shouldn't be missed is *Mok Pa* steamed fish in banana leaf. Most of the dishes are variations on two themes: fish and bird. *Laap*, also meaning 'luck' in Lao, is a traditional ceremonial dish made from (traditionally) raw fish or meat crushed into a paste, marinated in lemon juice and mixed with chopped mint. It is called *laap sin* if it has a meat base and *laap paa* if it's fish based. Beware of *laap* in cheap street restaurants. It is sometimes concocted from raw offal and served cold and should be consumed with great caution. Overall though *laap* is cooked well for the falang palate.

Restaurant food is, on the whole, hygienically prepared, and as long as street stall snacks have been well cooked, they are usually fine and a good place to sample local specialities. Really classy restaurants are only found in Vientiane and Luang Prabang. Good French cuisine is available in both cities. A better bet in terms of value for money are the Lao restaurants.

Far more prevalent are lower-end Lao restaurants, which can be found in every town. Right at the bottom end – in terms of price if not necessarily in terms of quality – are stalls that charge a US$1-2 for filled baguettes or simple single-dish meals.

Soft drinks are expensive as they are imported from Thailand. Bottled water is widely available and produced locally, so it is cheap (about 3000 kip for a litre). *Nam saa*, weak Chinese tea, is free. Imported beer can be found in hotels, restaurants and bars but is not particularly cheap. Beer Lao is a light lager (although the alcohol content is 5%). The local brew is rice wine (*lao-lao*) which is drunk from a clay jug with long straws.

Local customs and laws

Bargaining/haggling
While bargaining is common in Laos – in the market or in negotiating a trip on a *saamlor* or tuk-tuk, for example – it is not heavy-duty haggling. The Lao are extremely laid back and it is rare to be fleeced; don't bargain hard with them, it may force them to lose face and reduce prices well below their profit margin. For most things, you won't even really need to bargain. Approach bargaining with a sense of fun; a smile or joke always helps.

Clothing
It's polite to dress modestly: sleeveless shirts, short shorts or skirts are not ideal. When visiting wats, shoulders should be covered and shoes removed. One of the reasons for the tight controls on tourism in Laos is because of the perceived corrosive effects that badly dressed tourists were having on Lao culture. 'Scruffy' travellers are still frowned upon and officials are getting fed up with people wandering around skimpily clad, particularly in Vang Vieng and Siphandon. If bathing in public, particularly in rural areas, women should wear a sarong.

Conduct
Wats Monks are revered, don't touch their robes. If talking to a monk your head should be lower than his. Avoid visiting a wat around 1100 as this is when the monks have their morning meal. It is considerate to ask the abbot's permission to enter the *sim* and shoes should be removed before entry. When sitting down feet should point away from the altar and the main image. Arms and legs should be fully covered when visiting wats. A small donation is often appropriate (kneel when putting it into the box).

Greeting Lao people are addressed by their name, not their family name, even when a title is used. The *nop* or *wai* – with palms together below your chin and head bowed, as if in prayer – remains the traditional form of greeting. Shaking hands, though, is very widespread – more so than in neighbouring Thailand. This can be put down to the influence of the French during the colonial period (whereas Thailand was never colonized). '*Sabaidee*' (hello) is also a good way to greet. Avoid hugging and kissing to greet Lao people, as they tend to get embarrassed.

Eating etiquette In Laos, who eats when is important. At a meal, a guest should not begin eating until the host has invited him or her to do so. Nor should the guest continue eating after everyone else has finished. It is also customary for guests to leave a small amount of food on their plate; to do otherwise would imply that the guest was still hungry and that the host had not provided sufficient food for the meal. Sharing is a big thing at meal times, where plates of food are ordered and shared amongst everyone. Lao people often invite tourists to eat with them or share on buses, and it is a nice gesture if this is reciprocated (though Lao people tend to be shy so don't take any refusal as a rejection).

General Pointing with the index finger is considered rude. If you want to call someone over, gesture with your palm facing the ground and fingers waving towards you. In Lao your head is considered 'high' and feet are considered 'low'. So try to keep your feet low, don't point them at people or touch people with your feet. Don't pat children on the head (or touch people's heads in general), as it is considered the most sacred part of the body. If you visit a private home, remove your shoes. When seated on the floor, you should tuck your feet behind you.

Lao people have a passive nature. Yelling or boisterous people tend to freak them out and they go into panic mode. If a dispute arises, a smile and a few jokes will do the trick.

The Lao are proud people and begging is just not the done thing, so don't hand out money (or medicine) to local villagers. If you want to give a gift or a donation to someone, it is best to channel it through the village elder.

Festivals in Laos

The Lao celebrate New Year four times a year: international New Year in January, Chinese New Year in January/February, Lao New Year (Pi Mai) in April and Hmong New Year in December. The Lao Buddhist year follows the lunar calendar, so many festivals are movable.

Jan Boun Pha Vet (movable). To celebrate King Vessanthara's reincarnation as a Buddha. Sermons, processions, dance, theatre. Popular time for ordination.
1 Jan New Year's Day (public holiday). Celebrated by private *baci*.
6 Jan Pathet Lao Day (public holiday). Parades in main towns.
20 Jan Army Day (public holiday).
Jan/Feb Chinese New Year (movable). Many Chinese and Vietnamese businesses shut down for 3 days.

Feb Magha Puja (movable). Celebrates the end of Buddha's time in the monastery and the prediction of his death. Principally celebrated in Vientiane and at Wat Phou.
Apr Pi Mai (public holiday). The 1st month of the Lao New Year is Dec but festivities are delayed until Apr when days are longer than nights. By Apr it's also hotting up, so having hosepipes levelled at you and buckets of water dumped on you is more pleasurable. The festival also serves to invite the rains. Pi Mai is one of the most important annual

festivals, particularly in Luang Prabang (see page 59). There is usually a 3-day holiday. Similar festivals are celebrated in Thailand, Cambodia and Burma.

May Visakha Puja (movable). To celebrate the birth, enlightenment and death of Buddha, celebrated in local wats. **Boun Bang Fai** (movable). The 2-day rocket festival, is a Buddhist rain-making festival. Large bamboo rockets are built and decorated by monks and carried in procession before being blasted skywards. The higher a rocket goes, the bigger its builder's ego gets. Designers of failed rockets are thrown in the mud.

1 May Labour Day (public holiday). Parades in Vientiane.

Jun Khao Phansa (movable). The start of Buddhist Lent and a time of retreat and fasting for monks. The festival starts with the full moon in Jun/Jul and ends with the full moon in Oct. It all ends with the *Kathin* ceremony in Oct when monks receive gifts.

1 Jun Children's Day (public holiday).

Aug Ho Khao Padap Dinh (movable). Celebration of the dead.

13 Aug Lao Issara (public holiday). Free Lao Day.

23 Aug Liberation Day (public holiday).

Sep Boun Ok Phansa (movable). The end of Buddhist Lent when the faithful take offerings to the temple. It is in the '9th month' in Luang Prabang and the '11th month' in Vientiane, and marks the end of the rainy season. Boat races take place on the Mekong River with crews of 50 or more men and women. On the night before the race small decorated rafts are set afloat on the river.

12 Oct Freedom from the French Day (public holiday). Celebrated in Vientiane.

Nov Boun That Luang (movable). Celebrated in all Laos' *thats*, although most enthusiastically and colourfully in Vientiane, see page 37. As well as religious rituals, most celebrations include local fairs, processions, beauty pageants and other festivities.

Dec Hmong New Year (movable).

2 Dec Independence Day (public holiday). Military parades, dancing and music.

Shopping in Laos

Popular souvenirs from Laos include handicrafts and textiles, sold almost everywhere. The market is usually a good starting point, as are some of the minority villagers. The smaller, less touristy towns will sell silk at the cheapest price (at about 40,000 kip a length). The best place to buy naturally dyed silk in Laos is in Xam Neua. This high quality silk often makes its way to Luang Prabang and Vientiane but usually at much greater cost. Most markets offer a wide selection of patterns and embroidery though amongst the best places to go are **Talaat Sao** (Vientiane Morning Market) or, behind it, the cheaper **Talaat Kudin**, which has a textile section in the covered area. If you wish to have something made, most tailors can whip up a simple *sinh* (Lao sarong) in a day, but allow longer for adjustments or other items. **Ock Pop Tok** in Luang Prabang also has a fantastic reputation for producing top-shelf, naturally dyed silk. Vientiane and Luang Prabang offer the most sophisticated line in boutiques, where you can get all sorts of clothes from the utterly exquisite to the frankly bizarre. Those on a more frugal budget will find some tailors who can churn out a decent pair of trousers on Sisavangvong in Luang Prabang and around Nam Phou in Vientiane. If you get the right tailor, they can be much better than those found in Thailand both in terms of price and quality but you do need to allow time for multiple fittings. It is also a good idea to bring a pattern/picture of what you want.

    Silverware, most of it is in the form of jewellery and small pots (though they may not be made of silver), is traditional in Laos. The finest silversmiths work out of Vientiane and Luang Prabang. Chunky antique ethnic-minority jewellery, bangles, pendants, belts and earrings are often sold in markets in the main towns, or antique shops in Vientiane, particularly congregating around Nam Phou. Xam Neua market also offers a good range of ethnic minority-style silver jewellery. Look for traditional necklaces that consist of wide silver bands, held together by a spirit lock (a padlock to lock in your scores of souls). Gold jewellery is the preference of the Lao Loum (lowland Laos) and its bright yellow colour is associated with Buddhist luck (often it is further dyed to enhance its orange goldness), this is best bought in Vientiane. Craftsmen in Laos are still producing **wood carvings** for temples and coffins. Designs are usually traditional, with a religious theme.

Essentials A-Z

Accident and emergency
Ambulance T195, **Fire** T190, **Police** T191. Contact the relevant emergency service and your embassy. Obtain police/medical records in order to file insurance claims. If you need to report a crime visit your local police station, take a local who speaks English.

Customs and duty free
Duty-free allowance is 500 cigarettes, 2 bottles of wine and a bottle of liquor. Laos has a strictly enforced ban on the export of antiquities and all Buddha images.

Electricity
Voltage 220, 50 cycles in main towns. 110 volts in rural areas; 2-pin sockets. Blackouts are common outside Vientiane; many smaller towns are not connected to the national grid and only have power in the evening.

Internet
Internet cafés have been popping up all over Laos. The connections are surprisingly good in major centres. Fast, cheap internet is available in Vientiane, Luang Prabang, Vang Vieng and Savannakhet for around 100-200 kip per min. Less reliable and more expensive internet can be found in Phonsavanh, Don Khone, Don Deth, Luang Namtha, Thakhek, Savannakhet and Udomxai. Many internet cafés also offer international phone services.

Language
Lao is the national language but there are many local dialects, not to mention the ubiquitous languages of the minority groups. Lao is closely related to Thai and, in a sense, is becoming more so as the years pass. Though there are important differences between the languages, they are mutually intelligible – just about. French is spoken, though only by government officials, hotel staff and many educated people over 40. However, most government officials and many shopkeepers have some command of English. See also box, page 14.

Media
The *Vientiane Times*, is published 5 times a week and provides interesting cultural and tourist-based features, as well as quirky stories translated from the local press and wire service. Television is becoming increasingly popular as more towns and villages get electricity. The national TV station broadcasts in Lao. In Vientiane, **CNN**, **BBC**, **ABC** and a range of other channels are broadcast. Thailand's **Channel 5** subtitles the news in English. The **Lao National Radio** broadcasts news in English. The **BBC World Service** can be picked up on shortwave.

Money → *For up-to-the-minute exchange rates, see www.xe.com.*
The kip is the official currency. The lowest commonly used note is the 500 kip and the highest, the 50,000 kip. It is getting much easier to change currency and traveller's cheques. Banks are generally reluctant to give anything but kip in exchange for hard currency. US dollars and Thai baht can be used as cash in most shops, restaurants and hotels and the Chinese Yuan is starting to be more widely accepted in northern parts of Laos (closer to the Chinese border). A certain amount of cash (in US dollars or Thai baht) can also be useful in an emergency. Banks include the **Lao Development Bank** and **Le Banque pour Commerce Exterieur Lao (BCEL)**, which change most major international currencies (cash) and traveller's cheques denominated in US dollars and pounds sterling. Many of the BCEL branches offer cash advances on Visa/MasterCard. Note that some banks charge a hefty commission of US$2 per TC. While banks will change traveller's cheques and cash

Useful words and phrases

Hello/goodbye	*Suh-bye-dee/lah-gohn*	Where is the	*Sa ta ni lot*
Thank you	*Kop jai*	Is it far?	*Kai baw?*
Yes/No	*Men/baw*	Today	*Muh-nee*
How much is...?	*Tow-dai?*	Tomorrow	*Muh-ouhn*
That's expensive	*Pheng-lie*	Yesterday	*Muh-van-nee*

denominated in most major currencies into kip, some will only change US dollars into Thai baht, or into US dollars cash.

Thai baht are readily accepted in most towns but it is advisable to carry kip in rural areas (eg buses will usually only accept kip).

If you want to use an ATM, your best bet is the capital, Vientiane, where there are at least 15 now in operation – with many more due to be rolled out – accepting all major credit and debit cards. However, you can only get 700,000kip out at a time. There are also 1 or 2 machines in Luang Prabang. Our advice would be not to rely solely on ATMs as a source of cash when travelling in Laos.

Payment by credit card is becoming easier – although beyond the larger hotels and restaurants in Vientiane and Luang Prabang do not expect to be able to get by on plastic. American Express, Visa, Master Card/Access cards are accepted in a limited number of more upmarket establishments. Note that commission is charged by some places on credit card transactions. If they can route the payment through Thailand then a commission is not levied; but if this is not possible, then 3% is usually added.

Many BCEL banks will now advance cash on credit cards in Luang Prabang, Vientiane, Pakse, Phonsavanh, Savannakhet and Vang Vieng (not all cards are accepted at these banks, so it's better to check in advance).

Cost of travelling

The variety of available domestic flights means that the bruised bottoms, dust-soaked clothes and stiff limbs that go hand-in-hand with some of the longer bus/boat rides can be avoided by those with thicker

wallets. As the roads improve and journey times diminish, buses have emerged as the preferred (most reasonably priced) option. Budget accommodation costs US$3-10 with a mid-range hotel costing from US$20-30. Local food is very cheap and it is possible to eat well for under US$2. Most Western restaurants will charge between US$2-5.

Tipping is rare, even in hotels. However, it is a kind gesture to tip guides and, in some more expensive restaurants, a 10% tip is appreciated if service charge is not included on the bill. If someone offers you a lift, it is a courtesy to give them some money for fuel.

Opening hours

Banks Mon-Fri 0830-1600 (some close 1500). **Bars/nightclubs** Usually close around 2200-2300 depending on how strictly the curfew is enforced. In smaller towns, most restaurants and bars will be closed by 2200. **Offices** Mon-Fri 0900-1700; those that deal with tourists stay open later and many open at weekends. Government offices close at 1600.

Police and the law

If you are robbed insurers will require that you obtain a police report. The police may try to solicit a bribe for this service. Although not ideal, you will probably have to pay this fee to obtain your report. Laws aren't strictly enforced but when the authorities do prosecute people the penalties can be harsh, ranging from deportation through to prison sentences. If you are arrested seek embassy and consular support. People are routinely fined for drugs possession, having sexual relations with locals (when unmarried) and proselytizing. If you are arrested or encounter police, try to remain calm and friendly. Although drugs are available throughout the country, the police levy hefty fines and punishments if caught.

Post

The postal service is inexpensive and reliable but delays are common. As the National Tourism Authority assures: in Laos the stamps will stay on the envelope. Contents of outgoing parcels must be examined by an official before being sealed. Incoming mail should use the official title, Lao PDR. There is no mail to home addresses or guesthouses, so mail must be addresses to a PO Box. The post office in Vientiane has a poste restante service. EMS (Express Mail Service) is available from main post offices in larger towns. In general, post offices open 0800-1200, 1300-1600. In provincial areas, **Lao Telecom** is usually attached to the post office. **DHL, Fedex** and **TNT** have offices in Vientiane.

Safety

Crime rates are very low but it is advisable to take the usual precautions. Most areas of the country are now safe – very different from only a few years ago when foreign embassies advised tourists not to travel along certain roads and in certain areas. Today these risks have effectively disappeared. However, the government will sometimes make areas provisionally off-limits if they think there is a security risk – take heed!

There has been a reported increase in motorcycle drive-by thefts in Vientiane, but these and other similar crimes are still at a low level compared with most countries. If riding on a motorbike or bicycle, don't carry your bag strap over your shoulder – as you could get pulled off the bike if someone goes to snatch your bag. In the Siphandon and Vang Vieng areas, theft seems more common. Use a hotel security box if you can.

Road accidents are on the increase. The hiring of motorbikes is becoming more popular and consequently there are more tourist injuries – wear a helmet. The winding road from Luang Prabang to Vientiane (no 13) is now filled with huge trucks and bad drivers – be especially vigilant as there are plenty of accidents caused by run-away lorries.

Be careful around waterways, as drowning is one of the primary causes of tourist deaths. During the rainy season (May-Sep) rivers have a tendency to flood and can have extremely strong currents. Make sure if you are kayaking, tubing, canoeing, travelling by fast-boat, etc, that proper safety gear, such as life jackets, is provided. 'Fast-boat' river travel can be dangerous due to the risk of hitting something in the river and capsizing.

Xieng Khouang Province, the Boloven Plateau, Xam Neua and areas along the Ho Chi Minh Trail are littered with bombies (small anti-personnel mines and bomblets from cluster bomb units). There are also numerous, large, unexploded bombs; in many villages they have been left lying around. They are very unstable so DO NOT TOUCH. Only walk on clearly marked or newly trodden paths.

Tax
Airport tax

International departure tax is US$15, domestic tax is 5000 kip.

Telephone → *Country code +856.*

Public phones are available in Vientiane and other major cities. You can also go to **Lao Telecom** offices to call overseas. Call 178 in Vientiane for town codes. Most towns have at least one telephone box with IDD facility. The one drawback is that you must buy a phonecard. Because these are denominated in such small units, even the highest-value card will only get you a handful of minutes talk time with Europe. Most calls are between US$0.80 and US$2 per min. All post offices, telecoms offices and many shops sell phone cards. **Note** If ringing Laos from Thailand, dial 007 before the country code for Laos.

Mobile telephone coverage is now quite good. Pay-as-you-go Sim cards are available for 30,000 kip to 50,000 kip. Coverage is available in most provincial capitals.

Many internet cafés have set up call facilities that charge US$0.20 per min and under to make a call. In Vientiane, Pakse, Luang Prabang and Vang Vieng most internet cafés are equipped with Skype, including headphones and web-cam, which costs a fraction of the price for international calls (as long as you have already set up an account).

International operator: T170. Operator: T16. The IDD for Laos is 00856. Directory enquiries: T16 (national), T171 (international).

Time
7 hrs ahead of GMT.

Tourist information
The **Laos National Tourism Authority**, Lane Xang, Vientiane, T021-212248, www.tourism laos.gov.la, provides maps and brochures. The provincial offices are usually excellent and as long as you are patient they will usually come through with the information you need. There are particularly good tourist offices in Thakhek, Vieng Xai, Savannakhet, Xam Neua and Luang Namtha. The authority has teamed up with local tour operators to provide a number of ecotourism opportunities, such as trekking and village homestays, www.ecotourismlaos.com.

Useful websites
www.asean-tourism.com
www.ecotourismlaos.com
www.laohotelgroup.org
www.laopdr.com
www.mekongcenter.com
www.muonglao.com
www.travelfish.org
www.visit-laos.com
www.visitmekong.com

Visas and immigration
Visa on arrival
A 30-day tourist visa can be obtained on arrival at: Vientiane's Wattay Airport; Luang Prabang International Airport; Pakse International Airport; the Friendship Bridge crossing near Nong Khai/Vientiane, Chiang Khong/Houei Xai crossing; Chongmek/Vang Tao (near Pakse) crossing; Nakhon Phanom/Thakhek crossing; and Mukdahan/Savannakhet crossing. In China, Lao visas are available at the Mohan/Boten crossing. In Vietnam, they are available at: Lao Bao/Dansavanh in Savannakhet; Cau Treo/Nam Phao (Khammouane Province); and Nam Khan/Nam Can in Xieng Khouang Province.

Visa prices are based on reciprocity with countries and cost US$30-42. 'Overtime fees' are often charged if you enter after 1600 or at a weekend. To get a visa you need to provide a passport photograph and the name of your first hotel.

Visa extensions
Tourist visa extensions can be obtained from the Lao Immigration Office in the Ministry of the Interior opposite the Morning Market in Vientiane, T021-212529. They can be extended for up to a month at the cost of US$2 per day (although if you want to extend for a month it works out cheaper to cross the border); you will need 1 passport photo. It takes a day to process the extension and if you drop the paperwork off early in the morning it will often be ready by the afternoon. Travel agencies in Vientiane and other major centres can also handle this service for you for a fee (eg an additional US$1-2 per day). Visitors who overstay their visas are charged US$10 for each day beyond the date of expiration, they will be asked to pay this on departure from Laos.

Weights and measures
Metric.

Contents

Footprint features

Laos

Vientiane region

Vientiane's appeal lies in its largely preserved fusion of Southeast Asian and French colonial culture. Baguettes, plunged coffee and Bordeaux wines coexist with spring rolls, pho soup and papaya salad. Colourful tuk-tuks scuttle along tree-lined boulevards, past old Buddhist temples and cosmopolitan cafés. Hammer-and-sickle flags hang at 10-pin bowling discos and green and pink chickens wander the streets. But, as in the rest of Laos, the best thing about Vientiane is its people. Take the opportunity to stroll around some of the outlying bans (villages) and meet the wonderful characters who make this city what it is. Due to the US$31 million Mekong River Integrated Management Project, due for completion in 2013, the delightful riverfront foodstalls and beer shacks have been removed as land is reclaimed and prettified. Close to the city is Xieng Khuan, popularly known as the Buddha Park, a bizarre collection of statues and monuments, while, to the north, Vang Vieng, the adventure capital of Laos, attracts backpackers with a multitude of outdoor activities.

Arriving in Vientiane

Getting there by air Most visitors arrive in Vientiane by air, the great bulk on one of the daily connections from Bangkok, with **Thai Air** (www.thaiair.com) or **Lao Airlines** (www. laoairlines.com), which also runs international flights from Thailand, Cambodia, Vietnam, Singapore and China. **Vietnam Airlines** (www.vietnamairlines.com) runs flights from Hanoi and Ho Chi Minh City. **AirAsia** (www.airasia.com) flies from Kuala Lumpur. **Wattay International Airport** ① *T021-512012*, lies 6 km west of the town centre. Vientiane is the hub of Laos' domestic airline system and to travel from the north to the south or vice versa (except for the Pakse–Luang Prabang route) it is necessary to change planes here. Only taxis are allowed to pick up passengers at the airport, although tuk-tuks can drop off here. But tuk-tuks can be taken from the main road and sometimes lurk at the far side of the airport parking area, near the exit (40,000 kip to the centre). The taxi fare is fixed at 54,000 kip to the centre (15-20 minutes).

A cheaper alternative from Thailand is to fly from Bangkok to **Udon Thani** on a budget airline such as NokAir (www.nokair.com) or AirAsia (www.airasia.com) and then continue by road to Vientiane via the Friendship Bridge, which lies just 25 km downstream from the capital (allow three hours). Shuttle buses from Udon Thani, ฿80, run between the bus station and Vientiane. to the border after every flight. There are several flights a day between Udon Thani and Bangkok.

A new Laos-wide airline, **Lao Central Airlines** (T021-513099, www.flylaocentral.com, although at the time of publication this website was still under construction and it wasn't possible to book online), has launched a thrice-weekly from Vientiane to Bangkok.

Getting there by bus There are three public bus terminals in Vientiane. The **Southern bus station** (T021-740521) for destinations in the south of the country is 9 km north of the city centre on Route 13. Most international buses bound for Vietnam depart from here as well as buses to southern and eastern Laos. The station has a VIP room, restaurants, a few shops, mini-mart and there's a guesthouse nearby.

The **Northern bus station** (T021-261905) is on Route T2, about 3 km northwest of the centre before the airport, and serves destinations in northern Laos. Most tuk-tuks will take you there from the city for 10,000-20,000 kip; ask for *Bai Thay Song*. There are English-speaking staff at the help desk.

A third **bus station** (T021-216507) is across the road from the Morning Market, in front of Talaat Kudin, on the eastern edge of the city centre. This station serves destinations within Vientiane Province, buses to and from the Thai border and international buses to Nong Khai and Udon Thani in Thailand. It is also a good place to pick up a tuk-tuk. ➠ *See Transport, page 41.*

Getting around Vientiane is small and manageable and is one of the most laid-back capital cities in the world. The local catch phrase 'bopenyang' (no worries) has permeated through every sector of the city, so much so that even the mangy street dogs look completely chilled out. The core of the city is negotiable on foot and even outlying hotels and places of interest are accessible by bicycle. Cycling remains the most flexible way to tour the city. It can be debilitatingly hot at certain times of year but there are no great hills to struggle up. If cycling doesn't appeal, a combination of foot and tuk-tuk or small 110-125cc scooters take the effort out of sightseeing.

Vientiane can be rather confusing for the first-time visitor as there are few street signs and most streets have two names, pre- and post-revolutionary but, because Vientiane is so small and compact, it doesn't take long to get to grips with the layout. The names of major streets or *thanon* usually correspond to the nearest wat, while traffic lights, wats, monuments and large hotels serve as directional landmarks. When giving directions to a tuk-tuk it is better to use these landmarks, as street names leave them a little bewildered.

Vientiane

200 metres
200 yards

Where to stay 🛏
Auberge Sala Inpeng **1** *B1*
Beau Rivage
  Mekong **2** *B1*
Chanthapanya **40** *B2*
Day Inn **4** *B4*
Douang Deuane **5** *C2*
Dragon Lodge **39** *B2*
Green Park **38** *C6*

Inter City **8** *C1*
La Leela **3** *C5*
Lane Xang **22** *C3*
Lao Orchid **37** *B1*
LV City Riverine **11** *C2*
Mali Namphu Guesthouse
  29 *B3*
Saysouly **34** *C2*
Settha Palace **23** *A4*

Soukchaleun
  Guesthouse **24** *B2*
Syri II Guesthouse **36** *B1*
Vayakorn
  Guesthouse **28** *B2*
Villa Lao **7** *A1*
Villa Manoly **9** *C5*
Youth Inn **10** *C2*

Tourist information **Lao National Tourism Authority** ⓘ *Lane Xang (towards Patuxai), T021-212251 for information, www.tourismlaos.org*, can provide information regarding ecotourism operators and trekking opportunities. The **Tourist Police** ⓘ *0830-1200, 1300-1600*, are upstairs.

Background

Vientiane is an ancient city. There was probably a settlement here, on a bend on the left bank of the Mekong, in the 10th century but knowledge of the city before the 16th century

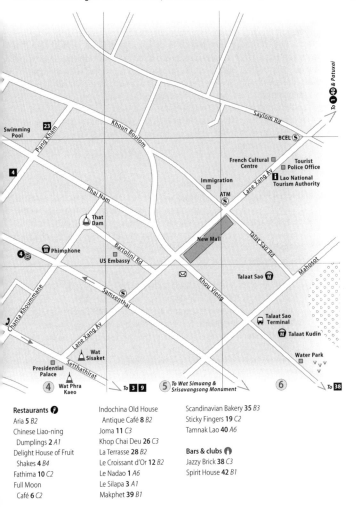

Restaurants 🍴
Aria **5** *B2*
Chinese Liao-ning
  Dumplings **2** *A1*
Delight House of Fruit
  Shakes **4** *B4*
Fathima **10** *C2*
Full Moon
  Café **6** *C2*

Indochina Old House
  Antique Café **8** *B2*
Joma **11** *C3*
Khop Chai Deu **26** *C3*
La Terrasse **28** *B2*
Le Croissant d'Or **12** *B2*
Le Nadao **1** *A6*
Le Silapa **3** *A1*
Makphet **39** *B1*

Scandinavian Bakery **35** *B3*
Sticky Fingers **19** *C2*
Tamnak Lao **40** *A6*

Bars & clubs 🍸
Jazzy Brick **38** *C3*
Spirit House **42** *B1*

is sketchy. From the chronicles, scholars do know that King Setthathirat decided to relocate his capital here in the early 1560s. It seems that it took him four years to build the city, constructing a defensive wall (hence 'Wiang', meaning a walled or fortified city), along with Wat Phra Kaeo and a much enlarged That Luang. Vieng Chan remained intact until 1827 when it was ransacked by the Siamese; this is why many of its wats are of recent construction.

The city was abandoned for decades and erased from the maps of the region. It was only conjured back into existence by the French, who commenced reconstruction at the end of the 19th century. They built rambling colonial villas and wide tree-lined boulevards, befitting their new administrative capital, Vientiane. At the height of American influence in the 1960s, it was renowned for its opium dens and sex shows.

For the moment, the city retains its unique innocence: DJs are officially outlawed (although this is not enforced); there is a 2330 curfew; a certain percentage of music played at restaurants and bars every day is supposed to be Lao (overcome by banging out the Lao tune quota at 0800 in the morning) and women are urged to wear the national dress, the *sinh*. However, to describe the Lao government as autocratic is unfairly negative. Vientiane's citizens are proud of their cultural heritage and are usually very supportive of the government's attempts to promote it. The government has tried, by and large, to maintain the national identity and protect its citizens from what it sees as harmful outside influences. This is already starting to change with the government reshuffle in 2006 came a gradual loosening of the cultural stranglehold.

Places in Vientiane

Most of the interesting buildings in Vientiane are of religious significance. All tour companies and many hotels and guesthouses will arrange city tours and excursions to surrounding sights but it is just as easy to arrange a tour independently with a local tuk-tuk driver; the best English speakers (and thus the most expensive tuk-tuks) can be found in the parking lot beside Nam Phou. Those at the Morning Market (Talaat Sao) are cheaper. Most tuk-tuk drivers pretend not to carry small change, so make sure you have the exact fare with you before taking a ride.

That Luang ① *That Luang Rd, 3.5 km northeast of the city centre; daily 0800-1200, 1300-1600 (except 'special' holidays), 5000 kip. A booklet about the wat is on sale at the entrance.* That Luang is Vientiane's most important site and the holiest Buddhist monument in the country. The golden spire looks impressive at the top of the hill, overlooking the city.

According to legend, a stupa was first built here in the third century AD by emissaries of the Moghul Emperor Asoka. Excavations on the site, however, have only located the remains of an 11th- to 13th-century Khmer temple, making the earlier provenance doubtful in the extreme. The present monument, encompassing the previous buildings, was built in 1566 by King Setthathirat, whose statue stands outside. Plundered by the Thais and the Chinese Haw in the 18th century, it was restored by King (Chao) Anou at the beginning of the 19th century.

The reliquary is surrounded by a square cloister, with an entrance on each side, the most famous on the east. There is a small collection of statues in the cloisters, including one of the Khmer king Jayavarman VII. The cloisters are used as lodgings by monks who travel to Vientiane for religious reasons and especially for the annual **That Luang Festival** (see page 37). The base of the stupa is a mixture of styles, Khmer, Indian and Lao – and each side has a *hor vay* or small offering temple. This lowest level represents the material world, while the second tier is surrounded by a lotus wall and 30 smaller stupas, representing the 30 Buddhist perfections. Each of these originally contained smaller golden stupas but they were stolen by Chinese raiders in the 19th century. The 30-m-high spire dominates the skyline and resembles an elongated lotus bud, crowned by a stylized banana flower and parasol. It was designed so that pilgrims could climb up to the stupa via the walkways around each level. It is believed that originally over 450 kg of gold leaf was used on the spire.

Patuxai (Victory Monument) ① *Junction of That Luang Rd and Lane Xang Av, daily 0800-1200, 1300-1630, 3000 kip.* At the end of That Luang is the Oriental answer to Paris's Arc de Triomphe and Vientiane's best-known landmark, the Victory Monument or Patuxai. It was built by the former regime in memory of those who died in the wars before the Communist takeover, but the cement ran out before its completion. Refusing to be beaten, the regime diverted hundreds of tonnes of cement, part of a US aid package to help with the construction of runways at Wattay Airport, to finish off the monument in 1969.

Wat Sisaket ① *Junction of Lane Xang Av and Setthathirat Rd, daily 0800-1200, 1300-1600, 5000 kip. No photographs in the sim.* Further down Lane Xang is the **Morning Market** or **Talaat Sao** (see page 37) and beyond, is one of Vientiane's two national museums, Wat Sisaket. Home of the head of the Buddhist community in Laos, **Phra Sangka Nagnok**, it is one of the most important buildings in the capital and houses over 7000 Buddha images. Wat Sisaket was built in 1818 during the reign of King Anou. A traditional Lao monastery, it was the only temple that survived the Thai sacking of the town in 1827-1828, making it the oldest building in Vientiane.

The main sanctuary, or **sim**, with its sweeping roof, shares many stylistic similarities with Wat Phra Kaeo (see below): window surrounds, lotus-shaped pillars and carvings of deities held up by giants on the rear door. The sim contains 2052 Buddha statues (mainly terracotta, bronze and wood) in small niches in the top half of the wall. There is little left of the Thai-style *jataka* murals on the lower walls but the depth and colour of the originals can be seen from the few remaining pieces.

The **cloisters** were built during the 1800s and were the first of their kind in Vientiane. They shelter 120 large Buddhas in the attitude of subduing Mara, plus a number of other images in assorted *mudras*, and thousands of small figures in niches, although many of the most interesting Buddha figures are now in Wat Phra Kaeo.

The whole ensemble is washed in a rather attractive shade of caramel and, combined with the terracotta floor tiles and weathered roof, is a most satisfying sight.

Wat Phra Kaeo ① *Setthathirat Rd, daily 0800-1200, 1300-1600, closed public holidays, 5000 kip. No photographs in the sim.* Almost opposite Wat Sisaket is Wat Phra Kaeo. It was originally built by King Setthathirat in 1565 to house the Emerald Buddha (Phra Kaeo), now in Bangkok, which he had brought from his royal residence in Chiang Mai. It was never a monastery but was kept instead for royal worship. The Emerald Buddha was removed by the Thais in 1779 and Wat Phra Kaeo was destroyed by them in the 1827 sacking of Vientiane. (The Thais now claim the Emerald Buddha as their most important icon in the country.) The whole building was in a bad state of repair after the sackings, the only thing remaining fully intact was the floor. The building was expertly reconstructed in the 1940s and 1950s and is now surrounded by a garden. During renovations, the interior walls of the wat were restored using a plaster made of sugar, sand, buffalo skin and tree oil.

The sim stands on three tiers of galleries, the top one surrounded by majestic, lotus-shaped columns. The tiers are joined by several flights of steps and guarded by nagas. The

Phou Khao Khouay National Protected Area

Phou Khao Khouay National Protected Area (pronounced *poo cow kway*) is one of Laos' premier national protected areas. The area extends across 2000 sq km and incorporates an attractive sandstone mountain range. It is crossed by three large rivers, smaller tributaries and two waterfalls at Tad Leuk and Tad Sae, which weave their way in to the Ang Nam Leuk reservoir, a stunning man-made dam and lake that sits on the outskirts of the park. Within the protected area is an array of wildlife, including wild elephants, gibbons, tigers, clouded leopards and Asiatic black bears.

Around the village of Ban Na the village's sugar cane plantations and river salt deposits attract a herd of wild elephants (around 30), which have, in the past, destroyed the villagers' homes and even killed a resident. This has limited the villagers' ability to undertake normal tasks, such as collecting bamboo, fearing that they may come across the wild elephants. To help compensate, the village, in conjunction with some NGOs, has constructed an elephant observation tower and has started running trekking tours to see these massive creatures in their natural habitat. The elephant tower is the primary attraction and it possible to stay over at the tower, 4 km from Ban Na, to try and catch a glimpse of the giant pachyderms who come to lap up salt from the nearby salt lick in the early evening hours. One-to three-day treks through the national park cross waterfalls, pass through pristine jungle and, with luck,

offer the opportunity to hear or spot the odd wild elephant. It is too dangerous to get close. This is an important ecotour that contributes to the livelihood of the Ban Na villagers and helps conserve the elephant population. Advance notice is required so it's advisable to book with a tour operator in Vientiane. If you are travelling independently you will need to organize permits, trekking and accommodation with the village directly. To do this, contact Mr Bounthanam, T020-220 8286. Visit www.trekkingcentrallaos.com and contact the **National Tourism Authority** in Vientiane or **Green Discovery Laos**. Visitors will need to bring drinking water and snacks. Do not try to feed the elephants, they are dangerous.

Ban Hat Khai is home to 90 families from the Lao Loum and Lao Soung ethnic groups. It is also a starting point for organized treks through mountain landscapes, crossing the Nam Mang River and the Phay Xay cliffs. Most treks take in the Tad Sae Falls. Homestay accommodation is available.

The park is northeast of Vientiane along Route 13 South. To get to Ban Na you need to stop at Tha Pabat Phonsanh, 80 km northeast of Vientiane; the village is a further 2 km. For Ban Hat Khai, 100 km northeast of Vientiane, continue on Route 13 to Thabok, where a *songthaew* or boat can take you 7-8 km to the village. Buses to Paksan from Vientiane's Talaat Sao bus station and That Luang market stop at Thabok.

main, central (southern) door is an exquisite example of Lao wood sculpture with carved angels surrounded by flowers and birds; it is the only notable remnant of the original wat. (The central door at the northern end, with the larger carved angels supported by ogres, is new.) The sim now houses a superb assortment of Lao and Khmer art and some pieces of Burmese and Khmer influence, mostly collected from other wats in Vientiane. Although people regularly come and pray here, the wat's main purpose is as a quasi-museum.

Lao National Museum ⓘ *Samsenthai Rd, opposite the Cultural Centre Hall, daily 0800-1200, 1300-1600, 10000 kip. No photography allowed.* Formerly called the Revolutionary Museum, in these post-revolutionary days it has been redesignated the National Museum. The museum's collection has grown over the last few years and now includes a selection of historical artefacts from dinosaur bones and pre-Angkorian sculptures to a comprehensive photographic collection on Laos' modern history. The rhetoric of these modern collections has been toned down from the old days, when photographic descriptions would refer to the 'running dog imperialists' (Americans). The museum features a dazzling array of personal effects from the revolutionary leader Kaysone, including his exercise machine and a spoon he once used. Downstairs there are ancient artefacts, including stone tools and poignant burial jars. Upstairs the museum features a range of artefacts and busts, as well as a small exhibition on various ethnic minorities. The final section of the museum comprises mostly photographs which trace, chronologically, the country's struggle against the 'brutal' French colonialists and American 'imperialists'.

Xieng Khuan ⓘ *Route 2 (25 km south of Vientiane), daily 0800-1630, 5000 kip, plus 5000 kip for cameras. Food vendors sell drinks and snacks.* Otherwise known as the **Garden of the Buddhas** or **Buddha Park**, Xieng Khuan is close to the border with Thailand. It has been described as a Laotian Tiger Balm Gardens, with reinforced concrete Buddhist and Hindu sculptures of Vishnu, Buddha, Siva and various other assorted deities and near-deities. There's also a bulbous-style building with three levels containing smaller sculptures of the same gods.

The garden was built in the late 1950s by a priest-monk-guru-sage-artist called Luang Pu Bunleua Sulihat, who studied under a Hindu *rishi* in Vietnam and then combined the Buddhist and Hindu philosophies in his own very peculiar view of the world. He left Laos because his anti-communist views were incompatible with the ideology of the Pathet Lao (or perhaps because he was just too weird) and settled across the Mekong near the Thai town of Nong Khai, where he proceeded to build an equally revolting and bizarre concrete theme park for religious schizophrenics, called Wat Khaek. With Luang Pu's forced departure from Laos his religious garden came under state control and it is now a public park.

To get there take the No 14 bus (one hour) from the Talaat Sao bus station, a tuk-tuk (100,000 kip), hire a private vehicle (US$15), or take a motorbike or bicycle because the road follows the river and is reasonably level the whole way.

Vang Vieng → *For listings, see pages 29-45.*

The drive from Vientiane to Vang Vieng, on the much-improved Route 13, follows the valley of the Nam Ngum north and then climbs steeply onto the plateau where Vang Vieng is located, 160 km north of Vientiane. The surrounding area is inhabited by the Hmong and Yao hill peoples and is particularly picturesque: craggy karst limestone scenery, riddled with caves, crystal-clear pools and waterfalls. In the early morning the views are reminiscent of a Chinese Sung Dynasty painting.

The town itself is nestled in a valley on the bank of the Nam Song River, amid a misty jungle. It enjoys cooler weather and offers breathtaking views of the imposing mountains of Pha Tang and Phatto Nokham.

The town's laid-back feel has made it a popular haunt for the backpacker crowd, while the surrounding landscape has helped to establish Vang Vieng as Laos' premier outdoor activity destination, especially for rock climbing, caving and kayaking. Its popularity in many ways has also become its downfall: neon lights, pancake stands, 'happy' this and 'happy' that, and pirated *Friends* DVDs now pollute this former oasis. Nevertheless, the town and surrounding area is still full of wonderful things to do and see.

Arriving in Vang Vieng Laos is a very safe country for tourists but a disproportionate number of accidents and crimes seem to happen in Vang Vieng. Theft is routinely reported, ranging from robberies by packs of kids targeting tubers on the river to the opportunist theft of items from guests' rooms. Most guesthouses won't take responsibility for valuables left in rooms, instead it is usually advisable to hand in valuables to the management. Otherwise, you will need to padlock your bag. Another major problem is the sale of illegal drugs. Police often go on sting operations and charge fines of up to US$600 for possession. Legal issues aside, numerous travellers have become seriously ill from indulging in the 'happy' supplements supplied by the restaurants. ▸ *For details of the significant safety risks involved in adventure activities, see What to do, page 38.*

Vang Vieng has become synonymous with tubing down the Nam Song. Tubes can be picked up from the Old Market area where the tubing company has formed a cartel. Without stops the 3-km tubing trip from the Organic Farm to town can take one to two hours if done quickly, but most people do it in three to four hours or take all day, choosing to stop along the way and drink, play volleyball or use the flying fox swings at the many bars dotted along the river. It's not for us to spoil the party but more than a handful of people have died while tubing. Drinks served along the riverbank are lethal mixtures. Watch your intake and go with friends. ▸ *See also Tubing, page 41.*

Many tour operators organize kayaking trips as well. Popular routes include kayaking down the Nam Song to incorporate the caves (especially Tham Nam – water cave), or the trip back to Vientiane via the drop-off point at Nam Lik. If you want to break the journey, there are several nice guesthouses at Nam Lik including the Nam Lik eco-village, south of the town. ▸ *See also Kayaking and rafting, page 40.*

Caves
ⓘ *Many caves have stalls where you can buy drinks and snacks. You can buy hand-drawn maps from the town but all the caves are clearly signposted in English from the main road so these are not really necessary.*
Vang Vieng is best known for its limestone caves, sheltered in the mountains flanking the town. Pretty much every guesthouse and tour operator offers tours to the caves (the best of these is **Green Discovery**, page 39) and, although some caves can be accessed independently, it is advisable to take a guide to a few as they are dark and difficult to navigate. Often children from surrounding villages will take tourists through the caves for a small fee. Don't forget to bring a torch, or even better a head-lamp, which can be picked up cheaply at the market both in Vang Vieng and Vientiane.

Of Vang Vieng's myriad caves, **Tham Chang** is the most renowned of all. Tham Chang penetrates right under a mountain and is fed by a natural spring: perfect for an early morning dip. From the spring it is possible to swim into the cave for quite a distance (bring a waterproof torch, if possible). The cave is said to have been used as a refuge during the 19th century from Chinese Haw bandits and this explains its name: *chang* meaning 'loyal' or 'steadfast'. Entrance is via Vang Vieng resort south of town. Although the cave is not the most magnificent, it serves as a superb lookout point.

Another popular cavern is **Tham Poukham** ⓘ *7 km from Vang Vieng, 10,000 kip.* The cave is often referred to as the cave of the Golden Crab and is highly auspicious. It's believed

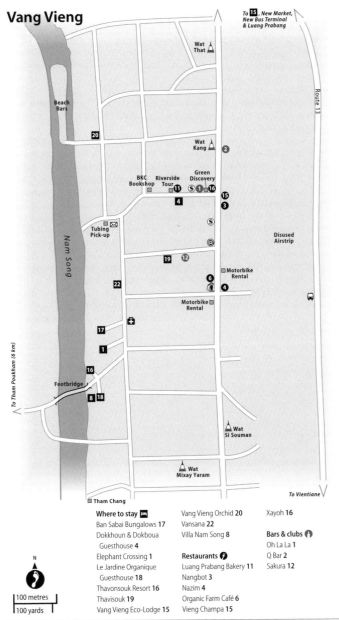

Vang Vieng

To **15**, New Market,
New Bus Terminal
& Luang Prabang

Route 13

Wat That

Beach Bars

20

Nam Song

Wat Kang **2**

BKC Bookshop Riverside Tour **11** Green Discovery Ⓢ **1** **16** **15**

4 **3**

Ⓢ

Tubing Pick-up @

19 **12**

22 **6** Motorbike Rental

4

Motorbike Rental

17 ✚

1

16

To Tham Poukham (6 km)

Footbridge

8 **18**

Wat Si Souman

Wat Mixay Yaram

To Vientiane

Disused Airstrip

Tham Chang

N

100 metres
100 yards

that if you catch a golden crab you will have a lifetime of fortune. To get there you need to cross the foot-bridge near the **Villa Nam Song**, and then follow the road for a further 6 km until you reach the village of Ban Nathong. From the village the cave is 1-km walk and a short climb up quite a steep hill. Mossy rocks lead the way into the main cavern area where a large bronze reclining Buddha is housed. Here there is an idyllic lagoon, with glassy green-blue waters, great for a swim.

Tham None ① *4 km north of Vang Vieng, 10,000 kip*, is known locally as the 'Sleeping Cave' because 2000 villagers took refuge there during the war. The large cave is dotted with stalagmites and stalactites, including the 'magic stone of Vang Vieng', which reflects light. Lots of bats reside in the grotto.

Tham Xang ① *14 km north of Vang Vieng on the banks of the Nam Song, 2000 kip*, also known as the 'Elephant Cave', is named after the stalagmites and stalactites that have created an elephant formation on a ledge. The cave also contains some Buddha images, including the Footprint of Buddha. Although the cave itself is relatively non-descript the bell used by monks is made of a former bomb. From this cave there is a signposted path that leads to **Tham Nam** (water cave) ① *15 km from town, 10000 kip*, a long spindly cave that is believed to stretch for at least 7 km. It takes about two hours to explore the cavern and at the entrance there is a crystal-clear pool. This is one of Vang Vieng's most interesting caves and in the wet season needs to be explored with an inner tube or by wading, while pulling yourself along a rope, although tour operators will also take you beyond the roped area. It's not an easy task and should not be attempted alone. At times the cavern is an extremely tight fit and commando-type crawling is required; a hard helmet with lamp attached is necessary. However, this is an incredible caving experience. To get to these two caves follow Route 13 north and turn left at Km 14, follow this dirt road for 1 km until you reach the river. Boats charge 10,000 kip to cross the river to see Tham Xang; from there you can walk to Tham Nam.

Vientiane region listings

For hotel and restaurant price codes and other relevant information, see pages 8-9.

🛌 Where to stay

Vientiane *p18, map p20*
There is very little quality accommodation in Vientiane under US$10 a night. There is a big difference in the quality of rooms between the US$10 and US$20-30 rooms, the extra US$10 is a worthwhile investment. Cheaper guesthouses will offer discounts in the wet season. Higher-end hotels offer better rates on the internet than the rack rate given if you walk in off the street. All of the guesthouses and boutique hotels, except for the most expensive, tend to get booked up, so reserve in advance as there is a shortage of accommodation in the capital. As a rule of thumb, hotels priced over US$50 accept major credit cards.

$$$$ Green Park Hotel, 12 Khou Vieng Rd, T021-264097, www.greenparkvientiane. com. Designed in a modern East-meets-West style, this hotel is set alongside Vientiane's primary park. Beautiful rooms with all the mod cons, Wi-Fi and super-duper bathtubs. Beautiful garden and excellent pool. The only drawback is that it is set a little further out from the city centre and river, but is still within walking distance. A fantastic luxury option.

$$$$ Settha Palace Hotel, 6 Pang Kham Rd, T021-217581/2, www.sethapalace.com. The stunning **Settha Palace** was built in 1936 and opened as a hotel in 1999. Its French architecture, impressive colonial decor, period furniture, plush rooms with black marble sinks and bathtubs and beautiful tropical gardens and pool sit more easily with the fundamental essence of Vientiane than the other top-level hotels. Often considered the best hotel in town. Recommended.

$$$ Chanthapanya, Nokeo Khoummane Rd, T021-244284, www.chanthapanyahotel. com. Fantastic modern Asian building.

The rooms are new and very comfortable. Beautifully furnished with modern Lao wooden furniture, comfy beds, fridge, TV, hot water, phone and a/c. Includes breakfast.

$$$ Lao Orchid Hotel, Chao Anou. T021-264134, www.lao-orchid.com. Beautiful spacious rooms with stunning modern furnishings, polished floorboards and large showers. Outstanding value for the price and very popular with business travellers. 4½-star accommodation for a 3½-star price. Very busy so advanced bookings essential. Includes breakfast and Wi-Fi. Café and zen fish pond. Visa and MasterCard accepted. Recommended.

$$$ Le Leela, Ban Phiawat 33, Unit 10, T021-214493, www.leleela.com. This beautiful white modernist home has been converted into a hip hotel. It's all zen-like and minimalist with a library, beautiful staircase, black lacquered wooden floors and doors and attractive furniture. Opt for a room with a 4-poster bed. Only one of the suites has a bathtub. Next to **Villa Manoly** in a quiet road just off-centre.

$$$-$$ Inter City Hotel, 24-25 Fa Ngum Rd, T021-242842, www.intercity-lao.com. This Singaporean-owned hotel is one of the oldest in Vientiane and has been operating for over 30 years. Renovations have made it sparkle: mosaics, relief sculptures and murals adorn the walls, and traditional shutters, silk hangings and furniture feature in every room. The a/c rooms are light and spacious, with slick bathrooms and fantastic balconies overlooking the Mekong. Lovely atrium and excellent gift shop with beautiful antique costumes. Wi-Fi available.

$$$-$$ Lane Xang Hotel, Fa Ngum Rd, T021-214100, www.lanexanghotel.com. la. This was the original 'luxury' hotel in Vientiane, built by the French in 1964. It has an indefinable charm, despite the fact that some of its retro-hip Soviet fittings and furniture have been ripped out to make way for a more contemporary look. One floor of the hotel has been remodelled (38 rooms) and the difference is remarkable compared to the rest of the rooms, which are looking shoddy and unloved. Go for a a junior suite de luxe room, with its own bar. Other facilities include a pool and bar.

$$$-$$ LV City Riverine Hotel, 48 Fa Ngum Rd, Mixay, T021-214643, www.lvcitylaos.com. A good central choice in the heart of town. The suite is sweet and cosy with a 4-poster bed, textile decor and a good-sized bathroom and stand-alone sink. The de luxe rooms have beds raised on small platforms but with smaller bathrooms; standard rooms are very nice with thoughtful extras like a clothes stand. Wi-Fi and breakfast is included.

$$ Auberge Sala Inpeng, 063 Unit 06, Inpeng St, T021-242021, www.salalao.com. 9 very attractive bungalows set in a small garden in a quiet street. The economy rooms don't come with TV. Opt for a standard or superior if available for the space and decor. Breakfast is included.

$$ Beau Rivage Mekong, Fa Ngum Rd, T021-243350, www.hbrm.com. One of the first Western-style boutique hotels in Vientiane, it is beautifully furnished, with artistic decoration and fantastic bathtubs. The pink exterior does not sit well with its surroundings but nonetheless this is a great hotel with superb Mekong river views. Its location, just out of the centre of town on the river, ensures peace and quiet but it's still only a 5-min walk to the hustle and bustle. Garden view rooms are cheaper. Includes breakfast.

$$ Douang Deuane, Nokeo Khoummane Rd, T021-222301, dd_hotel@hotmail.com. From the exterior, this dilapidated building looks like a classic Communist edifice, but the a/c rooms have charm and character: parquet wood floors, art deco furniture, excellent bathrooms with bathtubs (showers in single rooms) and satellite TV. Try and get a balcony room for lovely patchwork views of the roofs of the city. Although the room rates are no longer

competitive, it is a good centrally located option B if the others within this price range are fully booked. Good-value motorbike rentals, 70,000 kip per day.

$$ Hotel Day Inn, 59/3 Pang Kham Rd, T021-222985, www.day-inn-hotel.com. Run by a friendly Cambodian, this renovated villa is in a good position in a quiet part of town, just to the north of the main concentration of bars and restaurants. Attractive, airy, clean, large rooms, with a/c and excellent bathrooms; breakfast and complimentary airport transfer included. Wi-Fi available.

$$ Mali Namphu Guesthouse, 114 Pang Kham Rd, T021-215093, www.malinamphu.com. Difficult to spot as it looks like a small shopfront but the facade is deceiving, the foyer opens onto a beautifully manicured courtyard surrounded by quaint, terraced rooms. Clean, bright rooms are traditionally decorated with a modern twist and come with a/c, hot water, cable TV and a fantastic breakfast. The twin rooms are much nicer than the doubles. Friendly staff. Highly recommended. One of the best guesthouses in Laos in this price range.

$$ Vayakorn Guesthouse, 91 Nokeo Khoummane Rd, T021-241911, www.vayakorn.com. The rooms are clean, beautifully decorated with modern furniture and very comfortable. Polished floors, hot water, a/c and TV. Sadly breakfast is no longer included with rooms but it is still excellent value. Great value and centrally located. The new **Vayakorn Inn** has opened around the corner. Wi-Fi.

$$ Villa Manoly, Ban Phyavat, T021-218907, manoly20@hotmail.com. This is a wonderful ramshackle French colonial villa crowded with objets d'art, curios, books and ancient TV sets. It's like a rambling private house. There's a pool too in the garden. 12 rooms are in the main building and 8 rooms in a new block with small patios out front overlooking the pool. Monthly rates are US$650. Recommended.

$$-$ Dragon Lodge, 311-313 Samsenthai Rd, T021-250114, dragonlodge2002@yahoo.com. Somewhere between a guesthouse and a hotel. Fun, colourful downstairs restaurant area – good for a party; if you're looking for quiet this probably isn't the best choice. Nice, simply decorated rooms, with hot water, TV and a/c. 5-star service. Visa accepted. Fan rooms are cheaper.

$$-$ Villa Lao (formerly **Thongbay Guesthouse**), off Luang Prabang Rd, turn right before the **Novotel**, Ban Non Douang, T021-242292, www.villa-lao-guesthouse. com. Lovely traditional Lao house set in a lush tropical garden. Rooms have traditional-style fittings, mosquito nets and fan or a/c. Rooms with shared bath are cheapest. The guesthouse also runs cooking classes on request (150,000 kip), which include buying ingredients at the local market. The only drawback of this place is the distance from the city centre. Perfect if you want to relax.

$ Saysouly, 23 Manthathurath Rd, T021-218383, www.saysouly.com. A variety of rooms, a bit on the musty side. Parquet floors, cheap single fan rooms with shared bathroom. The shared bathrooms are excellent with powerful showers. Extra for a/c. The more expensive en suite rooms are quite good value.

$ Soukchaleun Guesthouse, 121 Setthathirat Rd, T021-218723, soukchaleun_gh@yahoo.com. Quaint guesthouse with a variety of rooms ranging from fan rooms with shared bathroom through to a/c en suite. Comfy, homely and very clean. The views are not scenic but the guesthouse is friendly and relatively good value.

$ Syri II Guesthouse, 63/6-7 Setthathirat Rd, T021-223178, syri2@hotmail.com. This is probably one of the best options within the cheaper price range. 3-storey guesthouse with a variety of rooms including fan rooms with shared bathroom and private bathroom. Clean and simply decorated with wooden furniture. Decorated with quirky curios from around Asia, with lounges and shared communal areas. Helpful staff. Recommended.

$ Youth Inn, 29 Fa Ngum Rd and on Francois Ngin Rd, T021-217130, youthinn@hotmail.com. A Vietnamese-run operation with 2 locations in the heart of things and a new addition to the budget scene. The standard-sized rooms are spotlessly clean and are compact with a/c. The owners are sometimes friendly and sometimes not!

Vang Vieng *p25, map p27*

The town's popularity has ensured a uniformity among almost all places catering to budget tourists: most restaurants feature the same menu and there isn't much individuality in the cheaper guesthouses either. The majority are geared to the needs of travellers and offer a laundry service, guides and bicycles. However, in the last 2 years a couple of higher-end hotels have cropped up, providing more attractive options. Although the accommodation in the centre of town is usually cheaper, try and get a room with a view of the river as it is simply stunning. A couple of new bamboo bridges have been constructed across the river to new bungalow developments; note though, that during the rainy season, the only bridge in operation is the Namsong bridge (4000 kip return, 6000 kip for bikes, 10,000 kip for motorbikes) as well as the high bridge leading past the **Vang Vieng Orchid** to the island bars.

$$$ Villa Nam Song, T023-511637, www.villanamsong.com. Quaint terracotta villas set in manicured gardens overlooking the Nam Song with parquet floors, hot water and separate shower compartments. Fan-cooled restaurant attached; breakfast included. Although this is an attractive hotel there is better value for money in town. Cheaper rooms lack river view. 2 rooms have wheelchair access.

$$$-$$ Ban Sabai Bungalow, on the banks of the river, T023-511088, www.xayohgroup.com. A lovely complex of bungalows with balconies in a spectacular location, with all the modern fittings but the rooms are not well lit, the water is not very hot, the bathroom is badly designed with the sink in the shower compartment and the breakfast service is very unpolished. Rooms 1-4 are near the laundry room and although not too noisy, light sleepers will be disturbed. Bungalows closer to the river are a bit more expensive.

$$$-$$ Thavonsouk Resort, on the river, T023-511096, www.thavonsouk.com. Offers 5 different styles of accommodation across a sprawling riverfront premises. Rooms are much more attractive on the outside than in; standard rooms come with tacky wood-imitation tiles. Some mid-range bungalows are great value with massive balconies fitted with sunbeds. There is a traditional Lao house, decorated with Lao furnishings, suitable for a family or big group, plus suites (TV, fridge, bath, a/c) and standard accommodation. Fantastic restaurant. Keep your eye out for local home-grown pop star, Aluna and her father, Alom, who run this family business.

$$ Elephant Crossing, on the Nam Song river, T023-511232, www.theelephant crossinghotel.com. A great, attractive mid-range option. Australian-owned riverfront hotel classically decorated with modern wooden furnishings. The big bathtub and sliding window between the bedroom and bathroom will be a big hit with romantics. All rooms except 6, have view, fridge, Wi-Fi and a/c. Breakfast included. There's a set of kids' swings in the garden. The owners are really lovely.

$$ Vansana, by the river, T023-511598, www.vansanahotel-group.com. Despite its soulless exterior this hotel boasts the best rooms and facilities in town. Large bedrooms fitted with all the mod cons have stunning mountain and river views. Modern wooden furniture, minibar and local handicrafts decorate the room. Beautiful pool and bar by the river with deckchairs. Ask for a room with a view; breakfast included. Recommended. Non-guests can use the pool for 20,000 kip per day.

$ Dokboua Guesthouse, T020-5614 4933. This newcomer, close to **Dokkhoun**, offers some of the best budget rooms in town.

Sparklingly clean rooms with taut white linens and good mattresses with huge attached bathrooms right in the centre. A/c rooms are more expensive; older rooms are cheaper. Friendly family owners. Highly recommended.

$ Le Jardine Organique Guesthouse, on the river, about 900 m from the centre of town, T023-511420. This set of bungalows and a guesthouse has been surrounded by 2 other properties owned by family members thus **Le Jardine** now offers no river view. The raised bungalows are smart and lovely with balconies attached. The guesthouse rooms are plain and clean. The **Bansuan Riverview** with rattan bungalows now hog the view while the **Vilayvong** facing **Le Jardine** bungalows offers smart wooden, floor-height bungalows with balconies. It is, thus, now like a compound of rooms but not unattractive with it. Cheaper rooms have fan only. The owners are lovely and don't suffer from the Vang Vieng jadedness quite often found in these cheaper bungalows.

$ Thavisouk, in the centre of town, T023-511658. If you are looking for a budget option in town, this is perfect. No frills but very clean. Rooms with en suite bathrooms and hot water, US$3-4. While the accommodation is good value, their tours, tickets and other services aren't.

$ Vang Vieng Orchid, on the river road, T023-511172. Comfortable fan or more expensive a/c rooms. Hot water in the bathrooms, clean tiled floors, very comfortable rooms. The rooms with the private balconies are well worth the few extra dollars because you will have your own personal piece of the phenomenal view. Unfortunately, they're not as friendly as they used to be.

Out of town

The places on the outskirts of town are great for those who wish to escape into a more natural landscape. The lack of facilities and transport in the area ensures tranquillity but also makes it quite difficult to get to town.

$$-$ Vang Vieng Eco-Lodge, 7 km north of town, T021-413370, www.vangvieng-eco-lodge.com. Although this isn't an eco-lodge it is still an exceptionally beautiful place to stay. Set on the banks of the river with stunning gardens and beautiful rock formations, it is a perfect place to get away from it all. The 11 chalet-style bungalows, which have been nicely decorated, with beautiful balconies, comfortable furnishings and a big hot-water bathtub; a bungalow of 4 rooms with sliding doors with great riverside views but small double bed and shower room; and a rattan longhouse (cheaper still, **$**) with 8 rooms and shared bath; breakfast included. Good Lao restaurant. Also arranges activities.

$ Vang Vieng Organic Farm, 3 km north of town in Ban Sisavang, T023-511174, www.laofarm.org. This mulberry farm has basic rooms with mosquito net, dorm accommodation and full board. If you volunteer (building a mudhouse, English teaching, working on the farm) you get a 20,000 kip per night discount. A new guesthouse with unappealing, very overpriced rooms with hard mattresses has opened (**$**). Hugely popular restaurant, serving great starfruit wine and famous mulberry pancakes (0600-2130). It is a very popular drop-off spot for tubers. The farm supports the **Equal Education for AllPproject** (www.eefaproject.com).

ⓧ Restaurants

Vientiane *p18, map p20*
Now that the Lao food stalls have gone from the banks of the Mekong along Fa Ngum, other Lao food stalls can be found at the **Dong Palane Night Market**, on Dong Palane, and the night markets near the corner of **Chao Anou** and **Khoun Boulom** Rd. There are various other congregations of stalls and vendors around town, most of which set up shop around 1730 and close down by 2100. Be sure to sample Lao ice cream with coconut sticky rice.

The **Chinese quarter** is around Chao Anou, Heng Boun and Khoun Boulom and is a lively spot in the evenings. There are a number of noodle shops here, all of which serve a palatable array of vermicelli, *muu daeng* (red pork), duck and chicken.

The **Korean-style barbeque**, *sindat*, is extremely popular, especially among the younger Lao, as it is a very social event and very cheap. It involves cooking finely sliced meat on a hot plate in the middle of the table, while forming a broth with vegetables around the sides of the tray. Reminiscent of a 1970s fondue evening. **Seendat** (see below) is a favourite amongst the older Lao.

$$$-$$ Le Nadao, Ban Donmieng (on the right-hand side of the Patuxai roundabout), T021-213174. Mon-Fri 1200-1330 and 1900-2230, Sat-Sun 1900-2230. This place is difficult to find but definitely worth every second spent searching the back streets of Vientiane in the dark. Sayavouth, who trained in Paris and New York, produces delectable French cuisine: soups, venison, lamb and puddings. The set lunch menu is one of the best lunches you will get in town. Fantastic.

$$$-$ Le Silapa, 17/1 Sihom Rd, T021-219689. Daily 1130-1400 and 1800-2200; closed for 1 month a year in the rain season and for a week over Lao New Year. Anthony and Frederick provide a fantastic French-inspired menu (tilapia with a vegetable marmalade, lime and black olive sauce). and intimate atmosphere for fine dining without blowing the budget. Innovative modern meals that would be as at home in the fine dining establishments of New York and London are here. Great value set lunch menu. Part of the profits (5000 kip per bottle of wine) is donated to disadvantaged families, usually for expensive but life-saving surgical procedures. Wine degustation evenings are occasionally held, US$75.

$$ Tamnak Lao Restaurant, That Luang Rd, T021-413562. 1200-2200. It's well worth deviating from the main Nam Phou area for a bite to eat here. This restaurant and its sister branch in Luang Prabang have a reputation for delivering outstanding Lao and Thai food, usually prepared with a modern twist.

$$-$ Aria, 8 Rue François Ngin, T021-222589, http://ariaorg.com. An outstanding addition to the Vientiane dining scene. Divine ice cream, a wine list 16 pages long, and a long mouth-watering menu of homemade pastas, ravioli, risottos and pizzas with real buffalo mozzarella. Dishes include mountain hunter's ravioli stuffed with slow fire-braised deer and mountain cheeses, barbera red wine and herb sauce. Service is ultra efficient and the owner, who is so friendly and welcoming, is an Italian returnee to Vientiane.

$$-$ La Terrasse, 55/4 Nokeo Koummane Rd, T021-218550. Mon-Sat 1100-1400, 1800-2200. This is the best European restaurant in terms of variety and price. Large fail-safe menu offering French, European, Lao and Mexican food. Good desserts, especially the rich chocolate mousse, and a good selection of French wine. Fantastic service. Reasonable prices with an excellent 'plat du jour' each day. Great 1970s-style comfort food.

$ Chinese Liao-ning Dumpling Restaurant, Chao Anou Rd, T021-240811. Daily 1100-2230. This restaurant is a firm favourite with the expats and it isn't hard to see why: fabulous steamed or fried dumplings and a wide range of vegetarian dishes. The place is spotlessly clean but the birds in cages outside are a bit off-putting. No one is ever disappointed by the meals here. Highly recommended.

$ Fathima, Th Fa Gnum, T021-219097. Without a doubt the best-value Indian in town. Ultra-friendly service and a large menu with a range of excellent curries.

$ Full Moon Café, Rue François Ngin, T021-243373. Daily 1000-2300. Delectable Asian fusion cuisine and Western favourites. Huge pillows, good lighting and great music make this place very relaxing. Fantastic chicken wrap and some pretty good Asian tapas. The Ladybug shake is a winner. Also a book exchange and music and movie shop for iPods. Free Wi-Fi available.

$ Khop Chai Deu, 54 Setthathirat Rd, on the corner of Nam Phou Rd. Daily 0800-2330, www.khopchaideu.com. This lively place housed in a former colonial building is one of the city's most popular venues. Garden seating, good atmosphere at night with soft lantern lighting, and an eclectic menu of Indian, Italian, Korean and international dishes (many of which come from nearby restaurants). While the food is okay most come for the bustling atmosphere. The best value are the local Lao dishes though, which are made on site and toned down for the falang palate. Also serves draft or bottled beer at a pleasant a/c bar. Excellent lunch buffet. Live performances.

$ Makphet, in a new location behind Wat Ong Teu, T021-260587, www.friends-international.org. Fantastic Lao non-profit restaurant that helps raise money for street kids. Run by the trainees, who are former street kids, and their teachers. Modern Lao cuisine with a twist. Selection of delectable drinks such as the iced hibiscus with lime juice. Beautifully decorated with modern furniture and painting by the kids. Also sells handicrafts and toys produced by the parents from vulnerable communities.

$ Seendat, Sihom Rd, T021-213855. Daily 1730-2200. This restaurant has been in existence for well over 20 years and is a favourite amongst the older Lao for its clean food (*sindat*) and good atmosphere. About US$1 per person more expensive than most other places but this is reflected in the quality.

$ Sticky Fingers, 10/3 François Ngin Rd, T021-215972. Mon-Fri 1700-2300, Sat and Sun 1000-2300. Very popular small restaurant and bar serving Lao and international dishes, including fantastic salads, pasta, burgers and such like. Everything from Middle Eastern through to modern Asian on offer. Fantastic comfort food and the best breakfast in town. Great cocktails, lively atmosphere, nice setting. Deliveries available. **Stickies** should be the first pit-stop for every visitor needing to get grounded quickly as, food aside, the expats who frequent the joint are full to the brim with local knowledge.

Cafés, cakeshops and juice bars

Pavement cafés are 10 a penny in Vientiane. You need not walk more than half a block for some hot coffee or a cold fruit shake.

Delight House of Fruit Shakes, Samsenthai Rd, opposite the **Asian Pavilion Hotel**, T021-212200. Daily 0700-2000. A wonderful selection of fresh shakes and fruit salads for next to nothing.

Indochina Old House Antique Café, 86/11 Setthathirat Rd, T021-223528. A delightful curio store where upstairs you can sip wholesome juices or coffee amid the artful clutter of antiques, propaganda work and knick-knacks. A real treat.

Joma, Setthathirat Rd, T021-215265. Daily 0700-2100. A very modern, chic bakery with efficient service. Wi-Fi and arctic-style a/c. However, it is starting to get a bit pricey and the iced coffee is better next door at **Dao Fa**.

Le Croissant d'Or, top of Nokeo Khoummane Rd, T021-223741, www.croissant-dor.com. Daily 0700-2100. French bakery, great for pastries.

Scandinavian Bakery 7174/1 Pang Kham Rd, Nam Phou Circle, T021-215199, www. scandinavianbakerylaos.com. Daily 0700-2000. Delicious pastries, bread, sandwiches and cakes. Great place for a leisurely coffee. Pricey for Laos but a necessary European fix for many expats. The Nam Phou Circle outlet is much better value and has a wider selection of cakes and sandwiches.

Vang Vieng *p25, map p27*

There is a string of eating places on the main road through town. Generally, the cuisine available are hamburgers, pasta, sandwiches and basic Asian dishes. Most of the restaurants offer 'happy' upgrades – marijuana or mushrooms in your pizza, cake or lassi, or opium tea. Although many people choose the 'happy' offerings, some wind up very ill.

$ Luang Prabang Bakery Restaurant, just off the main road, near BCEL. Excellent pastries, cakes and shakes and delicious breakfasts. Make sure you ask for the freshest batch as they have a tendency to leave cakes on the shelf well past their use-by date. Recommended.

$ Nangbot, on the main road, T023-511018. This proper sit-down restaurant is one of the oldest tourist diners in town and serves a few traditional dishes, such as bamboo shoot soup and *laap* with sticky rice, alongside the usual Western fare. However, the main road entrance is closed. Walk through to the disused airstrip side where all the action is taking place.

$ Nazim, on the main road, T023-511214. The largest and most popular Indian restaurant in town. Good range of South Indian and biryani specialities, plus a selection of vegetarian meals.

$ Organic Farm Café, further down the main road. Small café offering over 15 tropical fruit shakes and a fantastic variety of food. Mulberry shakes and pancakes are a must and the harvest curry stew is absolutely delicious. Try the fresh spring rolls with pineapple dipping sauce as a starter. The food is highly recommended, the service could do with a little work. The sister branch is at the **Organic Mulberry Farm**.

$ Vieng Champa Restaurant, on the main road, T023-511370. Refreshingly, this family-run restaurant seems to have a greater selection of Lao food than most other places on the street. Most meals are between 15,000 and 20,000 kip.

$ Xayoh, Luang Prabang Rd, T023-511088. Restaurant with branches in Vientiane and Luang Prabang offering good Western food in a comfy environment. Pizza, soups and roast dinners. **Xayoh** may have moved location by the time you read this.

🎵 Bars and clubs

Vientiane *p18, map p20*
Bars

There are a number of bar stalls, which set up in the evening along **Quai Fa Ngum** (the river roaay; a good place for a cold beer as the sun sets. Most bars will close at 2300 in accordance with the local curfew laws; some places seem to be able to stay open past this time although that varies on a day-to-day basis. Government officials go through phases of shutting down places and restricting curfews.

Jazzy Brick, Setthathirat Rd, near Phimphone Market. Very sophisticated, modern den, where delectable cocktails are served with jazz cooing in the background. Garish shirts banned. Decorated with an eclectic range of quirky and kitsch artefacts. Very upmarket. Head here towards the end of the night.

Khop Chai Deu, Setthathirat Rd (near the corner with Nam Phou). Probably the most popular bar for tourists in Vientiane. Casual setting with a nightly band.

Spirit House, follow Fa Ngum Rd until it turns into a dirt track, past the Mekong River Commission, T021-243795, www.thespirithouse laos.com. Beautiful wooden bar in perfect river location next to the **Hotel Beau Rivage**. Range of snacks and burgers but salads are overpriced. Good for those wanting to catch the sunset in style with some of the best cocktails in the city. Wi-Fi.

Sticky Fingers, Rue François Ngin, opposite the **Tai Pan Hotel**. A fantastic bar and restaurant run by 2 Australian women. Brilliant cocktails, especially the renowned Tom Yum. Also serves food (see page 34).

Sunset Bar, end of Fa Ngum Rd. Although this run-down wooden construction isn't much to look at, it is a firm favourite with locals and tourists hoping to have a quiet ale and take in the magnificent sunset.

Vang Vieng *p25, map p27*

The latest hotspot in Vang Vieng changes week to week. There's usually a nightly party right on the riverfront (accessed by crossing the bamboo bridges) with makeshift bars, hammocks and drunken antics.

Fluid Bar. A new addition to the riverbank bars, this bar is 3 km north of town, with great views. Kick back for a while on your tubing venture. The owners also run a helpful local website: www.vangviengbiz.com.

Oh La La Bar, off the main street. Very popular, open bar with pool table.

Sakura Bar, between the main road and the river, www.sakurabar.com. Big open bar with loud, blaring and often live music. The popular **Q Bar** (http://qbar-laos.com) on the main road diagonally opposite to Xayoh.

🎭 Entertainment

Vientiane *p18, map p20*
Films and exhibitions

Blue Sky Café, on the corner of Setthathirat and Chao Anou roads. Movies are shown on a 29-in TV on the 2nd floor.

COPE Visitors' Centre, National Rehabilitation Centre, Khou Vieng Rd (signposted), www.copelaos.org. Open 0900-1800, free. COPE (Cooperative Orthotic and Prosthetic Enterprise) has set up an exhibition on UXO (unexploded ordnance) and its effects on the people of Laos. The exhibition is very interesting and includes a small movie room, photography, UXO and a range of prosthetic limbs (some that are actually crafted out of UXO). The exhibition helps raise money for the work of COPE, which includes the production of prosthetic limbs and rehabilitation of patients.

French Cultural Centre, Lang Xang Rd, T021-215764, www.if-laos.org. Shows exhibitions, screens French films and also hosts the Southeast Asian film festival. Check the *Vientiane Times* for up-to-date details or pick up its quarterly programme.

Lao-International Trade Exhibition & Convention Center (**ITECC**), T4 Rd – Ban

Phonethane Neua, T021-416002, www.lao
itecc.info. Shows a range of international films.

Keep an eye in the *Vientiane Times* for
international performances at the **Lao
Cultural Centre** (the building that looks
like a big cake opposite the museum).

Karaoke
Could almost be the Lao national sport and
there's nothing like bonding with the locals
over a heavy duty karaoke session. Karaoke
places are everywhere. The more expensive,
upmarket **Don Chan Palace** (Piawat Village
(off Fa Gnum Quay), T021-244288,
www.donchanpalacelaodpdr.co6,
lets you hire your own room.

Traditional dance
Lao National Theatre, Manthaturath Rd,
T020-5550 1773. Daily shows of Lao dancing,
from 1730. Tickets, US$7. Performances
represent traditional dance of lowland Lao as
well as some minority groups. Performances
are less regular in the low season.

❀ Festivals

Vientiane *p18, map p20*
1st weekend in Apr Pi Mai (Lao New Year)
is celebrated with a 3-day festival and a
huge water fight.
12 Oct Freedom from the French Day.
Oct **Boun Souang Heua** is a beautiful
event on the night of the full moon at the
end of Buddhist Lent. Candles are lit in all
the homes and a candlelit procession takes
place around the city's wats and through
the streets. Then, thousands of banana-leaf
boats holding flowers, tapers and candles
are floated out onto the river. The boats
signify your bad luck floating away. On the
2nd day, boat races take place, with 50 or so
men in each boat; they power up the river in
perfect unison. Usually, a bunch of foolhardy
expats also tries to compete, much to the
amusement of the locals.
Nov (movable) **Boun That Luang** is
celebrated in all of Vientiane's *thats* but

most notably at That Luang (the national
shrine). Originally a ceremony in which
nobles swore allegiance to the king and
constitution, it amazingly survived the
Communist era. On the festival's most
important day, **Thak Baat**, thousands of
Lao people pour into the temple at 0600
and again at 1700 to pay homage. Monks
travel from across the country to collect
alms from the pilgrims. It is a really beautiful
ceremony, with monks chanting and
thousands of people praying. Women who
attend should invest in a traditional *sinh*. A
week-long carnival surrounds the festival
with fireworks, music and dancing.

⦿ Shopping

Vientiane *p18, map p20*
Bookshops
Kosila Books, Nokeo Khoummane Rd,
T021-241352. Small selection of second-
hand books.
Monument Books, 124/1 Nokeo
Khoummane Rd, T021-243708, www.
monument-books.com. The largest selection
of new books in Vientiane, **Monument** stock
a range of Southeast Asian speciality books
as well as coffee-table books. Good place to
pick up Lao-language children's books to
distribute to villages on your travels.
Vientiane Book Center, 32/05 Fa Ngum Rd,
T021-212031, vientianebookcenter@yahoo.
com. A limited but interesting selection of
used books in a multitude of languages.

Clothing and textiles
Couleur d'Asie, Nam Phou Circle, www.
couleurdasie.net. Modern-style Asian clothing.
Pricey but high-quality fusion fashion.
Lao Textiles by Carol Cassidy, Nokeo
Koummane Rd, T021-212123, www.lao
textiles.com. Mon-Fri 0800-1200, 1400-
1700, Sat 0800-1200. Exquisite silk fabrics,
including *ikat* and traditional Lao designs,
made by an American in a beautifully
renovated colonial property. Dyeing,
spinning, designing and weaving all

done on site (and can be viewed). It's expensive, but many of the weavings are real works of art; custom-made pieces available on request.

Mixay Boutique, Nokeo Khoummane, T021-2571 7943, contact@mixay.com. Exquisite Lao silk in rich colours. Clothing and fantastic photographs and artefacts.

Satri Laos, Setthathirat, T021-244387. If Vientiane had a Harrods this would be it. Upmarket boutique retailing everything from jewellery, shoes, clothes, furnishings and homewares. Beautiful stuff, although most of it is from China, Vietnam and Thailand.

Handicrafts and antiques

The main shops are along Setthathirat, Samsenthai and Pang Kham. The **Talaat Sao** (Morning Market) is also worth a browse, with artefacts, such as appliquéd panels, decorated hats and sashes, basketwork both old and new, small and large wooden tobacco boxes, sticky-rice lidded baskets, axe pillows, embroidered cushions and a wide range of silver work.

Camacraft, Nokeo Khoumman 660, T021-241217, www.camacrafts.org. NGO which retails handicrafts produced by the Hmong people. Beautiful embroidery, mulberry tea, Lao silk.

Oot-Ni Art Gallery, Samsenthai Rd, T021-214359, http://ootni-yenkham.laopdr.com. An Aladdin's Cave of serious objets d'art.

T'Shop Lai, Vat Inpeng St (behind Wat Inpeng), T021-223178, www.artisanslao.com. Mon-Sat 0800-2000, Sun 0800-1500. Has exhibitions of crafts made by disadvantaged people, as well as a shop.

Jewellery

Tamarind, Manthathurath, T021-243564. Great innovative jewellery designs, nice pieces. Also stocks a range of beautiful clothes made in stunning silk and organza.

Markets and shopping malls

Vientiane has several excellent markets. **Talaat Sao**, off Lane Xang Av. It's busiest in the mornings (from around 1000), but operates all day. There are money exchanges here (quite a good rate), and a good selection of foodstalls selling Western food, soft drinks and ice cream sundaes. It sells imported Thai goods, electrical appliances, watches, DVDs and CDs, stationery, cosmetics, a selection of handicrafts, an enormous choice of Lao fabrics, and upstairs there is a large clothing section, silverware, some gems and gold and a few handicraft stalls.

There is also the newer addition to the Morning Market – a modern shopping centre-style market. This is not as popular as it is much pricier and stocked with mostly Thai products sold in baht. Next to it is the new **Talat Sao Mall**.

There is an interesting produce section at **Talaat Kudin**, the ramshackle market on the other side of the bus stop. This market offers many of the same handicrafts and silks as the morning market but is a lot cheaper.

Supermarkets

Phimphone Market, Setthathirath Rd, opposite **Khop Chai Deu Restaurant**. This supermarket has everything a foreigner could ask for in terms of imported food, drink, magazines, translated books, personal hygiene products, household items and much more (and the price to go with it).

Simuang Minimart, Samsenthai Rd, opposite Wat Simuang. Supermarket with a great selection of Western products. Great place to pick up wine but check it is not past its use-by date.

◔ What to do

Vientiane p18, map p20
Cooking
Villa Lao (formerly **Thongbay Guesthouse**) (see page 31), T021-242292. Cooking classes, covering all of meal preparation, from purchasing the ingredients to eating the meal.

Cycling

Bicycles are available for hire from several places in town, see Transport, page 41. A good outing is to cycle downstream along the banks of the Mekong. Cycle south on Tha Deua Rd until Km 5 (watch the traffic) and then turn right down one of the tracks (there are a number) towards the riverbank. A path, suitable for bicycles, follows the river beginning at about Km 4.5. There are monasteries and drinks sellers en route to maintain interest and energy.

Gym

Sengdara, 77/5 Phonthan Rd, T021-414058. This is a very modern, well-equipped gym, with pool, sauna and massage.

Every afternoon at 1700 there is a free aerobics session in the outdoor gym on the river. Completely bizarre but lots of fun.

Kickboxing

Soxai Boxing Stadium, 200 m past the old circus in Baan Dong Paleb. Kickboxing is every Sat between 1400-1600.

Massage, saunas and spas

The best massage in town is given by the blind masseuses in a little street off Samsenthai Rd, 2 blocks down from Simuang Minimart (across from Wat Simuang). There are 2 blind masseuse businesses side-by-side and either one is fantastic: **Traditional Clinic**, T020-5565 9177, and **Porm Clinic** (no English spoken). They are marked by blue signs off both Khou Vieng and Samsenthai roads.
Mandarina, 74 Pang Kham, T021-218703. A range of upmarket treatments between US$5-30. Massage, facials, body scrubs, mini-saunas, oils, jacuzzi.
Papaya Spa, opposite Wat Xieng Veh, T020-5561 0565, www.papayaspa.com. Daily 0900-2000. Surrounded by beautiful gardens. Massage, sauna, facials. They also have a new branch that is more accessible on Lane Xang Av just up from the **Morning Market**.

Shooting

There is a shooting range in the Southern corner of the national stadium, US$1-2 for a few rounds.

Swimming and waterparks

Nongchan Water Park, Khou Vieng St, T021-219386. Open 1000-1800. 30,000 kip, children 20,000 kip.
Several hotels in town permit non-residents to use their fitness facilities for a small fee, including the **Tai Pan Hotel** (rather basic), the **Lao Hotel Plaza**, the **Lane Xang Hotel** and the luxurious **Settha Palace** (with a hefty entrance price to boot). **The Australian Embassy Recreation Club**, Km 3, Tha Deua Rd, T021-314921, has a fantastic saltwater pool with superb Mekong views.

Ten-pin bowling

Bowling is a very popular local pastime. Although it might sound quite sedate, the bowling alleys are often the only bars that are open after curfew.
The Lao Bowling Center, behind the Lao Plaza Hotel, T021-218661. Good value, shoe hire is included but bring your own socks.

Thak Baat

Every morning at day-break (around 0530-0600) monks flood out of the city's temples, creating a swirl of orange on the streets, as they collect alms. It is truly beautiful to see the misty, grey streets come alive with the robe-clad monks. Foreigners are more than welcome to participate, just buy some sticky rice or other food from the vendors and kneel beside others.

Tour operators

For general travel information for Phou Khao Khouay (www.trekkingcentrallaos.com), visit the **National Tourism Authority**. Most agents will use 'eco' somewhere in their title but this doesn't necessarily mean anything. **Asian Trails**, Unit 10, Ban Khounta Thong, Sikhottabong District, T021-263936, www.asiantrails.info.

Christophe Kittirath, No 15, Unit 01, Ban Savang, Chanthaboury District, T020-5550 4604, laowheels@yahoo.co.uk. Christophe runs tours all over the country with or without public transport, speaks English and French and is very helpful.

Exotissimo, 6/44 Pang Kham Rd, T021-241861, www.exotissimo.com. Tours and travel services. Excellent but pricey.

Green Discovery, Setthathirat Rd, next to Kop Chai Deu T021-223022, www.green discoverylaos.com. Specializes in ecotours and adventure travel.

Yoga

Vientiane Yoga Studio, Sokpaluang Rd, Soi 1 (first *soi* on the right after you turn onto Sokpaluang from Khou Vieng Rd), www.vientianeyoga.com.

Vang Vieng *p25, map p27*

Tour guides are available for hiking, rafting, visiting the caves and minority villages and can be booked at most travel agents and guesthouses. Safety issues need to be considered when taking part in any adventure activity. There have been fatalities in Vang Vieng from boating, trekking and caving accidents. The Nam Song River can flow very quickly during the wet season (Jul and Aug) and tourists have drowned here. Make sure you wear a life jacket during all water-borne activities and time your trip so you aren't travelling on the river after dark. A price war between tour operators has led to cost cutting, resulting in equipment that is not well maintained or does not exist at all. With all tour operators it is imperative you are given safety gear and that canoes, ropes, torches and other equipment are in a good state of repair. The more expensive, reputable companies are often the best option (see also Vientiane Tour operators, above). Reliable tour operators are listed below.

Ballooning

Ballooning above the beautiful karst landscape of Vang Vieng is awesome. Flights (US$70, child US$40) are 3 times a day and can be booked on T078-438690, fluid.partnership@gmail.com

Kayaking and rafting

See also tour operators, above. Kayaking is a very popular activity around Vang Vieng and competition between operators is fierce. There are a wide variety of trips available, ranging from day trips (with a visit to the caves and surrounding villages), to kayaking all the way to Vientiane via the stop-off point at Nam Lik, US$33-87, about 6 hrs, including a 40-min drive at the start and finish. All valuables are kept in a car, which meets kayakers at the end of their paddle. Be wary of intensive rafting or kayaking trips through risky areas during the wet season, as it can be very dangerous. Check equipment thoroughly before committing.

Rock climbing

Vang Vieng is the only really established rock climbing area in the country, with over 50 sites in the locality, ranging from grade 5 to 8A+. Almost all of these climbs have been 'bolted'. There are climbing sites suitable for beginners through to more experienced climbers. **Green Discovery** (see Tour operators, page 39) runs climbing courses almost every day in high season (US$20-45 per day, including equipment rental). The best climbing sites include: Sleeping Cave, Sleeping Wall and Tham Nam Them.

Tour operators

Green Discovery, attached to Xayo`h Café, T023-511440, www.greendiscoverylaoscom. By far the best tour operator in town. Caving, kayaking, hiking and rock climbing plus motorbike tours and mountain-bike tours from US$22-40 for 1 day. Very professional and helpful. Recommended. Also rents motorbikes from US$25-30 for 1 day. The office may have moved location by the time you read this.

Riverside Tour, T023-511137, www.riversidetourslaos.com. Kayaking and adventure tours. Also tour agency; friendly.

VLT Natural Tours, T023-511369, T020-55208283, www.vangviengtour.com. As well as all the usual tours, this company also offers cooking tours, fishing, camping trips, slow boat to Vientiane and a sunset barbecue on the river. Combined trekking, caving, tubing, kayaking is around 150,000 kip; a similar trip with **Green Discovery** is from US$52.

Trekking

Almost all guesthouses and agents offer hiking trips, usually incorporating a visit to caves and minority villages and, possibly, some kayaking or tubing. The best treks are offered through the major tour operators who will provide an English-speaking guide, all transport and lunch for US$10-15 per day.

Tubing

No trip to Vang Vieng is complete without tubing down the Nam Song. Floating slowly along the river is an ideal way to take in the stunning surroundings of limestone karsts, jungle and rice paddies. The drop-off point is 3 km from town near the **Organic Farm**, where several bars and restaurants have been set up along the river. Try and start early in the day as it's dangerous to tube after dark and the temperature of the water drops sharply. Women should take a sarong and avoid walking through town in a bikini; it is culturally unacceptable and highly offensive to the locals.

Tube operators have formed a cartel to benefit the 1555 families in town who have a stake in this activity. Thus there is only 1 place where you can pick up the tubes (marked on map, page 27). Tube collection is from 0830-1530 and costs 55,000 kip including the tuk-tuk ride to the drop-off point and a life jacket. A deposit of 60,000 kip is required. A rented dry bag costs 20,000 kip. For a lost tube the fine is US$7, a lost life jacket US$20 and a lost

dry bag US$15. The tube must be returned by 1800 or a fine of 20,000 kip is imposed (people may offer to return the tubes for you; it is best to decline this offer).

It is essential that you wear a life jacket as people have drowned on the river, particularly in the wet season (Jul and Aug) when the river swells and flows very quickly. Without stopping, expect the journey to take 2 hrs in the dry season and 1 hr in the wet season. Most people stop along the way and make a day of it.

⊙ Transport

Vientiane *p18, map p20*
Air

Lao Airlines, 2 Pang Kham Rd, T021-821 2054, www.laoairlines.com, also at Wattay Airport; T021-212051**. Thai Airways,** Head Office, Luang Prabang Rd, not far past the Novotel, T021-222527, www.thaiairways. com. **Vietnam Airlines,** Lao Plaza Hotel, T021-217562, www.vietnamairlines.com.vn, Mon-Fri 0800-1200, 1330-1630.

Prices and schedules are constantly changing, so always check in advance.

Lao Airlines to **Bangkok** (80 mins) and **Chiang Mai** in Thailand; to **Siem Reap** and **Phnom Penh** (1½ hrs); Singapore and **Kanning** in China. In Vietnam to **Hanoi** and **Ho Chi Minh City**. Domestic services include **Luang Prabang** (40 mins), **Houei Xai**, **Pakse** (50 mins), **Savannakhet**, **Oudomxay**, **Luang Namtha**, **Xieng Khouang** (**Phonsavan**) and **Sayaboury**.

A new Lao airline, **Lao Central Airlines** (T021-513099, www.flylaocentral.com, although at the time of publication this website was still under construction and it wasn't possible to book online), flies to **Luang Prabang**.

Bicycle and motorbike

For those energetic enough in the hot season, **bikes** are the best way to get around town. Many hotels and guesthouses have bikes available for their guests, expect to pay about 10,000 kip per day. There are also many bike hire shops around town. Markets, post offices and government offices usually have 'bike parks' where it is advisable to leave your bike. A small minding fee is charged.

Motorbikes are available for hire from US$5-10 per day and leave your passport as security. Insurance is seldom available anywhere in Laos on motorbikes but most places will also hire out helmets, a necessity. **PVO** also has a reliable selection of motorbikes from 70,000-250,000 kip per day. Often a driving licence can be used in lieu of a motorbike licence if the police pull you over.

Bus
Vientiane has 3 main public bus terminals: Northern, Southern and Talaat Sao (Morning Market).

Southern bus station Route 13, 9 km north of the city centre (T021-740521). Public buses depart daily for destinations in southern Laos. Prices change around every 3 months and also fluctuate (yes, they go down!) according to gas prices, so these prices are just a guide. The southern bus station has a range of stores, pharmacy and massage. To **Paksan**, at 0730, 1030, 1100, 1200, 1330, 150 km, 1 hr 30 mins, 25,000-40,000 kip. To **Lak Sao** (for the Vietnamese border), 335 km, 8 hrs, 50,000 kip, 3 daily at 0500, 0600, 0700, continuing to **Thakhek**, 360 km, 3 daily, 5-6 hrs, 50,000 kip; 1 VIP bus at 1300, 75,000 kip or take any southbound bus. To **Savannakhet**, 483 km, 8 daily (early morning), 8 hrs, 65,000 kip. Taking the overnight southbound VIP bus to Pakse costs 95,000 kip. To **Pakse**, 736 km, 8 daily, 13 hrs, 100,000 kip; express buses, 5 buses, 130,000 kip; there are also overnight express buses to Pakse, 11 hrs, 150,000 kip at 2030. **Thongli**, T021-242657, operates an overnight VIP service daily at 2030, which takes about the same time but has beds, water, snacks, etc, 135,000 kip. **KVT**, T021-213043, also runs VIP buses to Pakse at 2030.

Banag Saigon, T021-720175, runs buses to **Hanoi**, 24 hrs, 130,000 kip, **Vinh**, 1900,

160,000 kip, **Thanh Hoa**, 1900, 180,000 kip, **Hué**, 1900-1930, 150,000 kip, and **Danang**, 1900-1930, 200,000 kip. These services run on odd days so check in advance.

Northern bus station Route 2, towards the airport 3.5 km from the centre of town, T021-261905. Northbound buses are regular and have a/c. For the more popular routes, there are also VIP buses, which will usually offer snacks and service. To **Luang Prabang**, 400 km, standard buses, 8 daily, 10 hrs, 95,000 kip; VIP buses daily at 0800 and 0900, 8 hrs, 115,000 kip. To **Udomxai**, 550 km, standard buses 0645 and 1345, 13 hrs, 110,000 kip; a/c bus at 1700 daily, 130,000 kip; VIP bus at 1600, 155,000 kip. To **Luang Namtha**, 698 km, 0830 daily, 19 hrs, 140,000 kip. To **Phongsali**, 815 km, 0715 daily, 26 hrs, 160,000 kip. To **Houei Xai**, 895 km, daily 1730, 25-30 hrs, 180,000 kip. To **Sayaboury**, 485 km, standard at 0900 and 1630 daily, 12-15 hrs, 90,000 kip; a/c at 1830 daily, 110,000 kip. To **Xam Neua**, 850 km, at 0700, 0945, 1245, 30 hrs (it may go via Phonsavanh), 150,000 kip. To **Phonsavanh**, 365 km, standard at 0630, 0930, 1600, 10 hrs, 80,000 kip; a/c at 0800 and 1840 daily, 95,000 kip; VIP bus at 2000 daily, 115,000 kip.

Talaat Sao bus station (T021-216507) Across the road from Talaat Sao, in front of Talaat Kudin, on the eastern edge of the city centre. Destinations, distances and fares are listed on a board in English and Lao. Most departures are in the morning and can leave as early as 0400, so many travellers on a tight schedule have regretted not checking departure times the night before. There is a useful map at the station. However, it's likely you will need a bit of direction: staff at the ticket office only speak a little English so a better option is to chat to the friendly chaps in the planning office, who love a visit, T021-216506. The times listed below vary depending on the weather and the number of stops en route.

To the **Southern bus station**, every 30 mins, 0600-1800, 2000 kip. To the **Northern bus station**, catch the Nongping bus (5 daily) and ask to get off at 'Thay song' (1500 kip). To **Wattay Airport**, every 30 mins, 0640-1800, 3000 kip. Buses to Vang Vieng 5 daily, 3½ hrs, 15,000 kip.

There are numerous buses criss-crossing the province; most aren't very useful for tourists. To the **Friendship Bridge** (Laoside), every 30 mins, 0650-1710, 5000 kip. To **Nong Khai** (Thai side of the Friendship Bridge), 6 daily 0730-1800, about 1 hr including immigration, 15,000-80,000 kip.

Other private bus services To **Vang Vieng**, Green Discovery, from their office on Setthathirat, www.greendiscoverylaos.com, it also runs to Luang Prabang and Pakse.

There is also **Sabaidee Bus** for the same price. Both services will pick you up from your guesthouse if you arrange in advance. Other tour companies also offer this service. Sabaidee Bus to **Luang Prabang**, Tue and Thu, 130,000 kip, with a stopover in **Vang Vieng** on the way. Sabaidee also runs international buses to **Bangkok**, at 1700 with a change at Nong Khai leaving at 2000, arriving Bangkok 0600. **Green Discovery**, www.greendiscoverylaos.com, also runs international buses to **Udon Thani**, **Bangkok**, **Nong Khai**, **Chiang Mai** and **Pattaya** in Thailand and **Hanoi**, **Vinh**, **Hué**, **Danang** and **Ho Chi Minh City** in Vietnam.

Car hire
Europcar Laos (Asia Vehicle Rental), 354-356 Samsenthai Rd, T021-223 867, www.europcarlaos.com. Operates throughout Laos and across the border into Thailand, Vietnam and China..

Taxi
These are mostly found at the **Morning Market** (Talaat Sao) or around the main hotels. Newer vehicles have meters but there are still some ageing jalopies. Flag fall is 8000-12,000 kip. A taxi from the Morning Market to the **airport**, US$5-6; to **Tha Deua** (for the Friendship Bridge and Thailand), US$10-12, although you can usually get the trip much cheaper but some taxis are so

decrepit that you may as well take a tuk-tuk, 95,000 kip (see below). To hire a taxi for trips outside the city costs around US$20-30 per day. **Lavi Taxi**, T021-350 000 is the only reliable call-up service in town but after 2000 you may not get an answer.

Train
There is a train station at Thanaleng, beyond the Friendship Bridge, where trains cross the border into Thailand and run to Bangkok thus avoiding the need to get on and off transport to cross the border, but you still need to change trains in Nong Khai.

Tuk-tuks
Tuk-tuks usually congregate around **Nam Phou, Talaat Sao** and **Talaat Kudin**. Tuk-tuks can be chartered for longer out-of-town trips (maximum 25 km) or for short journeys of 2-3 km within the city (from 10,000-40,000 kip per person). Printed official prices are 55,000 kip to the airport; 40,000 kip to That Luang and Northern Bus Station; 60,000 kip to the Southern Bus Station; 95,000 kip to the Friendship Bridge; 150,000 kip return to the Beer Lao Factory; 195,000 kip return to the Buddha Park and 80,000 kip per hr sightseeing. An 8-hr charter is officially quoted at US$30. There are also shared tuk-tuks, which run on regular routes along the city's main streets.

Tuk-tuks are available around Nam Phou until 2330 but are quite difficult to hire after dark in other areas of town. The tuk-tuks that congregate on the city corners are generally part of a quasi cartel, it is thus much cheaper to travel on one that is passing through.

To stop a vehicle, simply flag it down. A good, reliable driver is Mr Souk, T020-7771 2220, who speaks good English and goes beyond the call of duty.

Vang Vieng *p25, map p27*
Bicycle and motorbike
There are many bicycles for rent in town (10,000 kip per day). There are also a few

motorbike rental places (60,000 kip per day); the best of these is diagonally opposite the **Organic Farm Café** in town.

Bus

Buses now leave from the new bus terminal at the New Market, 2 km north of town, T023-511657. Ticket office open daily 0530-1630; English is spoken and staff are helpful. There are toilets, shops and cafés. A tuk-tuk into town should cost around 10,000 kip per person. Minibuses leave from most guesthouses to both Vientiane and Luang Prabang. To **Vientiane** on local bus at 0530-0600, 0630, 0700, 1230 and 1400, 30,000 kip, 4 hrs; express bus at 1000, 1300, 60,000 kip, 3½ hrs; pick-ups every 20 mins, 30,000 kip, 4 hrs. To **Luang Prabang** express bus at 1000, 80,000 kip. To **Phonsovan** at 0930, 90,000 kip, 7 hrs.

Private minivan transport and VIP buses Tickets are usually sold by guesthouses and will include a pick-up at your hotel to the bus. Minivan to **Vientiane** 0900, 80,000 kip, 3½-4 hrs; drop off at Mekong riverside restaurants. Minibus to **Luang Prabang** 0900 and 1400, 90,000 kip (5-6 hrs). Every guesthouse and travel agent can book the VIP/minivans and they will pick up from your guesthouse.

Tour companies sell through tickets to **Pakse** and international tickets to **Vietnam** and **Bangkok** but there are better, more efficient and cost-effective ways to get back to the Thai capital.

Tuk-tuks

A day trip to the caves should cost US$10 but there have been reports of some drivers offering trips to the caves for 10,000 kip per person and then demanding an outrageous fee for the return leg. Make sure all prices are set in stone before setting off.

◑ Directory

Vientiane *p18, map p20*
Banks
See Money, page 13, for details on changing money in Laos. There are now around a dozen or more multicard Visa and MasterCard ATMs in the city. The **Banque Pour le Commerce Exterieur (BCEL)**, corner of Fa Ngum and Pang Kham roads, takes all the usual credit cards (maximum withdrawal 700,000 kip; much less on Sun). Other multicard ATMs can be found in front of the **Novotel**, and next to **Green Discovery** on and beside the petrol station near Wat Simuang. BCEL, 1 Pang Kham Rd, traditionally offers the lowest commission (1.5%) on changing US$ TCs into US$ cash; there is no commission on changing US$ into kip. **Joint Development Bank**, Lane Xane Ave, T021-213535, offers good rates on cash advances and has an ATM.

Embassies and consulates

Australia, Km 4 Thadeua Rd, T021-353800,www.laos.embassy.gov.au. **Britain**, no embassy; served by the Australian Embassy. **Cambodia**, Tha Deua Rd, Km3, T021-314952, visas daily 0730-1030. Cambodian visas US$20. **Canada**, no embassy; served by the Australian Embassy. **China**, Thanon Wat Nak Nyai T021-315105. Visas take 4 days. **France**, Setthathirat Rd, T021-2126 7400, www.ambafrance-laos.org. **Germany**, 26 Sok Paluang Rd, T021-312110. **Japan**, Sisavangvong Rd, T021-414400, www.la.emb-japan.go.jp. **Malaysia**, 23 Singha Rd, T021-414205. **Myanmar (Burma)**, Lao Thai St, Watnak, T021-314910, daily 0800-1200, 1300-1630. **Sweden**, Sok Paluang Rd, T021-315003, www.swedenabroad.se/vientiane. **Thailand**, Kaysone Phomivane Rd, T021-214581 (consular section has moved to Unit 15, Ban Phonsinaun, T021-415335 ext 605, http://vientiane.thaiembassy.org, 0830-1200 for visa extensions), Mon-Fri 0830-1200. If crossing by land, 30-day visas are also issued at the Friendship Bridge. **USA**,

Bartolonies St, Xieng Nyuen, T267000, http://
laos.usembassy.gov. **Vietnam**, 85, 23 Singha
Rd, T021-990986, www.mofa.gov.vn/vnemb.
la, visas 0800-1045, 1415-1615. 1-month
visa costs US$45 and you must wait 3 days.
An extra US$5 for the visa in 1 day.

Immigration

Immigration office, Phai Nam Rd (near
Morning Market), Mon-Thu 0800-1200, 1300-
1800. Visa extensions can be organized for
US$2 per day. Overstay, US$10 per day. For
visa information, see page 16.

Internet

Internet cafés have opened up all over the
city, many on Setthathirat and Samsenthai
roads. You shouldn't have to pay more than
100 kip per min. Internet phones are now
very popular, with most cafés providing
this service for under US$1 per min. Also,
most major internet cafés are fitted with
Skype and headphones. **Apollo Internet**,
Setthathirat Rd, Mon-Fri 0830-2300, Sat
and Sun 0900-2300.

Medical services

There are 2 pretty good pharmacies close
to the Talaat Sao Bus Station. **Australian
Embassy Clinic**, Australian Embassy, KM
4 Thadeua Rd, T021-353800/840, Mon-Fri
0830-1230, 1330-1700. **Mahosot Hospital**,
Fa Gnum, T021-214018, suitable for minor
ailments only. For anything major it is
advisable to cross the border to Nong Khai
and visit **AEK Udon International Hospital**,
T+66-4234 2555. In cases of emergency
where a medical evacuation is required,
contact **Lao West Coast Helicopter**, Hangar
703, Wattay International Airport, T021-
512023, www.laowestcoast.com. A charter

to Udon Thani costs from US$1550, subject
to availability and government approval.

Police

Tourist Police Office, Lang Xang Av (in
the same office as the National Tourism
Authority of Laos), T021-251128.

Post

Post Office, Khou Vieng Rd/Lane Xang Av
(opposite market), T021-216425, offers
local and international telephone calls.
Also a good packing service and a philately
counter. To send packages, use **DHL**, Nong
No Rd, near the airport, T021-214868, or
TNT Express, Thai Airways Building, Luang
Prabang Rd, T021-261918.

Telephone

The international telephone office is on
Setthathirat Rd, near Nam Phou Rd, 24 hrs.

Vang Vieng and around
p25, map p27
Banks BCEL, T021-511480, exchanges
cash, TCs and will also do cash advances on
Visa and MasterCard, 0830-1530. Visa and
MasterCard ATM. There are now a number of
ATMs in town. **Internet** There are a number
of internet cafés along the main drag; most
offer international internet calls from 3000 kip
per min. **Magnet** is the best of the internet
cafés and offers internet as well as music/
movie transfer to iPod and cash advances
from the EFTPOS facility for 3% commission.
Medical services Vang Vieng Hospital is
located on the road that runs parallel to the
river; it's terribly under-equipped. In most
cases it is better to go to Vientiane. **Post
office** The post office is next to the former
site of the old market, 0830-1600.

Luang Prabang and around

Anchored at the junction of the Mekong and Nam Khan rivers, the former royal capital of Lane Xang is now a UNESCO World Heritage Site. It is home to a spellbinding array of gilded temples, weathered French colonial facades and art deco shophouses. In the 18th century there were more than 65 wats in the city. Yet for all its magnificent temples, this royal 'city' feels more like an easy-going provincial town: at daybreak, scores of monks in saffron robes amble silently out of the monasteries bearing gold-topped wooden boxes in which to collect offerings from the town's residents; in the early evening women cook, old men lounge in wicker chairs and young boys play takraw in the streets. The famous Pak Ou Caves and the Kuang Si Falls are located near the town.

Arriving in Luang Prabang

Getting there Flying is still the easiest option with daily connections from Vientiane, plus flights from Bangkok and Chiang Mai to **Luang Prabang International Airport** (LPQ) ⓘ *4 km northeast of town, T071-212172/3*. The airport has a phone box, a couple of restaurants and handicraft shops. There is a standard US$6 charge for a tuk-tuk ride from the airport to the centre.

Route 13 is now safe, with no recent bandit attacks reported, and the road has been upgraded, shortening the journey from Vientiane to eight or nine hours. There are also overland connections with other destinations in northern Laos. Luang Prabang has two main bus stations: **Kiew Lot Sai Neua** (northern bus station), located on the northeast side of Sisavangvong Bridge, for traffic to and from the north; and **Naluang** (southern bus station) for traffic to and from the south. Occasionally buses will pass through the opposite station to what you would expect, so be sure to double-check. The standard tuk-tuk fare to/from either bus station is 10,000 kip. If there are only a few passengers, it's late at night or you are travelling to/from an out-of-town hotel, expect to pay 20,000 kip. These prices tend to fluctuate with the international cost of petroleum. Another option is to travel by river: a firm favourite is the two-day trip between Luang Prabang and Houei Xai (close to the Thai border), via Pak Beng (see page 68). Less frequent are the boats to Muang Ngoi Neua and Nong Khiaw, and Muang Khua. ➤*See Transport, page 62.*

Getting around Luang Prabang is a small town and the best way to explore is either on foot or by bicycle. Bicycles can be hired from most guesthouses for US$1 per day. Strolling about this beautiful town is a real pleasure but there are also tuk-tuks and *saamlors* for hire. Depending on the prevailing mood of the local government, motorbikes may or may not be available for hire. Motorbikes can be rented for about $15-20 per day.

Best time to visit Luang Prabang lies 300 m above sea level on the upper Mekong, at its confluence with the Nam Khan. The most popular time to visit the town is during the comparatively cool months of November and December but the best time to visit is from December to February. After this the weather is hotting up and the views are often shrouded in a haze, produced by shifting cultivators using fire to clear the forest for agriculture. This does not really clear until May or, sometimes, June. During the months of March and April, when visibility is at its worst, the smoke can cause soreness of the eyes, as well as preventing planes from landing.

In terms of festivals, on the October full moon, the delightful Lai Heua Fai fireboat festival takes place, see page 59.

Tourist information Luang Prabang Tourist Information Centre ① *Sisavang-vong, T071-212487*, provides provincial information and offers a couple of good ecotourism treks (which support local communities), including one to Kuang Si and one in Chompet District. The Chompet trek receives quite good reviews and includes visits to hot springs, villages and the chance to watch a traditional performance from Hmong performers.

Background

According to legend, the site of Luang Prabang was chosen by two resident hermits and was originally known as Xieng Thong – 'Copper Tree City'. Details are sketchy regarding the earliest inhabitants of Luang Prabang but historians imply the ethnic Khmu and Lao Theung groups were the initial settlers. They named Luang Prabang, Muang Sawa, which literally translates as Java, hinting at some kind of cross-border support. By the end of the 13th century, Muang Sawa had developed into a regional hub.

A major turning point in the city's history came about in 1353, when the mighty Fa Ngum travelled up the Mekong River, backed by a feisty Khmer army, and captured Muang Sawa. Here, the warrior king founded Lane Xang Hom Khao (Kingdom of a Million Elephants, White Parasol) and established a new Lao royal lineage, which was to last another 600 years. The name of the city refers to the holy Pra Bang, Laos' most sacred image of the Buddha, which was given to Fa Ngum by his father-in-law, the King of Cambodia.

The city had been significantly built up by the time King Visounarat came to power in 1512 and remained the capital until King Setthathirat, fearing a Burmese invasion, moved the capital to Vieng Chan (Vientiane) in 1563.

Luang Prabang didn't suffer as greatly as other provincial capitals during the Indochina wars, narrowly escaping a Viet Minh capture in 1953. During the Second Indochina War, however, the Pathet Lao cut short the royal lineage, forcing King Sisavang Vatthana to abdicate and sending him to a re-education camp in northeastern Laos where he, his wife and his son died from starvation. Despite the demise of the monarchy and years of revolutionary rhetoric on the city's tannoy system, Luang Prabang's dreamy streets have somehow retained the aura of old Lane Xang.

Places in Luang Prabang → *For listings, see pages 54-64.*

The sights are conveniently close together but, to begin with, it is worth climbing Phousi or taking a stroll along the river roads to get a better idea of the layout of the town. Most of Luang Prabang's important wats are dotted along the main road, Phothisarath.

Mount Phousi

ⓘ *The western steps lead up from Sisavangvong Rd, daily 0700-1800, admission at western steps 20,000 kip. If you want to watch the sun go down, get there early and jostle for position – don't expect to be the only person there.*

Directly opposite the Royal Palace is the start of the steep climb up Mount Phousi, the spiritual and geographical heart of the city and a popular place to come to watch the sunset over the Mekong, illuminating the hills to the east. Phousi is a gigantic rock with sheer forested sides, surmounted by a 25 m-tall *chedi*, **That Chomsi**. The *chedi* was constructed in 1804, restored in 1914 and is the designated starting point for the colourful Pi Mai (New Year) celebrations in April. Its shimmering gold-spired stupa rests on a rectangular base, ornamented by small metal Bodhi trees. Next to the stupa is a little sanctuary, from which the candlelit procession descends at New Year, accompanied by effigies of Nang Sang Kham, the guardian of the New Year, and Naga, protector of the city.

1 Luang Prabang

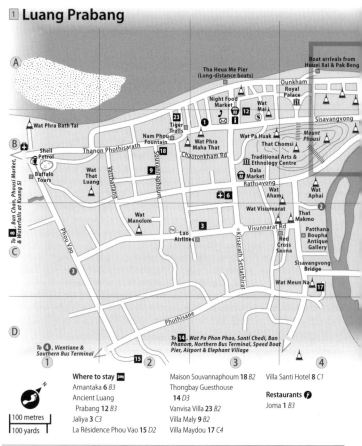

Where to stay 🛏	Maison Souvannaphoum 18 *B2*	Villa Santi Hotel 8 *C1*
Amantaka 6 *B3*	Thongbay Guesthouse	
Ancient Luang	14 *D3*	Restaurants 🍴
Prabang 12 *B3*	Vanvisa Villa 23 *B2*	Joma 1 *B3*
Jaliya 3 *C3*	Villa Maly 9 *B2*	
La Résidence Phou Vao 15 *D2*	Villa Maydou 17 *C4*	

100 metres
100 yards

Royal Palace

ⓘ *Sisavangvong Rd, daily 0800-1100, 1330-1600 (closed Tue), 80,000 kip, including a new audio tour and a map. Shorts, short-sleeved shirts and strappy dresses are prohibited; shoes should be removed and bags must be put in lockers. No photography.*

Also called the **National Museum**, the Royal Palace is right in the centre of the city on the main road and close enough to the Mekong to allow royal guests ready access by river. Unlike its former occupants, the palace survived the 1975 revolution and was converted into a museum the following year.

It was built by the French for the Lao King Sisavang Vong in 1904 in an attempt to bind him and his family more tightly into the colonial system of government. Later work saw the planting of the avenue of palms and the filling in of one of two fish ponds. Local residents regarded the ponds as the 'eyes' of the capital, so the blinding of one eye was taken as inviting bad fortune by leaving the city unprotected. The subsequent civil war seemed to vindicate these fears. The palace is Khmer in style, cruciform in plan and mounted on a small platform of four tiers. The only indication of French involvement can be seen in the two French lilies represented in stucco on the entrance, beneath the symbols of Lao royalty. There are a few Lao motifs but, in many respects, the palace is more foreign than Lao: it was designed by a French architect, with steps made from Italian marble; built by masons from Vietnam; embellished by carpenters from Bangkok, and funded by the largesse of the colonial authorities.

The small ornate pavilion of **Wat Ho Prabang** is located in the northeast corner of the palace compound, to the right of the entrance to the Royal Palace. The chapel contains four Khmer Buddhas, ivories mounted in gold, bronze drums used in religious ceremonies and about 30 smaller Buddha images from temples all over the city. The Pra Bang, see below, is due to be moved here.

The main **entrance hall** of the palace was used for royal religious ceremonies, when the Supreme Patriarch of Lao Buddhism would oversee proceedings from his gold-painted lotus throne. It now contains a collection of 15th- to 17th-century Buddha statues. The room to the immediate right of the entrance was the King's reception room, also called the **Ambassadors' Room**. It contains French-made busts of the last three Lao monarchs, a model of the royal hearse (which is kept in Wat Xieng Thong)

Mekong River

Tourist Boats to Pak Ou

Souvanna Khampong

Sakkaline

Nam Khan

Nam Khan

To Pak Ou, Northern Bus Terminal & Xang Hai

To Airport, & Ban Hat Hien

Wat Tao Hai

➡ Luang Prabang maps
1 Luang Prabang, page 48
2 Luang Prabang detail, page 50

Bars & clubs 🍸
Dao Fao Nightclub **4** *D1*
Muang Swa **2** *C4*
Utopia **3** *C1*

and a mural by French artist Alex de Fontereau, depicting a day in the life of Luang Prabang in the 1930s.

In comparison to the state rooms, the royal family's **private apartments** are modestly decorated. They have been left virtually untouched since the day the family left for exile in Xam Neua Province. To the rear of the entrance hall, the **Coronation Room** was decorated between 1960 and 1970 for Crown Prince Sisavong Vatthana's coronation, an event which was interrupted because of the war. The walls are a brilliant red with Japanese glass mosaics embedded in a red lacquer base with gilded woodwork and depict scenes from Lao festivals.

To the left of the entrance hall is the reception room of the **King's Secretary**, and beyond it, the **Queen's reception room**, which together house an eccentric miscellany of state gifts from just about every country except the UK.

To the far right of the entrance to the palace is a room (viewed from the outside) in which sits the **Pra Bang**, or **Golden Buddha**, from which the city derived its name. The Buddha is in the attitude of Abhayamudra or 'dispelling fear'. Some believe that the original image is kept in a bank vault, though most dispel this as rumour. It is 90% solid gold. Reputed to have originally come from Ceylon, and said to date from any time between the first and ninth centuries, the statue was moved to Cambodia in the 11th century, given to King Phaya Sirichanta, and was then taken to Lane Xang by King Fa Ngum, who had spent some time in the courts of Angkor and married into Khmer royalty. An alternative story has the Pra Bang following Fa Ngum to the city: it is said he asked his father-in-law, the King of Angkor, to send a delegation of holy men to assist him in spreading the Theravada Buddhist faith in Lane Xang. The delegation arrived bringing with them the Pra Bang as a gift from the Cambodian King. The Pra Bang's arrival heralded the capital's change of name, from Xieng Thong to Nakhon Luang Prabang, 'The city of the great Buddha'. In 1563

② Luang Prabang detail

Where to stay 🛏
3 Nagas **14** *B3*
Ammata Guesthouse **20** *A3*
Apsara Rive Droite **15** *B4*
The Belle Rive **3** *A3*
Le Calao Inn **5** *A4*
Oui's Guesthouse **21** *B5*
Pa Phai **8** *A2*

Pack Luck **7** *A3*
Sala Luang Prabang **9** *A1*
Sayo Guesthouse **11** *A1*
Silichit Guesthouse **12** *A2*

Restaurants 🍴
Blue Lagoon **21** *A1*
Café Ban Vat Sene **1** *B2*

Coconut Garden **13** *B1*
Couleur Café **6** *A2*
Dao Fa **3** *B2*
Dyen Sabai **12** *B2*
Khemkhan Food
Garden **5** *B2*
L'Éléphant **7** *A3*
L'Étranger **8** *B1*

100 metres
100 yards

King Setthathirat took the statue to Lane Xang's new capital at Vientiane. Two centuries later in 1779 the Thais captured it but it was returned to Laos in 1839. The Pra Bang is revered in Laos as its arrival marked the beginnings of Buddhism in Lane Xang.

Wat Mai

ⓘ *Sisavangvong Rd, daily 0800-1700, 10,000 kip.*

Next to the Royal Palace is Wat Mai. This royal temple, inaugurated in 1788, has a five-tiered roof and is one of the jewels of Luang Prabang. It took more than 70 years to complete. It was the home of the Buddhist leader in Laos, Phra Sangkharath, until he moved to That Luang in Vientiane. During Pi Mai (New Year), the Pra Bang is taken from the Royal Palace and installed at Wat Mai for its annual ritual cleansing, before being returned to the palace on the third day.

The facade is particularly interesting: a large golden bas-relief tells the story of Phravet (one of the last reincarnations of the Gautama or historic Buddha), with several village scenes, including depictions of wild animals, women pounding rice and people at play. Inside, the interior is an exquisite amalgam of red and gold, with supporting pillars similar to those in Wat Xieng Thong.

Wat Sene (Wat Saen)

Further up the promontory, Wat Sene was built in 1718 and was the first sim in Luang Prabang to be constructed in Thai style, with a yellow and red roof. The exterior may lack subtlety, but the interior is delicate and rather refined, painted red, with gold patterning on every conceivable surface. Sen means 100,000 and the wat was built with a local donation of 100,000 kip from someone who discovered 'treasure' in the Khan River.

Wat Xieng Thong

ⓘ *Xiengthong Rd, daily 0800-1700, 20,000 kip.*

Wat Xieng Thong Ratsavoraviharn, usually known as just Wat Xieng Thong, is set back from the road, at the top of a flight of steps leading down to the Mekong. It is arguably the finest example of a Lao monastery, with graceful, low-sweeping eaves, beautiful stone mosaics and intricate carvings. The wat has several striking chapels, including one that houses a rare bronze reclining Buddha and another sheltering a gilded wooden funeral chariot. Inside, resplendent gold-stencilled pillars support a ceiling with *dharma* wheels. The striking buildings in the tranquil compound are decorated in gold and post-box red, with imposing tiled roofs and mosaics, making this the most important and finest royal wat in Luang Prabang. It was built by King Setthathirat in 1559, and is one of the few buildings to have survived the successive Chinese raids that marked the end of the 19th century.

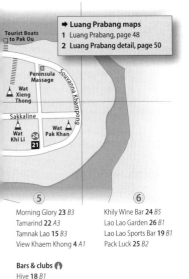

➡ **Luang Prabang maps**
1 Luang Prabang, page 48
2 Luang Prabang detail, page 50

The **sim** is a perfect example of the Luang Prabang style. Locals believe the roof has been styled to resemble a bird, with wings stretched out to protect her young. The eight central wooden pillars have stencilled motifs in gold and the facade is finely decorated. The beautiful gold-leaf inlay is predominantly floral in design but a few images illustrate *Ramayana*-type themes and the interior frescoes depict *dharma* wheels and the enigmatic King Chantaphanit. At the rear of the sim is a mosaic representation of the thong copper 'Tree of Life' in glass inlay.

Behind the sim are two red *haw song phra* (**side chapels**): the one on the left is referred to as **La Chapelle Rouge** (the Red Chapel) and houses a rare Lao reclining Buddha in bronze, dating from the 16th century. The exterior mosaics which relate local tales, were added in 1957 to honour the 2500th anniversary of the Buddha's birth, death and enlightenment. The other *haw song phra*, to the right of the sim, houses a standing image of the Buddha which is paraded through the streets of the city each New Year and doused in water.

The **Chapel of the Funeral Chariot** is diagonally across from the sim and was built in 1962. The centrepiece is the grand 12-m-high gilded wooden hearse, with its seven-headed serpent, which was built for King Sisavang Vong, father of the last sovereign, and used to carry his urn to the stadium next to Wat That Luang where he was cremated in 1959. It was built on the chassis of a six-wheel truck by the sculptor, Thid Tan. On top of the carriage sit several sandalwood urns, none of which contain royal ashes. Originally the urns would have held the bodies of the deceased in a foetal position until cremation. The mosaics inside the chapel were never finished but the exterior is decorated with some almost erotic scenes from the *Phalak Phalam* (the local version of the *Ramayana*), sculpted in enormous panels of teak wood and covered with gold leaf.

Wat Visunnarat (Wat Wisunarat) and That Makmo
① *Daily 0800-1700, 20,000 kip.*
This is better known as Wat Visoun and is on the south side of Mount Phousi. It is a replica of the original wooden building, constructed in 1513, which had been the oldest building in Luang Prabang, until it was destroyed by marauding Chinese tribes. The sim is virtually a museum of religious art, with numerous 'Calling to the Rain' Buddha statues: most are more than 400 years old and have been donated by locals. Wat Visoun also contains the largest Buddha in the city and old stelae engraved with Pali scriptures (called *hin chaleuk*). The big stupa, commonly known as That Makmo ('melon stupa'), was built by Queen Visounalat in 1504. It is of Sinhalese influence with a smaller stupa at each corner, representing the four elements.

Wat Phra Maha That
Close to the **Hotel Phousi** on Phothisarath, this is a typical Luang Prabang wat, built in the 1500s and restored at the beginning of this century. The ornamentation of the doors and windows of the sim merit attention, with their graceful, golden figures from the Phalak phalam (the *Ramayana*). The pillars, ornamented with massive nagas, are also in traditional Luang Prabang style and reminiscent of certain styles adopted in Thailand.

Wat Manolom
South of Wat That Luang, Wat Manolom was built by the nobles of Luang Prabang to entomb the ashes of King Samsenthai (1373-1416) and is notable for its large armless bronze Buddha statue, one of the oldest Lao images of the Buddha, which dates back to 1372 and weighs two tonnes. Locals maintain that the arm was removed during a skirmish

between Siamese and French forces during the latter part of the 19th century. While it is not artistically significant, the temple – or at least the site – is thought to be the oldest in the city, dating back, so it is said, to 1375 and the reign of Fa Ngum.

Wat Pa Phon Phao and Santi Chedi

ⓘ *3 km northeast of town, near Ban Phanom, daily 0800-1000, 1300-1630, donation expected.*
Outside town, Wat Pa Phon Phao is a forest meditation centre renowned for the teachings of its famous abbot, Ajahn Saisamut, one of the most popular monks in Lao history. More famous to tourists, though, is Santi Chedi, known as the Peace Pagoda. It looks as though it is made of pure gold from a distance but is rather disappointing close up. The wat was started in 1959 but was only completed in 1988; the names of donors are inscribed on pillars inside. It is modelled on the octagonal Shwedagon Pagoda in Yangon (Rangoon) and its inner walls are festooned with gaily painted frescoes of macabre allegories. Less grotesque paintings, extending right up to the fifth floor, document the life of the Buddha. On the second level, it is possible to duck through a tiny opening to admire the Blue Indra statues and the view of Luang Prabang.

Traditional Arts and Ethnology Centre

ⓘ *Ban Khamyong, T071-253364, www.taeclaos.org, Tue-Sun 0900-1800, 20,000 kip.*
A fantastic museum dedicated to the various ethnic groups in Laos. This non-profit centre has a permanent exhibition featuring fantastic photographs, religious artefacts, clothing, household objects and handicrafts. Within the exhibition there is a focus on the Hmong and their New Year celebrations; the Khmu and their baskets and art of backstrap looms; the Mien Yao embroidery and Lanten Taoist religious ceremonies, the Tai Dam bedding and Tai Lue culture. Truly this museum is a must-see in Luang Prabang – particularly for those that are venturing further north to go trekking. Attached to the centre is a handicraft shop that directly supports ethnic artisan communities. There's also a café and a small library.

Around Luang Prabang

Pak Ou caves

ⓘ *20,000 kip, free for children. Torches are available but candles make it possible to see reasonably well after your eyes have become accustomed to the dark. A boat trip from Luang Prabang is the best way to reach the caves. Rest houses, tables and a basic toilet are available.*
The Pak Ou Caves are perhaps the most popular excursion from Luang Prabang and are located 25 km upstream from the city, set in the side of a limestone cliff opposite the mouth of the Mekong's Nam Ou tributary (Pak Ou means 'Mouth of the Ou'). The two caves are studded with thousands of wooden and golden Buddha images – 2500 in the lower cave and 1500 in the upper – and are one of the main venues for Pi Mai in April, when hundreds make the pilgrimage upriver from Luang Prabang.

The two sacred caves were supposedly discovered by King Setthathirat in the 16th century but it is likely that the caverns were associated with spirit (*phi*) worship before the arrival of Buddhism in Laos. For years the caves, which locals still believe to be the home of guardian spirits, were inhabited by monks.

Kuang Si Falls

ⓘ *30 km south Luang Prabang, 20,000 kip, parking 2500 kip. There are public toilets and changing rooms. Travel agents run tours or you can charter a tuk-tuk for about US$15 return.*

Slow boats take 1 hr down and 2 hrs back upriver, via Ban Ou (a pretty little village), where it is necessary to take a tuk-tuk for the last 6 km or so to the falls.

These waterfalls are on a tributary of the Mekong. The trip to the falls is almost as scenic as the cascades themselves, passing through small Hmong and Khmu villages and vivid, green, terraced rice paddies. The falls are stunningly beautiful, misty cascades flowing over limestone formations, which eventually collect in several tiered, turquoise pools. Best of all, and despite appearances, it's still possible to take the left-hand path halfway up the falls and strike out through the pouring torrents and dripping caves to the heart of the waterfall. Note that swimming is only permitted in designated pools and, as the Lao swim fully clothed, you should wear modest swimwear and bring a sarong.

Hoy Khoua Waterfall (Tad Hoy Khoua)

ⓘ *14 km west of Luang Prabang in Ban Pakleung.*

Beautiful two-tiered cascades that plummet 50 m, with a deep pool at the bottom. There are several Hmong and Khmu villages in the vicinity. To get to the falls cross the Mekong by boat at Tha Heua (boat station) in Luang Prabang to Xiang Men Village and then travel the rest by road. There are three bungalows here at **Tad Hoy Khoua Guesthouse**, T020-5557 0825.

Luang Prabang and around listings

For hotel and restaurant price codes and other relevant information, see pages 8-9.

🍽 Where to stay

Luang Prabang *p46, maps p48 and p50*
Accommodation in Luang Prabang continues to expand at the rate of knots.
$$$$ 3 Nagas, http://3-nagas.com. Housed in a beautifully restored building, with an annexe across the road, this boutique hotel is a running contender for best room in town. Attention to detail is what sets this hotel apart: from the 4-poster bed covered with local fabrics, to the large deep-set bathtub with natural handmade beauty products. Private balconies or rooms leading onto a stunning courtyard. There's a lovely sitting area in each room, plus traditional *torchis* walls and teak floors. Breakfast (included) is served in the fantastic café downstairs. Internet facilities available for those travelling with laptop.
$$$$ Amantaka, Kingkitsarath Rd, T071-860333, www.amanresorts.com. For those on the ultimate splurge, slip into one of the Pool Villas (complete with private plunge pool) in this latest addition to the Aman Resort chain.

Minimalist decor and top-notch gym and spa now grace the old buildings of the French colonial hospital at the foot of Phousi hill. Try the Four Hands Massage for a supremely relaxing experience.
$$$$ The Belle Rive, Souvannakhamphong Rd, T071-260733, www.thebellerive.com. Elegant rooms occupy refurbished structures facing the Mekong on a quiet end of the peninsula. The hotel's restaurant garden patio offers fine views of boats drifting by.
The attraction of this hotel lies in its charm; you would almost expect to find Graham Greene or Noel Coward staying here.
$$$$ La Résidence Phou Vao, T071-212 5303, www.residencephouvao.com. Best hotel in town by a mile. Every little detail in this plush hotel is perfect, from the fragrance of frangipani that wafts through the foyer, to the carefully lit pool with lines of lamps. Massive, beautiful rooms with lounge area, fresh fruit and a simply divine bathroom. A luxury hotel through and through. In the low season they drop their rates by about US$200.
$$$$ Villa Maly, T071-253902, www.villa-maly.com. This is a gorgeous boutique hotel set around a pool with ivory umbrellas in

a leafy garden. The former royal residence has been lavished with attention: it's stylish and petite and the rooms are plush; the bathrooms, however, are small with serious practical flaws. Service is impeccable.

$$$$ Villa Santi Hotel, Sisavangvong Rd, T071-252157, www.villasantihotel.com. Almost an institution in Luang Prabang, this is a restored house from the early 20th century that served as the private residence of the first King Sisavangvong's wife and then Princess Manilai. It's a charming place, full of character and efficiently run and has just received a much-needed facelift. There are 6 heavenly suites in the old building, and 14 newer rooms, with baths and showers, in a stylishly built annexe. The daughter of the official royal cook rustles up mouthwatering French cuisine in the Princess Restaurant and there are attractive seating areas in the garden, lobby or on the balcony.

$$$$-$$$ Sala Luang Prabang, 102/6 Ounkham Rd, T071-252460, www.salalao. com. Very chic, renovated 100-year-old building several of which overlook the Mekong. Nice use of exposed beams and stone inlay in communal areas. Rooms have a minimalist, up-to-date edge with a/c, modern bathrooms, and doors either opening onto a small courtyard or river balcony (more expensive). Bus, car and bicycle hire available.

$$$$-$$$ Villa Maydou, set very close to the grounds of Wat Meun Na, T071-254601, www.villamaydou.com. Slightly on the expensive side but beautiful nonetheless. The hotel has a very evocative Buddhist feel due to its location right on the doorstep of Wat Meun Na. The French-owned hotel is set in restored government buildings, originally built in 1925. Spacious airy a/c rooms simply decorated in a modern style with bathtub and minibar.

$$$$-$$ The Apsara, Kingkitsarath, T071-254670, www.theapsara.com. Ivan Scholte, wine connoisseur and antique collector, has done a perfect job on this establishment. It oozes style. The stunningly beautiful rooms are themed by colour, with 4-poster beds, changing screen, big bathtub and lovely

balcony. Very romantic with a modern twist. The rooms in the 2nd building are equally magnificent and have large terrazzo showers you could fit an elephant in. The foyer and lovely restaurant (see Restaurants) are decorated with Vietnamese lanterns, Burmese offering boxes and modern art. Room rate includes breakfast. Get in early, this popular place gets booked up in advance.

$$$$-$$ The Apsara Rive Droite, Ban Phanluang, T071-254670, www.theapsara. com. The Apsara's 9-room cousin across the Khan River is accessible by boat from the other Apsara. Spacious, well-appointed rooms sport a unique French-Lao vibe and have balconies that have striking views of the city. This hotel also has the first salt-water pool in Luang Prabang, if not the country.

$$$ Ancient Luang Prabang, Sisavangvong Rd, T071-212264, www.ancientluangprabang. com. 12 fantastically designed open-plan rooms featuring a big modern bathtub (separate toilet). The perfect romantic retreat for couples but not the place to bunk down with your mother. Rooms facing the road can be a bit noisy as the night market carries on down below. These rooms represent good value though. Lovely wooden furnishings. Café downstairs with Wi-Fi and a good range of coffees including frappés.

$$$ Le Calao Inn, River Rd, T071-212100, www.calaoinn.laopdr.com. Enclosed by yellow walls, this Portuguese/French colonial (1902) building boasts beautiful rooms in an incomparable position overlooking the Mekong. The balcony view is a real plus, so ensure you ask for a room with water views.

$$$ Maison Souvannaphoum, Phothisarath, T071-212200, www.angsana.com. Formally Prince Souvannaphouma's residence, this place really is fit for royalty. There are 4 spacious suites and 23 rooms, with a/c, aromatherapy burners and special treats left in the rooms. The service is top-notch.

$$$ Pack Luck, T071-253373, www. packluck.com. This boutique hotel has 5 rooms that you couldn't swing a cat in but are tastefully decorated with beautiful fabrics and have bathrooms with deep slate bathtubs.

$$$-$$ Riverside Guesthouse, T071-212664, http://guesthouse-riverside.com. Small, attractive guesthouse in a quiet part of town. There are 5 rooms on the 1st floor (1 with a great balcony) but walls are thin and so the concrete ground floor rooms are a better option. The owner is really friendly and helpful. Wi-Fi available.

$$$-$$ Sayo Guesthouse, Sotikoumman Rd, http://sayoguesthouse.free.fr.com. A lovely hotel set in colonial mansion. The front rooms are beautifully and tastefully decorated with local fabrics and woodwork, polished wooden floors and furniture, and they boast a fantastic view over Wat Xieng Mouan – you can watch the monks carving, painting and woodworking. The back rooms aren't as good value but are still recommended. This hotel also has branches on the Mekong and near the post office.

$$ Ammata Guesthouse, T071-212175, phetmanyp@yahoo.com.au. Very popular guesthouse with largish rooms decorated simply and stylishly with wooden furniture and polished floorboards. Hot water and en suite bathroom.

$$ Oui's Guesthouse, at the end of the peninsula in Ban Khili on Sukkaserm, T071-252374, www.oui-guesthouse.com. Charming little guesthouse with sparkling new rooms with polished floorboards, hot water, TV and fridge. Nicely decorated with local artefacts. Fantastic wine bar next door.

$$-$ Silichit Guesthouse, just off Ounkham Rd, T071-212758. Despite the dubious sounding name, this clean guesthouse is excellent value and well located. Comfortable rooms with fan, en suite bathroom and hot water. The very friendly owners speak English and French, and often invite guests to sit down for a family dinner or have a Beer Lao. As with most budget places, prices drop dramatically in the low season.

$ Jaliya, Phamahapasaman Rd, T071-252154. The ever-popular Jaliya has a range of bungalow-type rooms on offer, with varied facilities, from shared bathrooms and fan through to a/c and TV, so take a look around. Relaxing garden area. Bicycle and motorbike rental.

$ Pa Phai, opposite Wat Pa Phai. This guesthouse is run by an elderly lady who speaks good English and French. It is a bit run down but classic Laos: an attractive little wooden place with a shady garden and a veranda on the 1st floor. 10 clean rooms (separated only by rattan walls – which don't leave much to the imagination), very clean bathrooms, bikes for rent and same day laundry service. Recommended.

$ Vanvisa Villa, T071-212925, www.vanvisa-guesthouse.com. Brightly coloured guesthouse down a quaint street. This is a little gem, with teak floors, large, characterful and immaculate rooms and friendly owners. The downstairs has beautiful handicrafts and antiques. It's a bit run down but has a homely feel.

Hotels out of Luang Prabang

$$$$ Shangri-Lao, Ban Xiem Lom, T071-252417, www.shangri-lao.com. A luxury tented camp where guests can play at explorer on 5 expedition tours (from half-day to 2-day). Learn to be a *mahout* (elephant keeper) and elephant trek through the jungles, some 15 km outside of Luang Prabang. There's also a conservation angle with some proceeds of the explorers' camp going to reforestation.

$$$$-$$$ Xiengthong Palace, Kounxoau Rd, T071-213200, www.xiengthongpalace.com. Next to Wat Xieng Thong this hotel, housed in restored buildings of the last royal residence in Laos, boasts a spa and all 26 rooms feature great in-room facilities such as Wi-Fi, iPod dock and artwork on the walls. The 2 suites have private plunge pools.

$$ Thongbay Guesthouse, Ban Vieng May, 3 km southeast of the centre of Luang Prabang, T071-253234, www.thongbay-guesthouses.com. Absolutely stunning set-up of modern bungalows overlooking the Nam Khan. 12 bungalows including

2 extra large family-sized ones. Beautiful tropical garden with a small pond as a centrepiece. The rooms overlooking the river are the best, affording fantastic views of the laid-back rural life. Bungalows have a fridge, 4-poster bed and hot water. Popular with tour groups so advanced booking is necessary. Recommended.

🍴 Restaurants

Luang Prabang *p46, maps p48 and p50*
Note that, as Luang Prabang has a curfew; most places won't stay open past 2200.

The most famous local delicacy is *khai pehn*, dried river weed, mainly from the Nam Khan, which is mixed with sesame, fried and eaten nationwide. *Cheo bong*, a spicy, smoky purée made with buffalo hide, is also popular throughout the country. Other delicacies include: *phak nam*, a watercress that grows around waterfalls and is commonly used in soups and salads; *mak kham kuan*, tamarind jam, and *mak nat kuan,* pineapple jam.

One of the best local culinary experiences is to grab some Lao takeaway food from the night market that runs off **Sisavangvong Rd**, 1600-2200. Here you can pick up fresh spring rolls (*nem dip*), papaya salad (*tam som*), sticky rice (*khao niao*), the local delicacy Luang Prabang sausage (*Sai Oua*), barbecue chicken on a stick (*gai*) or fish (*pa*), dried buffalo (*sin savanh*) and dried river weed. There are also a number of cheap buffets where you can get a selection of local curries and dishes. If you don't want your food too spicy ask for '*bo pet*'.

$$$-$$ L'Éléphant, Ban Vat Nong, T071-252482, www.elephant-restau.com. About as fine as dining gets in Luang Prabang. Very upmarket and utterly delectable cuisine. Pan-fried fillet of snapper, with capers and basil-flavoured mash is delicious, as are the simmered scallops. Also a number of Lao dishes. There are 3 set menus and an extensive wine list.

$$-$ The Apsara, see Where to stay. Beautifully decorated restaurant offering modern Lao/Thai/Western fusion cuisine. Try their delicious red curry cream soup with lentils and smoked duck or braised beef shin Chinese style. Great fish cakes. Good value.

$$-$ Blue Lagoon, beside the Royal Palace, www.blue-lagoon-cafe.com, T071-253698. This restaurant offers a great selection of delicious hearty European meals – especially Swiss-inspired meals such as the fondue chinoise. Great steaks, beef stroganoff, pasta and ice creams. Indoor and outdoor seating in comfortable candlelit garden setting.

$$-$ Coconut Garden, Sakkaline Rd, T071-252482, www.elephant-restau.com/coconutgarden. A hip spin-off of L'Elephant and centrally located on main street. Similar French and Lao menu but affordable prices. The chic bar and excellent service make this a place not to miss.

$$-$ Couleur Café/Restaurant, Ban Vat Nong, T020-5562 1064. The French expats in town have nothing but praise for this place with its French and Lao meals and ambient setting. Good wine. This is the place for the carnivores as it has become renowned for its steaks.

$$-$ Dyen Sabai, Ban Phan Luang, T020-5510 4817. In the dry season, this cosy, prettily lit spot is accessible via bamboo bridge (4000 kip 0800-1700, 1700-2330 free) across the Khan River (around mid-Nov to late May). From late May to mid-Nov the restaurant offers free paddle boat rides to and fro across the river. The original cocktails (happy hour 1200-1900) and Lao food are not to be missed. Amazing sunset views! This is a highly recommended spot.

$ Dao Fa, Sisavangvong Rd, T071-215651, www.daofa-bistro.com. Great selection of teas and coffees, fab ice creams and tasty home-made pasta. The latter is the real draw and is recommended. Brightly decorated space with pavement seating.

$ Morning Glory, Sakkaline Rd. 0800-1600. Small but cosy Thai restaurant decorated with the proprietor's photographs and paintings. Intimate open-style kitchen serving up fantastic home-style meals –

great juices, breakfasts and curries. Try the *Tom Kha Gai* and zesty juice.

$ Tamarind, facing Wat Nong, T020-7777 0484, www.tamarindlaos.com. Mon-Sat 1100-1800. Brilliant restaurant offering modern Lao cuisine; an utterly exceptional dining experience. Try the 5-bites (the Lao equivalent to tapas), the pumpkin soup is to die for and the tamarind juice is exceptional. Even better than their à la carte menu are the 'dining experiences' such as the traditional Lao Celebration meal *Pun Pa*, which includes succulent marinated fish and purple sticky rice dessert, or the Adventurous Lao Gourmet degustation menu, which comes with clear explanations of what each dish is. They also do **market tours** with in-depth explanations of Lao delicacies (advance booking is essential) and can organize picnics. You also can't go wrong drinking a chilli-watermelon granita, watching the colours of the temple take on a surreal glow at sunset. The owners Joy and Caroline have been receiving accolades from around the region.

$ Tamnak Lao, Sisavangvong Rd, opposite **Villa Santi**, T071-252525, www.tamnaklao. net. Brilliant restaurant, serving modern Lao cuisine, with a strong Thai influence. Very popular with tour groups. The freshest ingredients are used: try fish and coconut wrapped in banana leaf or pork-stuffed celery soup. Atmospheric surroundings, particularly upstairs, yet service can be a bit spotty. Best for dinner. They also run a book exchange which raises money for Lao children's health and education.

$ View Khaem Khong, Ounkham Rd, T071-212726. The most popular of the dining establishments along the river with consistently excellent food. Good for a beer at sunset. Tasty Luang Prabang sausage, curry spaghetti and *laap*.

Cafés and bakeries
Café Ban Vat Sene, Sakkaline Rd. Great French food, more of a restaurant than a café, upmarket, great for breakfast.

Joma, Sisavangvong Rd, T071-252292. Serves an utterly delicious array of comfort foods. If you're planning a trek or boat trip get yout picnic food here.

L'Étranger, Kingkitsarath Rd, T020-5547 17036. This is a great little bookshop-cum-café. Outstanding breakfasts. Books are rented here for 5000 kip per day. A movie is shown daily at 1900.

🎶 Bars and clubs

Luang Prabang *p46, maps p48 and p50*
Dao Fa nightclub on the way to the South Bus Station. Extremely popular with locals, plays Asian dance music.
Hive Bar, Kingkitsarath Rd, next to L'Étranger. Luang Prabang's most happening bar-club is good for a dance, though it has become quieter now that the competition around it has started to grow.
Icon Klub, Just off of Sisavangvong Rd near the Khan River. For bohemians, poets and lovers, this Hungarian-owned bar is perfect for an eclectic drink. Signature cocktails and a worldly clientele make for interesting evenings of conversation. Open from 1730 until the bar runs dry!
Khily Wine Bar, tucked away next door to **Oui's Guesthouse** at the end of the peninsula. A secret hotspot for locals. This intimate bar has high chairs and a long bar stocked with an extensive selection of *lao-lao* and wine. Great for a quiet drink.
L'Éléphant, **La Résidence Phou Vao** and **Apsara**, provide attractive settings for a drink. A sunset beer at the restaurants overlooking the river is divine. After everything closes between 2200 and 2300 most locals either head to Dao Fa or have a bowl of soup and a cold beverage on Phou Vao Rd at one of the many *pho* noodle shops.
Lao Lao Garden, Kingkitsarath Rd. A tiered landscaped terrace, with low lighting, that's become a favourite backpacker haunt with cheap, delicious cocktails. A bonfire keeps you cozy in the winter months. The Lao-style barbecue is the best in town.

Lao Lao Sports Bar, Kingkitsarath Rd, opposite **Hive Bar** (formerly known as **Khob Jai**). This bar fills up during football matches, televised on a big screen.

Muang Swa, Phouvao Rd. Local style nightclub decked out with low couches and alternates between Thai pop, Lao traditional music and occasional western oldies. Practice your Lamvong (circle dance) moves. Part 50s prom, part 70s disco. Highly recommended.

Pack Luck, Sisavangvong Rd. For a more upmarket drink, this cosy wine bar has a great selection of tipples and well-selected wines. This modern establishment is high on atmosphere, with comfy beanbags, modern art adorning its walls and candlelit tables.

Utopia, on the Khan River in Ban Aphay, www.utopialuangprabang.com. Landscaped gardens, a sand volleyball court and a long wooden deck overlook the Khan. Great for a drink at sunset, but there are better places in town for food.

Entertainment

Luang Prabang *p46, maps p48 and p50*
Cinema
The annual **Luang Prabang Film Festival** (http://luangprabanglao.com/) is held every Dec.

Theatre and dance
Traditional dance performances are held Mon, Wed and Sat at 1800, at the **Royal Palace**; US$6-15.

Festivals

Luang Prabang *p46, maps p48 and p50*
Apr Pi Mai (Lao New Year; movable) is the time when the tutelary spirits of the old year are replaced by those of the new. It has special significance in Luang Prabang, with certain traditions celebrated in the city that are no longer observed in Vientiane. It lasts 11 days.

May Vien Thiene (movable). Candlelit festival.

Sep Boat races. Boats are raced by the people living in the vicinity of each wat.

Oct Lai Heua Fai (Fireboat Festival). Each village creates a large boat made of bamboo and paper and decorated with candles and offerings. These are paraded down main street to Wat Xieng Thong where they are judged and sent down into the Mekong to bring atonement for sins. All of the temples and most houses are decorated with paper lanterns and candles. People also make their own small homemade floats, similar to Loy Krathong in Thailand, to release in the Mekong River.

Dec Luang Prabang Film Festival, www.lpfilmfest.org. The country's 1st and only major film festival, this new annual event held in early Dec showcases Southeast Asian cinema. The project also produces ongoing educational activities for young Lao relating to media literacy.

Shopping

Luang Prabang *p46, maps p48 and p50*
Caruso Gallery, Sisavangvong Rd (towards the **Three Nagas Boutique Hotel**) stunning but expensive wood furniture and artefacts.

Naga Creations, Sisavangvong Rd, T071-212775. A large collection of jewellery and trinkets, combining Lao silver with quality semi-precious stones. Both contemporary and classic pieces. Some truly innovative work by the jeweller **Fabrice**, including beautiful use of beetle wings (the same style that were once used to adorn royal clothing).

Ock Pop Tok, near L'Éléphant restaurant, T071-253219. **Ock Pop Tok**, which literally translates as 'East meets West', truly incorporates the best of both worlds in beautiful designs and fabrics. It specializes in naturally dyed silk, which is of a much better quality than synthetically dyed silk as it doesn't run. Clothes, household items, hangings and custom-made orders are also available (if ordered well in advance). Check out the **Fibre2Fabric** gallery next door to see the stories behind the fabulous creations.

Patthana Boupha Antique Gallery, Ban Visoun, T071-212262. This little gem can be found in a partitioned-off area in a fantastic colonial building. Antique silverware and jewellery, Buddhas, old photos and fine textiles. Less common are furniture and household items. Reasonable prices. Often closed, so ring beforehand.
Satri Lao Silk, Sisavangvong Rd, T071-219295. Truly beautiful silks and handicrafts for sale. Can sometimes be slightly over-priced, but definitely worth a look.

Markets
Night market, sprawls down several blocks off Sisavangvong Rd (this market has been moving around the last few years but is expected to return to Sisavangvong Rd). Daily 1700-2230. Hundreds of villagers flock to the market to sell their handicrafts, ranging from silk scarves through to embroidered quilt covers and paper albums. The market shouldn't be missed.
Phousy market, 1.5 km from the centre of town. This market is a real gem: aside from the usual fruit and vegetables, it is a fantastic place to pick up quality silk garments. Pre-made silk clothes are sold here for a fraction of the price of the shops in town. Make sure that you are very detailed with instructions and ensure the same colour thread is used.
Talat Dala, housed in a market building in the middle of town on the corner of Setthathirat and Chao Sisophon roads, has been recently revamped to become a major market for artisans and jewellers to sell their wares.

Silver
There are several Lao silversmiths around the Nam Phou area (fountain), where you can watch the artisans ply their trade. **Thit Peng**, signposted almost opposite Wat That, is a workshop and small shop.

What to do

Luang Prabang *p46, maps p48 and p50*
Cookery classes
There are a number of classes offered in Luang Prabang. The cooking classes are ordered in preference below.
Tamarind, www.tamarindlaos.com, facing Wat Nong, T020-7777 0484. This successful restaurant has been running specialized classes for groups in their enchanting jungle garden school outside of town. Recommended.
Tamnak Lao, T071-252525, www.tamnaklao. net. US$305 per person for 1-day cooking class, including shopping at the markets.
Tum Tum Cheng, Sakkaline Rd, T071-253187, tumtumcheng@yahoo.com. Mon-Sat. Popular cooking classes operating since 2001. 1 day, US$25; 2 days, US$45; 3 days, US$60. Advanced bookings are required.

Elephants tours and activities
Elephant Village, 15 km from Luang Prabang (visits and activities can be organized through their office on Sisavangvong Rd, www.elephantvillage-laos.com, T071-252417).This was originally established in conjunction with **Tiger Trails** in Luang Prabang. They have bought old elephants that were chained up in Hongsa as they were no longer useful for hauling timber. In order to keep the old elephants active, the operators run a number of activities. Tourists can participate in up to 25 activities at the elephant park, including experiencing life as a *mahout* (elephant keeper), washing the elephants or trekking with them. There are a few other similar elephant park projects but these are pale imitations.

Exhibitions and galleries
Fibre2Fabric, 71 Ban Vat Nong (next door to **Ock Pop Tok**), T071-254761, www.fibre2fabric.org. A fantastic gallery exhibiting textiles and a display on the culture surrounding the textiles of different

ethnic groups. Exhibition with photography, weaving and explanations of local ethnic customs and cultures associated with textile production. Local weavers often on hand to explain.

Kinnaly Gallery, Sakkaline Rd, T020-5555 7737. Gallery featuring black and white photographic work.

Kop Noi, Ban Aphay, www.kopnoi.com. This little shop has a rotating exhibition. They also exhibit photographs from renowned Lao photographer Sam Sisombat.

Spa and massage

Aroma Spa, Sisavangvong Rd, T020-77611255. Another mid-priced spa offering aromatherapy, facials, body scrubs, etc.

Khmu Spa, Sisavangvong Rd, T071-212092. A range of cheaply priced massages including the Khmu massage (gentler, lighter strokes), Lao massage (stretching, cracking and pressure points) and foot massage. Also has herbal sauna. Open until 2200.

Maison Souvannaphoum (see Where to stay). A spa with a range of luxurious and expensive treatments. For sheer indulgence.

Red Cross Sauna, opposite Wat Visunnarat, reservations T071-212303. Daily 0900-2100 (1700-2100 for sauna). Massage 30,000 kip per hr, traditional Lao herbal sauna 10,000 kip. Bring your own towel or sarong. Profits go to the Lao Red Cross.

The Spa at La Residence Phou Vao, www.residencephouvao.com, T071-212530. Offers 3-hr massage course0 for 2 people. This includes a 1-hr massage for each person, the class, a handbook and oils.

Spa Garden, Ban Phonheauang, T071-212325, www.spagardenlpb.com. More upmarket. Offers a wide selection of massage and beauty treatments including aromatherapy massage, sports body massage, facial treatments and skin detox. The best value for money in luxury massages, pedicure, manicure all set in a relaxing building with oil burners, wind

chimes and dolphin-esque sounds playing in the background.

Tour operators
Asia Pacific Travel, 88/07 Ban Phonpheng Rd, T071-224473, www.laosvoyage.com. Good operator running tours throughout the region.

All Laos Service, Sisavangvong Rd, T071-253522, www.alllaoservice.com. Large successful travel agency organizing ticketing and travel services.

Buffalo Tours, 8/40 Ban Nongkham, T071-254395, www.buffalotours.com. New player on the block in Laos organizes tours that delve into local culture in conjunction with tours around Southeast Asia. Very helpful, knowledgable and very efficient.

Green Discovery, T071-212093, www.green discoverylaos.com. Rafting and kayaking trips on grade 1 and 2 rapids. Cycling trips around Luang Prabang. Homestays, trips to Pak Ou caves, etc.

Luxury Travel, 03 Ban Viengxay-Kithsarath Rd, T071-260567, www.luxurytravelvietnam. com. Asian specialist in luxury private guided and fully bespoke holidays in Vietnam, Laos, Cambodia, Myanmar and Thailand.

Tiger Trail, T071-252655, www.laos-adventures.com. Adventure specialists: elephant treks, trekking, rafting, mountain biking tours, rock climbing, etc.

Weaving
Weaving Centre, 2 km out of town on the river (bookings at **Ban Vat Nong Gallery**, T071-253219, www.ockpoptok.com/index. php/weaving-centom). The team behind the fabulous creations at Ock Pop Tok have opened a weaving centre. Half-day dyeing classes introduce students to the world of silk dyes (US$45). A variety of 1- to 3-day weaving classes are also offered. Classes are run by professional weavers and their English-speaking assistants. A small café is also open, serving amazing renditions of Lao favorites as well as some original signatures, such as Silkworm Poo Tea.

⊖ Transport

Luang Prabang *p46, maps p48 and p50*
Air
Luang Prabang International Airport (LPQ) about 4 km from town, T071-212172/3.
Lao Airlines, Phamahapasaman Rd, T071-212172, has daily connections with **Vientiane**, 40 mins, **Houei Xai**, **Pakse** and **Phonsavanh**, and a service to **Chiang Mai**, **Siem Reap**, **Udon Thani** and **Hanoi**. It also runs daily flights to **Bangkok**. These flights are notoriously prone to change so check schedule well in advance. Bangkok Airways runs daily flights to **Bangkok**.

Early morning departures are often delayed during the rainy and cool seasons, as dense cloud can make the airport inoperable until about 1100. Airline tickets are more often than not substantially cheaper from travel agents (see Tour operators, above) than from the actual airline. Confirm bookings a day in advance and arrive at the airport early, as flights have been known to depart as soon as they're full.

Bicycle
Bikes can be rented for about US$1 per day from most guesthouses.

Boat
Tha Heua Mea Pier is the most popular departure point and has a blackboard listing all the destinations and prices available (daily 0730-1130 and 1300-1600). Prices are largely dependent on the price of gasoline. There is also a dock at **Ban Don** (15 mins north of town by tuk-tuk, US$1-2).
To Houei Xai/Pak Beng The 2-day boat trip down the Mekong between Houei Xai and Pak Beng has become a rite of passage for travellers in Southeast Asia. There are a range of boat options to suit the flashpacker to the backpacker.

The **slow boat** to Houei Xai, leaves from the boat pier on Khem Khong Rd called the Tha Heua Mea pier, 2 days, with a break in Pak Beng after 6-7 hrs on the 1st day. It is

US$25 for each leg of the trip and almost all travel agents sell tickets. It's often packed to the brim so wear something comfortable and bring some padding to sit on. Seats are usually basic wooden benches though you may luck out with one that has bus seats. The trip from Luang Prabang to Houei Xai (via Pak Beng overnight) is usually less busy than in the other direction. (If the boat to Pak Beng is full, you can charter your own for about US$400-500.) Tickets for the onward trip to Houei Xai, can be purchased in Pak Beng. Take a good book and a grab some goodies from one of the bakeries to take on board. Most boats will have a vendor selling basic drinks. The boat usually leaves between 0800 and 0900 (changeable so check) but it is necessary to get there early to secure yourself a good seat.

The most luxurious way to make the trip is on the **Luangsay Cruise**, office on Sisavangvong Rd, T071-252 553, www.luangsay.com, which makes the trip in 2 days and 1 night, stopping over at Pak Ou Caves en route and staying overnight at their luxurious lodge in Pak Beng. The boat is extra comfortable and has lounges and a well-stocked bar and small library. Food and drinks are more than ample. Very popular in high season and will need to be booked 6 months in advance. Departure days from Houei Xai and Luang Prabang, and frequencies vary between high and low season (prices from US$305) for the 2-day trip.

Speedboats (which are not recommended) depart from Ban Don to **Houei Xai** (on the Thai border; see page 67), US$30, around 6 hrs, with a short break in **Pak Beng**. Tickets are available from most travel agents. The boats are horribly noisy and dangerous (numerous fatalities have been reported from boats jack-knifing when hitting waves). Ear plugs are recommended and ensure boatmen provide a helmet and life jacket.

A few boats travel up the Nam Ou to **Nong Khiaw**. However, these are infrequent, especially when the river is low. The journey usually takes 6 hrs to Nong Khiaw, 150,000 kip. The Nam Ou joins the Mekong near the Pak Ou Caves, so it is possible to combine a journey with a visit to the caves en route. The irregular travel dates to Nong Khiaw are posted on a board outside the boat pier or ask one of the travel agents on Sisavangvong Rd when the next departure is. It is possible to charter a boat for 1-6 people for US$200. Speedboats to Nong Khiaw sometimes leave from Ban Don, expect to pay 200,000 kip. These boats are hazardous, uncomfortable and not environmentally friendly.

Bus/truck

The northern bus terminal is for north-bound traffic and the southern for traffic to/from the south. Always double-check which terminal your bus is using, as unscheduled changes are possible.

From the northern terminal To **Luang Namtha**, daily 0900 and 1730, 10 hrs, usually via Udomxai, 80,000 kip. The roads are reasonable and paved but quite hilly. The 1730 bus has usually come from Vientiane and is often full. An alternative is to break the journey by catching the bus to **Udomxai**, 0900 and 1130 daily, 5 hrs, 50,000 kip, and then continuing on to Luang Namtha in the afternoon. There are also daily departures (usually in the morning) to **Houei Xai** on the Thai/Lao border, 110,000 kip, 11-12 hrs. A VIP bus to Houei Xai passes through daily, 1000, 10 hrs, 155,000 kip. There is a very long bus journey to **Xam Neua**, 1630, they say it takes 14 hrs but it can be up to 20 hrs, 120,000 kip. **Phongsali**, 1600, 13-15 hrs 110,000 kip. To Nong Khiaw, by *songthaew*, regular departures usually in the morning 35,000 kip.

From the southern terminal There are up to 8 daily buses to **Vientiane**, although scheduled departures tend to decline in the low season, 10-11 hrs, 950,000 kip; most of these services stop in **Vang Vieng**, 6 hrs, 80,000 kip. VIP buses to Vientiane depart 0800 and 0900, 9 hrs,

115,000 kip; both these services stop in Vang Vieng, 115,000 kip.

To **Phonsavanh**, daily 0830, 8-9 hrs, 75,000 kip. It should cost 10,000-15,000 kip to get to the centre of town from the station.

Minibus

Minibuses with driver are available from several hotels and the tour companies, US$50 per day around Luang Prabang, US$60 per day if travelling further afield. Check out the notice boards for services to **Vang Vieng**, 5 hrs, and **Vientiane**, 7 hrs; quicker than the bus, but more expensive. If you have a big group you can organize independent minivan rental.

Saamlor and tuk-tuk

Lots around town which can be hired to see the sights or to go to nearby villages. A short stint across town should cost about 10,000 kip per person, but expect to pay 20,000 kip for anything more than 1 km. Most of the nearby excursions will cost US$5-10.

● Directory

Luang Prabang *p46, maps p48 and p50*
Banks There's now a healthy scattering of ATMs around Luang Prabang. **Lao Development Bank**, 65 Sisavangvong Rd, Mon-Sat 0830-1200, 1330-1530, will change US$/Thai TCs into kip, but doesn't accept credit cards. **Banque pour le Commerce Exterieur Lao** (BCEL), Sisavangvong Rd, Mon-Sat 0830-1200, 1330-1530; all transactions in kip, will exchange Thai baht, US$, AU$, UK£, Euros and TCs, also offers cash advances on Visa cards. They also have an ATM. Many of the jewellery stalls in the old market, plus restaurant and tourist shop owners, will change US$ and Thai baht. Many of the travel agencies will do credit card advances if you get stuck after hours without money but charge a whopping 6-8% commission. **Internet** There are a concentration of places on Sisavangvong Rd. Wi-Fi is now available in a good number of hotels, guesthouses and cafés. Non-guests can access Wi-Fi for a fee in certain areas; in other places, it's free. **Medical services** The main hospital, is about 3 km outside of town, T071-252049, and is only useful for minor ailments. For anything major you're better off getting a flight to Bangkok. There are a few reasonably well-equipped pharmacies towards Villa Santi on Sisavangvong Rd. **Post and telephone** The post and telephone office is on the corner of Chau Fa Ngum and Setthathirat, Mon-Fri 0830-1730, Sat 0830-1200, express mail service, international telephone facilities. Hotels and some guesthouses allow international calls from reception (about US$5 a min). It is dramatically cheaper to make international calls from one of the internet cafés, which usually have Skype.

Far north

The misty, mountain scenery of the far north conjures up classic Indochina imagery of striking rice terraces, golden, thatched huts and dense, tropical forests, all dissected by a cross-hatching of waterways. Here, life is beautifully interwoven with the ebb and flow of the rivers. The mighty Mekong forges its way through picturesque towns, such as Pak Beng and Houei Xai, affording visitors a wonderful glimpse of riverine life, while, to the east, the Nam Ou attracts visitors to Nong Khiaw and, the latest traveller hot spot, Muang Ngoi Neua. The wonderful upland areas are home to around 40 different ethnic groups, including the Akha, Hmong, Khmu and Yao, and it's not surprising that the country's best trekking is also found here.

Luang Namtha and around → For listings, see pages 71-78.

This area has firmly established itself as a major player in Laos' ecotourism industry, primarily due to the **Nam Ha Ecotourism Project**, which was established in 1993 by NTA Lao and UNESCO to help preserve Luang Namtha's cultural and environmental heritage in the Nam Ha National Protected Area. The Nam Ha NPA is one of the largest protected areas in Laos and consists of mountainous areas dissected by several rivers. It is home to at least 38 species of large mammal, including the black-cheeked crested gibbon, tiger and clouded leopard, and over 300 bird species, including the stunning Blythe's kingfisher.

Udomxai
Heading northwest from Luang Prabang, travellers will reach Udomxai, the capital of Udomxai Province. It's a hot and dusty town that is used as a pit-stop and a brothel stop but the local tourist board, with the help of a German NGO are keen to promote the area's other attractions. However, the town does make a decent stop-off point at a convenient junction; it's one of the biggest settlements in northern Laos and has excellent facilities. One only has to look around at the presence of Chinese flags on shop fronts to get an inkling of the large presence of Chinese workers and businesses in town.

Luang Namtha
Luang Namtha Province has witnessed the rise and decline of various Tai Kingdoms and now more than 35 ethnic groups reside in the province, making it the most ethnically diverse in the country. Principal minorities include Tai Lu, Tai Dam, Lanten, Hmong and Khmu. The provincial capital was obliterated during the war and the concrete structures erected since 1975 have little charm but there are a number of friendly villages in the area. As with all other minority areas it is advisable to visit villages with a local guide or endorsed tourism organization.

The **Luang Namtha Museum** ① *near the Kaystone Monument, Mon-Fri 0800-1130, 1300-1600, 10,000 kip,* houses a collection of indigenous clothing and artefacts, agricultural tools, weapons, textiles and a collection of Buddha images, drums and gongs.

In the centre of town is a **night market** with a range of food stalls. It is only in its infancy but the local authorities have aspirations to expand the market to include ethnic handicrafts, making it similar to the one in Luang Prabang.

Surrounding villages

Ban Nam Chang is a Lanten village, 3 km along a footpath outside town; **Ban Lak Khamay** is quite a large Akha village 27 km from Luang Namtha on the road to Muang Sing. The settlement features a traditional Akha entrance; if you pass through this entrance you must visit a house in the village, or you are considered an enemy. Otherwise you can simply pass to one side of the gate but don't touch it. Other features of interest in Akha villages are the swing, located at the highest point in the village and used in the annual swing festival (you must not touch the swing), and the meeting house, where unmarried couples go to court and where newly married couples live until they have their own house. **Ban Nam Dee** is a small bamboo papermaking Lanten village about 6 km northeast of town. The name of the village means 'good water' and not surprisingly, if you continue on 1 km from Ban Nam Dee there's a waterfall. The trip to the village is stunning, passing through verdant rice paddies dotted with huts. A motorbike rather than a bicycle will be necessary to navigate these villages and sights, as the road can be very rocky. Villagers usually charge 5000 kip for access to the waterfall.

The small Tai Lue village of **Ban Khone Kam** is also worth a visit. The villagers offer **homestays** here (30,000 kip per night, includes meals), for one or two nights.

Ban Vieng Nua is a Tai Kolom village, 3 km from the centre of town, famous for its traditional house where groups can experience local dancing and a good luck *baci* ceremony (150,000 kip per person). Contact the tourist information office to make a booking. Dinner can also be organized here at a cost of 42,000 kip per head.

Nam Ha National Protected Area

Both Luang Namtha and Vieng Phouka are great bases from which to venture into the Nam Ha National Protected Area, one of a few remaining places on earth where the rare black-cheeked gibbon can be found. If you're lucky you can hear the wonderful singing of the gibbons in the morning. See also the Gibbon Experience, page 67. The 222,400-sq-km conservation area encompasses more than 30 ethnic groups and 37 threatened mammal species. Organizations currently lead two- and three-day treks in the area for small groups of four to eight culturally sensitive travellers. Treks leave three to four times a week; check with the **Luang Namtha Guide Service Unit** or Vieng Phouka Eco Guide Service or **Green Discovery** (see Tour operators, page 74) for departure days; an information session about the trek is given at the Guide's Office. The price will cover the cost of food, water, transportation, guides, lodging and the trekking permit. All the treks utilize local guides who have been trained to help generate income for their villages. Income for conservation purposes is also garnered from the fees for trekking permits into the area. ▶▶ *See What to do, page 74.*

Muang Sing and around

Many visitors consider this peaceful valley to be one of the highlights of the north. The only way to get to Muang Sing is by bus or pickup from Luang Namtha. The road is asphalt and the terrain on this route is mountainous with dense forest. Muang Sing itself is situated on an upland plateau among misty, blue-green peaks. The town features some interesting old wooden and brick buildings and, unlike nearby Luang Namtha and several other towns in the north, it wasn't bombed close to oblivion during the struggle for Laos. Numerous hill peoples come to the market to trade, including Akha and Hmong tribespeople, along with Yunnanese, Tai Dam and Tai Lu. The **Muang Sing Tourism Office** ① *T086-400015, www. luangnamtha-tourism.org*, offers treks.

Muang Sing Ethnic Museum ① *in the centre of town, daily 0800-1200 and 1300-1600, 5000 kip*, is a beautiful building housing a range of traditional tools, ethnic clothes, jewellery, instruments, religious artefacts and household items. The building was once the royal residence of the Cao Fa (Prince), Phaya Sekong.

The population of the district is said to have trebled between 1992 and 1996, due to the resettlement of many minorities, either from refugee camps in Thailand or from highland areas of Laos and, as a result, it is one of the better places in northern Laos to visit ethnic villages. The town is predominantly Tai Lu but the district is 50% Akha, with a further 10% Tai Nua. The main activity for visitors is to hire bicycles and visit the villages that surround the town; several guesthouses have maps of the surrounding area and trekking is becoming increasingly popular. However, do not undertake treks independently as it undermines the government's attempts to make tourism sustainable and minimize the impact on local villages. ▶▶ *See What to do, page 74.*

From Muang Sing, trek uphill past **Stupa Mountain Lodge** for 7 km up an 886-m hill to reach **That Xieng Tung**, the most sacred site in the area. The stupa was built in 1256 and is believed to contain Buddha's Adam's apple. It attracts lots of pilgrims in November for the annual full moon festival. There is a small pond near the stupa, which is also believed to be very auspicious: if it dries up it is considered very bad luck for Muang Sing. It is said that the pond once dried up and the whole village had no rice and starved.

Along the Mekong → *For listings, see pages 71-78.*

The slow boat along the Mekong between Houei Xai and Luang Prabang is a favourite option for visitors travelling to and from the Thai border. It's a charming trip through lovely scenery.

Houei Xai

Located southwest of Luang Namtha on the banks of the Mekong, Houei Xai is a popular crossing point to and from Thailand. Few people spend more than one night in the town. Boats run between here and Luang Prabang, two days' journey downstream, via Pak Beng. Most passengers arrive close to the centre at the passenger ferry pier. The vehicle ferry pier is 750 m further north (upstream). Although the petite, picturesque town is growing rapidly as links with Thailand intensify, it is still small and easy enough to get around on foot.

Most visitors who do stick around in Houei Xai do so to visit the **Gibbon Experience** ① *T084-212021, www.gibbonexperience.org, from US$180-290 (price includes tree house accommodation, transport, food, access to Bokeo Nature Reserve and well-trained guides)*. This is a thrilling, exciting and unmissable three-day trip into Bokeo Nature Reserve, where a number of tree houses have been built high up in the jungle canopy and linked by interconnected zip-lines. Staying in the trees and waking to the sound of singing gibbons is a truly awe-inspiring experience, as is zip-lining high above the jungle canopy, through the mist. In the morning well-trained guides take visitors hiking to see if they can spot the elusive gibbons as well as other plant and animal species. Others to look out for are the giant squirrel, one of the largest rodents in the world, and the Asiatic black bear, whose numbers are in decline as they are hunted for their bile and gall bladders. First and foremost this is a very well-run conservation project. The Gibbon Experience was started to help reduce poaching, logging, slash-and-burn farming and the destruction of primary forest by working with villagers to transform the local economy by making a non-destructive living from their unique environment. Already the project has started to pay dividends: the forest conservation and canopy visits generate as much income year on year as the local logging comany could do only once.

Pak Beng

This long thin strip of a village is perched halfway up a hill, with fine views over the Mekong. Its importance lies in its location at the confluence of the Mekong and the Nam Beng. There is not much to do here but it's the obligatory place to stop en route between Houei Xai and Luang Prabang (or vice versa). The village is worth a visit for its traditional atmosphere and the friendliness of the locals, including various minorities. There are also a couple of monasteries in town. The locals are now organizing guided treks to nearby villages; check with the guesthouses.

Northeast of Luang Prabang → *For listings, see pages 71-78.*

In recent years the settlements of Nong Khiaw and Muang Ngoi Neua in the north of Luang Prabang Province have become firm favourites with the backpacker set. In fact, idyllic Muang Ngoi Neua is often heralded as the new Vang Vieng, surrounded by stunning scenery and the fantastic ebb of life on the river. It is far more pleasant to travel between Luang Prabang and Nong Khiaw/Ban Saphoun, just south of Muang Ngoi Neua, by long boat, than by bus. The Nam Ou passes mountains, teak plantations, dry rice fields and a movable waterwheel mounted on a boat, which moves from village to village and is used for milling. But with the improvements that have been made to Route 13, road travel has now become the preferred option for many – partly because it is cheaper, and partly because it is quicker. Route 13 north runs parallel with the river for most of the journey to Nam Bak. There are trekking and activities around Nong Khiaw and Muang Ngoi Neua.

Nong Khiaw and Ban Saphoun

Nong Khiaw lies 22 km northeast of Nam Bak and is a delightful, remote little village on the banks of the Nam Ou, surrounded by limestone peaks and flanked by mountains, the largest aptly named Princess Mountain. It is one of Laos' prettiest destinations. There are, in fact, two settlements here: Ban Saphoun on the east bank of the Nam Ou and Nong Khiaw on the west. Of the two, Ban Saphoun offers the best views and has the best riverside accommodation. Confusingly, the combined village is sometimes called one name, sometimes the other and sometimes Muang Ngoi, which is actually another town to the north (see below) and the name of the district.

One reason why the area has become a popular stopping place for travellers is because of its pivotal position on the Nam Ou, affording river travel from Luang Prabang to the north. It is also on the route between Udomxai and Xam Neau, which is one of the most spectacular in Laos, passing through remote villages. Despite its convenience as a staging post, this village is a destination in its own right. It is a beautiful spot, the sort of place where time stands still, journals are written, books read and stress is a deeply foreign concept. It is possible to swim in the river (women should wear sarongs) or walk around the town or up the cliffs. If you go to the boat landing it is also possible to organize a fishing trip with

Phongsali

High up in the mountains at an altitude of about 1628 m, this northern provincial capital provides beautiful views and an invigorating climate. It is especially stunning from January to March, when wildflowers bloom in the surrounding hills. The town can be cold at any time of the year, so take some warm clothes. Mornings tend to be foggy and it can also be very wet. There is an end of an earth feel in the areas surrounding the main centre, with dense pristine jungle surrounded by mountains.

Phongsali was one of the first areas to be liberated by the Pathet Lao in the late 1940s. The old post office (just in front of the new one), is the sole physical reminder of French rule. The town's architecture is a strange mix of Chinese post-revolutionary concrete blocks, Lao wood-and-brick houses, with tin roofs, and bamboo or mud huts, with straw roofs. The town itself is home to about 20,000 people, mostly Lao, Phou Noi and Chinese, while the wider district is a mixture of ethnicities, with around 28 minorities inhabiting the area.

It is not possible to hire bikes, tuk-tuks or even ponies here so walking is the only way to explore the fantastic landscapes of this region. Many paths lead out of town over the hills; the walking is easy and the panoramas are spectacular. Climb the 413 steps to the top of Mount Phoufa for humbling views of the surrounding hills. The **Provincial Tourism Office**, on the way to Phou Fa Hotel (now simply a restaurant), T088-210098, (http://phongsali.net) Monday-Friday 0730-1130, 1330-1630, can arrange guided ecotreks, including village homestays, for up to five nights. The rates depend on the number of people. Some people trek north from Phongsali to **Uthai**, staying in Akha villages en route. Uthai is probably as remote and unspoilt as it gets.

Where to stay Viphahone Hotel, next to the post office, T088-210111. A three-storey building with restaurant and 24 very clean, large and airy twin and double rooms, with hot-water bathrooms, some with Western flush toilets.

Sensaly Guesthouse, up the hill and around the bend from the market, T088-210165. Worn but comfortable rooms, with squat toilets and scoop showers.

Restaurants Yu Houa Guesthouse, across the road from the market. Has a short Lao and Chinese section on an English menu; cheap and good. The Phongsaly Hotel is also a good bet and has a larger variety of dishes, including a few Thai, Chinese and Lao.

Transport You can travel from Muang Khua to Phongsali either by truck or by boat. Trucks also depart from Pak Nam Noi (near Muang Khua); buy lunch from the market before departure. The ride is long and difficult when the pickup is full, but it's a great experience and the scenery near Phongsali is utterly breathtaking. Alternatively, catch a boat from Muang Khua to Hat Xa, 20 km or so to the northeast of Phongsali, five to six hours, 100,000 kip. In the low season there may not be any scheduled boats so it might be necessary to gather a few extra tourists and charter a boat, US$80-100. Depending on the season, the river is quite shallow in places, with a fair amount of white water. It can be cold and wet so wear waterproofs and take a blanket. Note that you may find yourself stuck in Hat Xa, as there are no onward buses to Phongsali after mid-afternoon. Alternative routes to Phongsali are by bus to/from Udomxai, nine to 10 hours, 60,000 kip. From Phongsali to Hat Xa buses leave in the morning from a bus station 500 m from the centre on the road to Hat Xa.

one of the local fishermen for very little money. You might need someone to translate for you. The bridge across the Nam Ou offers fine views and photo opportunities. There are caves in the area and the Than Mok waterfall.

Tham Pha Thok cave ① *2.5 km southeast of the bridge, 10,000 kip*, was a Pathet Lao regional base during the civil war. It was divided into sections – the hospital section, a police section and a military section. Old remnants exist like campfires and ruined beds but other than that there is little evidence of it being the PT headquarters until you see the bomb crater at the front. To get there you walk through beautiful rice paddies. There is a second cave about 300 m further down on the left, **Tham Pha Kwong**, which was the Pathet Lao's former banking cave. The cave is a tight squeeze and is easier to access with help from a local guide. It splits into two caves, one of which was the financial office and the other the accountant's office. A further 2 km along the road, at Ban Nokien is the **Than Mok** waterfall, also accessible by boat.

Muang Ngoi Neua

The town of Muang Ngoi Neua lies 40 km (one hour) north of Nong Khiaw, along the Nam Ou. This small town surrounded by ethnic villages has become very popular with backpackers over the last few years. The town is a small slice of utopia, set on a peninsula at the foot of Mount Phaboom, shaded by coconut trees, with the languid river breeze wafting through the town's small paths. Most commonly known as Muang Ngoi, the settlement has had to embellish its name to distinguish it from Nong Khiaw, which is also often referred to as Muang Ngoi (see above). It's the perfect place to go for a trek to surrounding villages, or bask the day away swinging in your hammock. A market is held every 10 days and villagers come to sell produce and handicrafts. There are also caves and waterfalls in the area.

Muang Khua

Muang Khua is nestled into the banks of the Nam Ou, close to the mouth of the Nam Phak, in the south of Phongsali Province. Hardly a destination in itself, it's usually just a stopover between Nong Khiaw and Phongsali and the first town of significance for those crossing in from Vietnam from Dien Bien Phu, a relatively new border crossing. It only has electricity from 1900 to 2200 nightly. The Akha, Khmu and Tai Dam are the main hilltribes in the area. The nearest villages are 20 km out of town and you will need a guide if you want to visit them (tourist office, T020-2284 8020). Trekking around Muang Khua is fantastic and still a very authentic experience, as this region remains largely unexplored by backpackers (see What to do, page 74). The friendly villages are very welcoming to foreigners, as they don't see as many here as in somewhere like Muang Sing. For these reasons, it is very important to tread lightly and adopt the most culturally sensitive principles: don't hand out sweets and always ask before taking a photograph. Treks usually run for one to three days and involve a homestay at a villager's house (usually the Village Chief).

Far north listings

For hotel and restaurant price codes and other relevant information, see pages 8-9.

⊖ Where to stay

Udomxai *p65*

$ Litthavixay Guesthouse, about 100 m before the turning onto the airport road, T081-212175, litthavixay@yahoo.com. This place has some of the best rooms in town, large single, double and triple rooms and all very clean. Rooms with lots of facilities. Hot-water shower attached; bathrooms on the small side. Opt for the nicer upstairs rooms. Fan rooms are cheaper. Best-value internet (Wi-Fi available) in town. The restaurant has a small but good selection of foreign breakfast dishes. Car hire possible.

$ Villa Keoseumsack, 2 doors down from the Siinphet restaurant, T081-312170, seumsack@hotmail.com. Not quite a villa but this is definitely the classiest place to stay in town and extremely good value with 17 rooms with polished floors, large comfy double beds, desks, wardrobes and spacious hot-water showers. Fan rooms are cheaper.

Luang Namtha *p65*

$$$-$$ Boat Landing Guesthouse & Restaurant, T086-312398, www.theboat landing.com. Further out of town than most, this place is right on the river. Time stands still here. It's an eco-resort that's got everything just right: pristine surroundings, environmentally friendly rooms, helpful service and a brilliant restaurant serving traditional northern Lao cuisine.

$ Manychan Guesthouse, on main road in centre opposite the smaller bus station, T086-312209, ath.phongsavanh@yahoo. com. One of the most popular places, probably due to the location and restaurant. Decent, clean rooms with fan and hot-water bathrooms. The staff are very friendly.

$ Thoulasith Guesthouse, T086-212166, thoulasithguesthouse@gmail.com. The

newbie in town set off the main road in a compound with a garden, tables and chairs. Rooms come with TV, desk, hot-water bathrooms (3 rooms have bathtubs) and free Wi-Fi. Friendly management. Restaurant too.

$ Zuela Guesthouse, T020-5588 6694. Fantastic value guesthouse in a beautiful, modern, wooden building with immaculate fan rooms. Extremely comfortable beds, en suite hot-water bathrooms and linen provided. This family-run guesthouse is truly a league apart from other budget options in town. Restaurant attached. Highly recommended.

Muang Sing *p66*

$ Phou lu Bungalows, at the southern end of town, T030-5511 0326, www.muang-sing. com. This is the best accommodation in town by a long way. There are great spacious double ground-floor bungalows with 4-poster beds, small balconies with bamboo seats, set around a grassy compound with restaurant and massage service.

$ Taileu Guesthouse, on the main road, T030-511 0354. Above the restaurant, 8 very basic rattan rooms with bamboo-style, 4-poster beds (the rickety backpacker version not the romantic type), squat toilets and temperamental hot water via solar power. The owners are lovely, lovely people.

Houei Xai *p67*

$ BAP Guesthouse, on the main Sekhong Rd, T084-211083, bapbiz@live.com. One of the oldest guesthouses in town consisting of a labyrinth of additions and add-ons as their business has grown over the years. A range of rooms, though the newer tiled ones with hot-water bathrooms are the best. Rooms with TV are more expensive; rooms with shared bath are cheaper. The female proprietor here is hard as nails but has loads of charisma and a wily sense of humour. She's also super helpful.

$ Taveensinh Guesthouse, northwest end of the town, T084-211502. The best value in town with fan, TV hot-water bathrooms; a/c costs more. Great communal balconies overlooking the river and friendly family in charge.

Pak Beng *p68*
During peak season, when the slow boat arrives from Luang Prabang, about 60 people descend on Pak Beng at the same time. As the town doesn't have an endless supply of great budget guesthouses, it is advisable to get someone you trust to mind your bags, while you make a mad dash to get the best room in town.
$$$$-$$$ Pakbeng Lodge, T081-212304, www.pakbenglodge.com. A wooden and concrete construction, built in Lao style, this stunning guesthouse sits perched on a hillside above the Mekong and includes 20 rooms with fan, toilet and hot water. Good restaurant and wonderful views. Breakfast is included. Wi-Fi available. Elephant activities arranged.
$ Salika, T081-212306. This is an elegant structure on the steep cliff overlooking the river. 15 big, clean rooms with toilet and shower en suite (mostly cold), tiled floors. There is a great restaurant, serving reasonably priced meals (see Restaurants). Fantastic service.

Nong Khiaw and Ban Saphoun *p68*
$$-$ Nong Kiau Riverside, turn-off left just over the bridge in Ban Saphoun, T020-5570 5000, www.nongkiau.com. Stunning bungalows and restaurant. Beautifully decorated rooms with 4-poster beds, mosquito nets and hot-water bathrooms. For those looking for something upmarket this exquisite place fits the bill perfectly. The restaurant has a great selection of wines and access to the internet. Book in advance as it is a favourite with tour groups. Recommended.
$ CT Guesthouse (formerly Phanoy Guesthouse), just past the bridge, Ban Saphoun, T071-253919. Guesthouse has 7 basic but clean and comfortable thatched bungalows with mosquito nets and squat

toilets. Inside bathroom. Fantastic verandas overlooking the river. Very nice family-owned business with a great atmosphere.
$ Sunset Guesthouse, down a lane about 100 m past the bridge, Ban Saphoun, T071-810033, sunsetgh2@hotmail.com. Slap bang on the bank of the river – you couldn't ask for a more picturesque setting from which to watch the sunset. The charming, sprawling bamboo structure looks out onto tables and sun umbrellas liberally arranged over the various levels of decking that serve as a popular restaurant in the evenings. 13 wood and brick bungalows with decent bathrooms with Western toilet and hot water shower outside. The twins are more attractive than the doubles; breakfast included. Internet access.

Muang Ngoi Neua *p70*
The accommodation in town is dirt cheap and of the same standard: bungalows with extremely welcoming hammocks on their balconies. Most offer a laundry service for around 10,000 kip per kg and all have electricity 1800-2200. Theft has become a bit of a problem in Muang Ngoi Neua. Secure all windows and doors and do not leave any valuables in your room. Bring earplugs for the wat gong at 0500 and the cockerels from 0400.
$ Lattanavongsa Guesthouse 2, T030-514 0770. Close to the river, these 4 bungalows are fenced in around a small garden, cluster bomb and picnic table and are just beyond the main Lattanvongsa restaurant near the dock. Decent-sized bathrooms.
$ Ning Ning Guesthouse, T030-514 0863, behind the boat landing with a restaurant with a great ringside view for sunset. Double and twin bungalows, with separate Western toilet and hot shower; the smarter rooms have large comfy double beds and super-white linens and mosquito nets; breakfast included. The food in the adjoining restaurant is great and the owner speaks good English. A popular spot.

$ Phet Davanh Guesthouse, T020-2214 8777, on the main road, near the boat landing. Concrete guesthouse, with 7 double and twin rooms. Comfy mattresses on the floor; 3 shared Western toilets and shower. There's a well-positioned balcony on the 2nd floor complete with hammocks.

Muang Khua p70
$ Nam Ou Guesthouse & Restaurant, follow the signs at the top of the hill, T081-210844. Looking out across the river where the boats land, this guesthouse is the pick of the ultra-budget bunch in Muang Khua. Singles, twins and doubles, some with hot-water en suites, and 3 newer rooms with river views. Good food (see Restaurants, below). A popular spot. Go for an upstairs room.
$ Sernnali Hotel, in the middle of town, near the top of the hill, T021-414214. By far the most luxurious lodging in town. 18 rooms with large double and twin beds, hot-water scoop showers and Western-style toilets, immaculately clean. Balconies overlook the Nam Ou. Chinese, Vietnamese and Lao food served in the restaurant.

❷ Restaurants

Udomxai p65
$ Litthavixay Guesthouse (see Where to stay.) Can whip up some good dishes, including Western-style pancakes and breakfasts.
$ Sinphet Restaurant, opposite Linda Guesthouse. One of the best options in town. English menu, delicious iced coffee with ovaltine, great Chinese and Lao food. Try the curry chicken, *kua-mii* or yellow noodles with chicken.

Luang Namtha p65
The night market, though small, offers an interesting array of local cuisine.
$$-$ Boat Landing Guesthouse & Restaurant (see Where to stay, page 71), T086-312398. The best place to eat in town, with innovative cuisine. Serves a range

of northern Lao dishes made from local produce, thereby supporting nearby villages. Highly recommended.
$ Banana Restaurant, main road, T020-5558 1888. This restaurant is gaining favour with the locals and tourists for its good fruit shakes and Lao food. Also serves a few Western dishes.
$ Coffee House, off the main road around the corner from **Green Discovery**, T030-525 7842. This fantastic little Thai restaurant with a range of delicious meals all under 12,000 kip. The meals are served on brown rice imported from Thailand and include Massaman curry, Tom Yum soup and a variety of other Thai staples. Fantastic coffees. Mr Nithat, the owner's husband, is good for a chat. Recommended.
$ Yamuna Restaurant, on the main road, T020-5557 1579. Delicious Indian restaurant with vegetarian, non-vegetarian and halal dishes. Extensive, predominantly south Indian menu.

Muang Sing p66
$ Muang Sing View Restaurant. A bamboo walkway leads to this rustic restaurant which enjoys the best views in Muang Sing overlooking the paddy fields and the valley. All the usual Lao staples are served.
$ Sengdeuane Guesthouse & Restaurant. Korean barbecue only (*sindat*). Popular with the locals.
$ Taileu Guesthouse & Restaurant (see Where to stay), T081-212375. The most popular place to eat due to its indigenous Tai Leu menu. Tasty meals, including baked aubergine with pork, soy mash and fish soup. One of the few places in the country where you can sample northern cuisine. Try their local piña colada with *lao-lao*, their *sa lo* (Muang Sing's answer to a hamburger) or one of the famous *jeow* (chilli jam) dishes. The banana flower soup is fantastic. Stand-out option in town and an eating experience you won't find elsewhere in Laos. Noi, the owner, is very friendly. Highly recommended.

Houei Xai p67
$ Bar How? A cute little place with fresh spring rolls, soups, sarnies, and other Western and Lao offerings. There's a warm atmosphere with paper lanterns and wooden tables. Breakfasts are a little expensive.

$ Khemkhong Restaurant, across from the immigration stand. Good option for those who want a drink after the cross-border journey. Lao and Thai food.

$ Nutpop, on the main road, T084-211037. The fluorescent lights and garish beer signs don't give a good impression. However, this is a pleasant little garden restaurant, set in an atmospheric lamp-lit building, with good Lao food including fried mushrooms and curry. The fish here is excellent.

$ Riverview Garden Restaurant. Its streetside view and tables have become a firm favourite with the backpacker set. There's a mixed menu of sandwiches, pizzas, stir fries, barbecue and noodles. It's conveniently next to the **Gibbon Experience** office.

Pak Beng p68
There are dozens of restaurants lining the main road towards the river; all seem to have the same English menu, basic Lao dishes, eggs and freshly made sandwiches.

$ Kopchaideu Restaurant, overlooking the Mekong. This restaurant has a large selection of Indian dishes with a few Lao favourites thrown in. Great shakes and fantastic service.

Nong Khiaw and Ban Saphoun p68
Most of the guesthouses have cafés attached. For some fine dining the restaurant at the **Riverside** is absolutely fantastic, with an extensive wine menu. For those on a budget the **CT Guesthouse** does reasonably good food. Ask for dishes to be served with *jeow*, which is delicious.

Muang Ngoi Neua p70
$$-$ Sainamgoi Restaurant & Bar, centre of town. Tasty Lao food in a pleasant atmosphere, with good background music. The bar, the only one in town, is in the next room.

$ Nang Phone Keo Restaurant, on the main road. All the usual Lao food, plus some extras. Try the 'Falang Roll' for breakfast (a combination of peanut butter, sticky rice and vegetables).

$ Sengdala Restaurant & Bakery, on the main road. Very good, cheap Lao food, terrific pancakes and freshly baked baguettes.

Muang Khua p70
The **Nam Ou Guesthouse & Restaurant** (see Where to stay) is up the mud slope from the beach. An incomparable location for a morning coffee overlooking the river; it has an English menu and friendly staff.

⏣ What to do

Luang Namtha and around p65
Tour operators
Green Discovery, T086-211484, www.greendiscoverylaos.com. Offers 1- to 7-day kayaking/rafting, cycling and trekking excursions into the Nam Ha NPA.
Luang Namtha Provincial Tourism Office and Eco Guide Unit, T086-211534, www.luangnamtha-tourism.org. Information on treks to Nam Ha NPA.
Vieng Phouka Eco Guide Service Unit, T084-212400, mpvpk@laotel.com.

Muang Sing p66
Trekking
This activity has become a delicate issue around Muang Sing as uncontrolled tourism was beginning to have a detrimental effect on some of the surrounding minority villages. Some sensible procedures and protocols have been put in place to ensure low impact tourism which still benefits the villages concerned.
Exotissimo, www.exotissimo.com (T086-400016, akhaexp@gmail.com in Muang Sing). In cahoots with **GTZ**, a German aid agency, have launched more expensive but enjoyable treks such as the **Akha Experience**, which include tasty meals prepared by local Akha people. Closed on weekends.

Muang Sing Tourism Office, T086-213021, www.luangnamtha-tourism.org. Mon-Fri 0800-1130 and 1330-1700, Sat-Sun 0800-1000 and 1500-1700. Offers 1-, 2- and 3-day treks from 300,000 kip per person (minimum 2 people). Most treks have received glowing reports from tourists, particularly the *Laosee Trek*.

Nong Khiaw *p68*
Check out www.nongkiauclimbing.com in association with **Green Discovery**. **Lao Youth Travel**, www.laoyouthtravel.com, at the boat landing offer trekking, fishing, tubing, boat trips and kayaking. **Tiger Trails**, www.laos-adventure.com. Runs trips to the 100 waterfalls and organizes trekking.

Muang Ngoi Neua *p70*
Trekking, hiking, fishing, kayaking, trips to the waterfalls and boat trips can be organized through most of the guesthouses. **Lao Youth Travel**, T030-514 0046, www.laoyouthtravel.com. Daily 0730-2000. Half-day, day, overnight or 2-night treks. Also kayaking trips.

Muang Khua *p70*
Mr Boun Ma, T020-606 5501. Mr Boun Ma works at the local school and runs treks into the valleys. He speaks reasonable English and takes guests to villages and areas relatively unexplored by tourists.

⊖ Transport

Udomxai *p65*
Air
There are flights to **Vientiane**, 3 times a week. **Lao Airlines** has an office at the airport, T081-312047.

Bus/truck/songthaew
Udomxai is the epicentre of northern travel. If arriving into Udomxai to catch a connecting bus, it's better to leave earlier in the day as transport tends to peter out in the afternoon.

The bus station is 1 km east of the town centre. Departures east to **Nong Khiaw**, 3 hrs, trucks are fairly frequent, most departing in the morning. If you get stuck on the way to Nong Khiaw it is possible to stay overnight in **Pak Mong** where there are numerous rustic guesthouses. The bus to **Nong Khiaw** leaves at 0900. **Pak Mong**, 1400 and 1600, 2 hrs, 22,000 kip. To **Luang Prabang**, 0800, 1100 and 1400, 5 hrs direct, 48,000 kip. Direct bus to **Vientiane**, 1530 and 1800, 15 hrs, 100,000 kip. Vientiane VIP bus, 1600 and 1800, 121,000 kip (also runs via **Luang Prabang**). **Xam Neua**, Tue-Sat 1230, 100,000 kip. **Luang Namtha**, 0800, 1130 and 1500, 4 hrs, 32,000 kip. **Boten** (the Chinese border), 0800, 28,000 kip. It is possible for some nationalities to obtain Chinese visas at the border, check eligibility in advance (at the time of publication UK citizens could, but US citizens could not).

There are services north on Route 4 to **Phongsali**, 0800, 9 hrs, 60,000 kip; this trip is long so bring something soft to sit on and try to get a seat with a view.

There are plenty of *songthaew*s waiting to make smaller trips to destinations like **Pak Mong** and **Nong Khiaw**, if you miss one of the earlier buses it is worth bargaining with the drivers, as if they can get enough money or passengers they will make the extra trip.

Luang Namtha *p65*
Air
The airport is 6 km south of town There are flights 3 times a week to **Vientiane**. **Lao Airlines**, T086-212072, has an office south of town on the main road.

Bicycle/motorbike
Bicycles for hire from Namtha Vehicle Rental Service, next door to the **Manychan Guesthouse**, T086-312172 for 8000-20,000 kip a day. Motorbikes for hire for US$30-50 a day from **Zuela guesthouse**.

Boat

Slow boats are the best and most scenic option but their reliability will depend on the tide and in the dry season (Jan-May) they often won't run. There isn't really a regular boat service from Luang Namtha, so you will have to either charter a whole boat and split the cost or hitch a ride on a boat making the trip already. If you organize a boat it should cost around 1,900,000 kip to **Houei Xai**. It is cheaper to go from Luang Namtha to Houei Xai than vice versa. The **Boat Landing Guesthouse** is a good source of information; if arrangements are made for you, a courtesy tip is appreciated.

Bus/truck/songthaew

The main inter-provincial bus station and its ticket office have moved to 10 km south of town. A new intra-provincial bus station is close to the **Panda Restaurant**, on the main road.

To **Udomxai**, 0830, 1200, 1430, 100 km, 4 hrs, 32,000 kip, additional services will leave in the early afternoon if there is demand, otherwise jump on a bus to Luang Prabang.

To **Houei Xai**, 0900 and 1330, 55,000 kip, 4 hrs. Take this service for Vieng Phouka. To **Luang Prabang**, 0930 daily, 8 hrs, 65,000 kip. To **Vientiane**, 0830, 1430, 21 hrs, 140,000 kip. To get to **Nong Khiaw**, you need to go via Udomxai (leave early).

From the intra-provincial (unsigned) bus station: to **Muang Sing**, 3 daily, 1½ hrs, 20,000 kip, additional pickups may depart throughout the rest of the day, depending on demand.

Muang Sing p66
Bicycle

Available for rent from **Tiger Man** trekking agency on the main road.

Bus/truck

The bus station is across from the new morning market, 500 m from the main road. To **Luang Namtha**, by bus or pickup, 0800, 0930, 1100, 1300, 1400, 1500, 2 hrs,

20,000 kip. To charter a *songthaew* or tuk-tuk to Luang Namtha costs at least 250,000 kip.

Houei Xai p67

Lao National Tourism State Bokeo, on the main street up from immigration, T084-211162, can give advice on the sale of boat, bus, pickup and other tickets. Numerous travel agencies congregate around the immigration centre offering bus and boat ticket sales. See below for information on boat travel between Houei Xai and Luang Prabang.

Air

Houei Xai airport is located 2 km south of town and has flights to **Vientiane**, 3 times a week.

Boat

The **BAP Guesthouse** in Houei Xai is a good place to find out about boat services.

The 2-day trip to Luang Prabang has become part of the Southeast Asian rite of passage. The slow boat to **Pak Beng** is raved about by many travellers. However, in peak season the boat can be packed extremely uncomfortable. Bring something soft to sit on, a good book and a packed lunch. The boat leaves from a jetty 1.5 km north of town, daily 1100, 6-7 hrs, around 250,000 kip for the 2-day trip (usually you buy the ongoing ticket at Pak Beng). If you can get enough people together it is possible to charter a boat, 1,765,000 kip although ask for advice at the tourist office as they quote much cheaper. The trip, done in reverse, usually has fewer passengers.

For those looking for a luxury option there is the **Luangsay Cruise**, T084-212092, www. luangsay.com, which undertakes a 2-day/ 1-night cruise down the river in extreme comfort with cushioned deckchairs, a bar and games on board. Guests stay at the beautiful **Luangsay Lodge** in Pak Beng.

Speedboats are a noisy, nerve-wracking, dangerous alternative to the slow boats; they leave from the jetty south of town, to **Pak Beng**, 0900, 3 hrs, 180,000 kip and to

Luang Prabang, 360,000-400,000kip. There have been reports of unscrupulous boatmen claiming there are no slow boats in the dry season to encourage travellers to take their fast boats. This is usually untrue. To **Luang Namtha** by longtail boat, 1,750,000 kip, max 5 people, 2 days.

Bus/truck/songthaew
The bus station is located at the Morning Market, 3 km out of central Houei Xai, a tuk-tuk to the centre costs 10,000 kip. Trucks, buses and minivans run to **Vieng Phouka**, daily 0830, 1230, 5 hrs, 35,000 kip; to **Luang Namtha**, daily 0830, 1230, 1700, 170 km, 7 hrs, 55,000 kip (there are also more regular minivans to Luang Namtha); to **Udomxai**, daily 0900, 1200, 1700, 12 hrs, 120,000 kip; to **Luang Prabang**, 0900, 1200, 1700, 12 hrs, 120,000 kip; to **Vientiane**, daily 1130, 20 hrs, 200,000 kip.

Pak Beng *p68*
Boat
The times and prices for boats are always changing so check beforehand. The slow boat to **Houei Xai** leaves 0900 from the port and takes all day, 110,000 kip. The slow boat to **Luang Prabang** leaves around the same time. Get in early to get a good seat. Speedboats to Luang Prabang (2-3 hrs) and Houei Xai leave in the morning, when full.

Bus/truck/songthaew
Buses and *songthaews* leave about 2 km from town in the morning for the route to **Udomxai**, 6-7 hrs, 40,000 kip. Direct *songthaews* to **Udomxai** are few, so an alternative is to take one to **Muang Houn** to catch the more frequent service from there.

Nong Khiaw and Ban Saphoun *p68*
Boat
Boat services have become irregular following road improvements, although you may find a service to **Muang Noi Neua**, 1 hr, 20,000 kip, from the boat landing. Likewise, boats to Luang Prabang only run if there are

enough people, so you might find yourself waiting a couple of days. 100,000 kip per person, minimum 10 people or charter the whole boat, 7-8 hrs. Some vessels also head upriver to **Muang Khua**, 5 hrs, 100,000 kip per person, minimum 10 people. The river trips from Nong Khiaw are spectacular.

Bus/truck
Buses en route from surrounding destinations stop in Nong Khiaw briefly. As they usually arrive from Vientiane or Luang Prabang, the timetables are unreliable. Basic timetables are offered but buses can be early or late, so check details on the day. It is often a matter of waiting at the bus station and catching the bus on its way. Waiting in a restaurant on the main road usually suffices but you will need to flag down the bus. To **Luang Prabang**, 0830 and 1100, 3-4 hrs, by *songthaew* at 0900 and 1100, 35,000 kip; minibus at 1300, 50,000 kip. Also several departures daily to **Nam Bak**, 30 mins, 10,000 kip and on to **Udomxai** 1100, 4 hrs, 40,000 kip. Alternatively, there are more regular *songthaews* to **Pak Mong**, 1 hr, 20,000 kip, where there is a small noodle shop-cum-bus station on the west side of the bridge, and from there travel on to Udomxai/Vientiane.

Travelling east on Route 1, there are buses to **Vieng Kham**, 0900, 2 hrs, 25,000kip, and a village 10 km from **Nam Nouan**, where you can change and head south on Route 6 to **Phonsavanh** and the **Plain of Jars**. There are direct buses north to **Xam Neua** and the village near Nam Nouan, which can be caught from the toll gate on the Ban Saphoun side of the river when it comes through from Vientiane at around 2000-2200, 100,000 kip; it's usually quite crowded. If you miss a bus to/from Nong Khiaw you can always head to **Pak Mong** which is a junction town sitting at the crossroads to Luang Prabang, Nong Khiaw and Udomxai. Aim to get here earlier in the day to catch through traffic otherwise you may have to stay overnight. (If you do, try the **Pak Mong Guesthouse Restaurant**, T020-5579 5860, or any of the other places in town.)

Muang Ngoi Neua p70
Boat

From the landing at the northern end of town, slow boats travel north along the beautiful river tract to **Muang Khua**, 5 hrs, per person, minimum 10 people. Slow boats also go south (irregularly) to **Nong Khiaw**, 1 hr, 25,0000 kip per person (minimum 10 people), and **Luang Prabang**, 8 hrs, US$100 per boat. Departure times vary and whether they depart at all depends on demand. For more information and tickets, consult the booth at the landing.

Muang Khua p70
Boat

Road travel is now more popular but irregular boats still travel south to **Muang Ngoi Neua/Nong Khiaw**, 3 hrs to Muang Ngoi Neua, 100,000 kip. Also north to **Phongsali** via Hat Xa, 100,000 kip. Boats can be charted to Phongsali 4-6 hrs, 90,000-100,000 kip per person, minimum 10 people at 0900 and 1000. A truck transports travellers on from Hat Xa to Phongsali, 20 km, 2 hrs along a very bad road, 10,000 kip at 1000 and 1430. Alternatively, charter what other limited transport is available.

Songthaew/truck

To get to **Phongsali**, take a *songthaew* to **Pak Nam Noi**, 0800, 1 hr, 10,000 kip, then the *songthaew* or bus that passes through from Udomxai at around 1000, 50,000 kip.

To **Udomxai**, buses leave 0800, 1200 and 1530 from the bus station alongside the market, 3 hrs, 30,000 kip and **Luang Prabang**, 8 hrs, US$7.

Buses also now travel to **Sop Hun** for the border crossing to Vietnam at Tay Trang.

● Directory

Udomxai p65
Banks Lao Development Bank, Udomxai, just off the road on the way to Phongsali, changes US$, Thai ฿ and Chinese ¥. The BCEL Bank, on the main road,

offers the same services. ATM available. **Internet** Litthavixay Guesthouse.

Luang Namtha p65
Banks Mon-Fri only. Lao Development Bank, changes US$ and Thai ฿, also TCs but charges a sizeable commission. The BCEL changes US$ and Thai ฿ and does cash advances on Visa. ATM available. **Internet** KNT Computers. **Telephone** Lao Telecom.

Muang Sing p66
Banks The small Lao Development Bank opposite the market will exchange Thai ฿, US$ and Chinese ¥. **Internet** Muang Sing Tourism Office, offers internet.

Houei Xai p67
Banks Mon-Fri only. BCEL, and has an ATM. **Immigration** At the boat terminal, daily 0800-1800, a small overtime fee is charged Sat and Sun and after 1600. Quite possibly the most friendly immigration post in the country. **Internet** There is internet opposite Sabaydee hotel.

Pak Beng p68
Bank There is no bank in Pak Beng, but most of the guesthouses and restaurants will exchange Thai ฿ and US$ cash at a hefty commission. **Internet** Available at the ferry office.

Nong Khiaw and Ban Saphoun p68
Internet Sunset Guesthouse and Riverside Guesthouse.

Muang Khua p70
Bank Lao Development Bank, near the truck stop, Mon-Fri 0800-1130, 1300-1630, changes US$, Thai ฿ and Chinese ¥ at bad rates. Won't change TCs or do cash advances, so make sure you have plenty of cash before you come here. **Electricity** 1830-2200. **Telephone** International calls from the Telecom office, a small hut with a huge satellite, halfway up the road, behind the bank.

Plain of Jars, Vieng Xai and the northeast

Apart from the historic Plain of Jars, Xieng Khouang Province is best known for the pounding it took during the war. Many of the sights are battered monuments to the plateau's violent recent history. Given the cost of the return trip and the fact that the jars themselves aren't that spectacular, some consider the destination oversold. However, further east, and near border crossings with Vietnam, are the Vieng Xai caves, the Pathet Lao subterranean headquarters during the Secret War. For those interested in modern history, it's the most fascinating area of Laos and helps one to gain an insight into the resilient nature of the Lao people. The countryside, particularly towards the Vietnam frontier, is beautiful – among the country's best – and the jars, too, are interesting by dint of their very oddness: as if a band of carousing giants had been suddenly interrupted, casting the jars across the plain in their hurry to leave. The cave history is fascinating and brought to life by brand new audio tours.

Background

Xieng Khouang Province has had a murky, blood-tinted, war-ravaged history. The area was the most bombed province in the most bombed country, per capita, in the world as it became a very important strategic zone that both the US and Vietnamese wanted to retain control of. The town of Phonsavanh has long been an important transit point between China to the north, Vietnam to the east and Thailand to the south and this status made the town a target for neighbouring countries. What's more, the plateau of the Plain of Jars is one of the flatter areas in northern Laos, rendering it a natural battleground for the numerous conflicts that ensued from the 19th century to 1975. While the enigmatic Plain of Jars is here, this region will also hold immense appeal for those interested in the modern history of the country.

Once the French departed from Laos, massive conflicts were waged in 1945 and 1946 between the Free Lao Movement and the Viet Minh. The Pathet Lao and Viet Minh joined forces and, by 1964, had a number of bases dotted around the Plain of Jars. From then on, chaos ensued, as Xieng Khouang got caught in the middle of the war between the Royalist-American and Pathet Lao-Vietnamese. The extensive US bombing of this area was to ensure it did not fall under the Communist control of the Pathet Laos. The Vietnamese were trying to ensure that the US did not gain control of the area from which they could launch attacks on North Vietnam.

During the 'Secret War' (1964-1974) against the North Vietnamese Army and the Pathet Lao, tens of thousands of cluster bomb units (CBUs) were dumped by the US military on Xieng Khouang Province. Other bombs, such as the anti-personnel plastic 'pineapple' bomblets were also used but by and large cluster bombs compromised the majority dropped. The CBU was a carrier bomb, which held 670 sub-munitions the size of a lemon. As the CBU was dropped each of these smaller bombs was released. Even though they were the size of a tennis ball, they contained 300 metal ball-bearings that were propelled hundreds of metres. As 30% of the original bombs did not explode, these cluster bombs continue to kill and maim today. The Plain of Jars was also hit by B-52s returning from abortive bombing runs to Hanoi, who jettisoned their bomb loads before heading back to the US air base at Udon Thani in northeast Thailand. Suffice it to say that, with over 580,944 sorties flown (1½ times the number flown in Vietnam), whole towns were obliterated and the area's geography was permanently altered. Today, as the Lao Airlines plane begins its descent towards the plateau, the meaning of the term 'carpet bombing' becomes clear. On the final approach to the town of Phonsavanh, the plane banks low over the cratered paddy fields, affording a T-28 fighter-bomber pilot's view of his target, which in places has been pummelled into little more than a moonscape. Some of the craters are 15 m across and 7 m deep. Testament to the Lao people's resilience, symbolically, many of these craters have been turned into tranquil fish ponds; the bombs transformed into fences and the CBU carriers serving as planter pots. Because the war was 'secret', there are few records of what was dropped and where and, even when the unexploded ordnance (UXO) have been uncovered, their workings are often a mystery – the Americans used Laos as a testing ground for new ordnance so blueprints are unavailable. The UK-based **Mines Advisory Group (MAG) UXO Visitor Information Centre** ① *on the main road in the centre of town, Mon-Fri 0800-2000, Sat and Sun 1600-2000,* is currently engaged in clearing the land of UXO. They have an exhibition of bombs, photographs and information on the bombing campaign and ongoing plight of Laos with UXO. Usually there are staff on hand to explain exactly how the bombs were used. All T-shirts sold here help fund the UXO clearance of the area and are a very worthwhile souvenir.

Xieng Khouang remains one of the poorest provinces in an already wretchedly poor country. The whole province has a population of only around 250,000, a mix of different ethnic groups, predominantly Hmong, Lao and a handful of Khmu.

Trekking and biking opportunities have opened up in the area with the help of a German NGO. Contact the **Xieng Khouang Provincial Tourism Department** ① *2 km from the town centre, T061-312217, xkgtourism@yahoo.com*, for the Xieng Khouang Discovery Guide or local tour operators.

Plain of Jars and Phonsavanh → *For listings, see pages 84-86.*

The undulating plateau of the Plain of Jars (also known as Plaine de Jarres or **Thong Hai Hin**) stretches for about 50 km east to west, at an altitude of 1000 m. In total there are 136 archaeological sites in this area, containing thousands of jars, discs and deliberately placed stones, but at the moment only three principal sites are open to tourists. The plateau can be cold from December to March. **Phonsavanh** is the main town of the province today – old Xieng Khouang having been flattened – and its small airstrip is a crucial transport link in this mountainous region. It's the only base from which to explore the Plain of Jars, so it has a fair number of hotels and guesthouses. Note that travel agents and airlines tend to refer to Phonsavanh as Xieng Khouang, while the nearby town of 'old' Xieng Khouang is usually referred to as Muang Khoune.

Visiting the Plain of Jars and Phonsavanh

Getting there Phonsavanh Airport (aka Xieng Khouang airport) is 4 km west of Phonsavanh – there are flights from Vientiane. A tuk-tuk to town costs 20,000 kip per person. The most direct route by road from Luang Prabang to Xieng Khouang is to take Route 13 south to Muang Phou Khoun and then Route 7 east. An alternative, scenic, albeit convoluted, route is via Nong Khiaw (see page 68), from where there are pickups to Pak Xeng and Phonsavanh via Vieng Thong on Route 1 or Nam Nouan.

The bus station is 4 km west of Phonsavanh on Route 7; a tuk-tuk to/from the centre costs 10,000 kip.

Getting around Public transport is limited and sporadic. Provincial laws have occasionally banned tuk-tuks and motorbikes from ferrying customers around the area. It should be possible to drive from Phonsavanh to the Plain of Jars, see Site one below, and return to town in two hours. Expect to pay in the region of US$30 for an English-speaking guide and vehicle for four people, or US$60 for seven people and a minivan. A tuk-tuk to Site one costs approximately US$7 per person. Alternatively, guesthouses and tour companies in Phonsavanh run set tours to the Plain of Jars. If you arrive by air, the chances are you'll be inundated with official and unofficial would-be guides as soon as you step off the plane. Note that it is not possible to walk from the airport to Site one, as there is a military base in between. It is recommended that you hire a guide, for at least a day, to get an insight into the history of the area. The cost of admission to each site is 10,000 kip. The sites are open October-February 0800-1600, March-September 0700-1700. ▶▶ See What to do and Transport, page 85.

Background

Most of the jars are between 1 m and 2.5 m high, around 1 m in diameter and weigh about the same as three small cars. The largest are about 3 m tall. The jars have long presented an

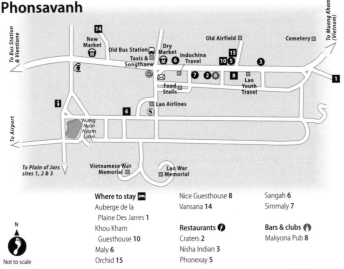

Phonsavanh

Where to stay 🛏️
Auberge de la
  Plaine Des Jarres **1**
Khou Kham
  Guesthouse **10**
Maly **6**
Orchid **15**

Nice Guesthouse **8**
Vansana **14**

Restaurants 🍴
Craters **2**
Nisha Indian **3**
Phonexay **5**

Sangah **6**
Simmaly **7**

Bars & clubs 🎵
Maliyona Pub **8**

N
Not to scale

archaeological conundrum, leaving generations of theorists nonplussed by how they got there and what they were used for. Local legend relates that King Khoon Chuong and his troops from Southern China threw a stupendous party after their victory over the wicked Chao Angka and had the jars made to brew outrageous quantities of *lao-lao*. However, attractive as this alcoholic thesis is, it is more likely that the jars are in fact 2000-year-old stone funeral urns. The larger jars are believed to have been for the local aristocracy and the smaller jars for their minions. Tools, bronze ornaments, ceramics and other objects have been found in the jars, indicating that a civilized society was responsible for making them but no one has a clue which one, as the artefacts seem to bear no relation to those left behind by other ancient Indochinese civilizations. Some of the jars were once covered with round lids and there is one jar, in the group facing the entrance to the cave, which is decorated with a rough carving of a dancing figure.

The sites

More than 334 jars survive, mainly scattered on one slope at so-called 'Site one' or **Thong Hai Hin**, 10 km southwest of Phonsavanh, entry 10,000 kip. This site hosts the largest jars. A path, cleared by MAG, winds through the site, with a warning not to walk away from delineated areas as UXO are still around. Each of the jars weighs about a tonne, although the biggest, called **Hai Cheaum**, is over 2 m tall and weighs over six tonnes.

True jar lovers should visit Site two, known as **Hai Hin Phu Salatao** (literally 'Salato Hill Stone Jar Site') and Site three called **Hai Hin Laat Khai** – entry to both is 7000 kip each

Site two is 25 km south of Phonsavanh and features 90 jars spread across two hills. The jars are set in a rather beautiful location, affording scenic 360 degree views. Most people miss this site but it is in fact the most atmospheric because of the hilltop location. On the second hill, trees have grown through the centre of the jars, splitting them four ways; butterflies abound.

A further 10 km south of Site two, Site three is the most peaceful, set in verdant green rolling hills, Swiss-cheesed with bomb craters. To get there you have to walk through some rice paddies and cross the small bamboo bridge. There are more than 130 jars at this site, which are generally smaller and more damaged than at the other sites. There's also a very small, basic restaurant, serving *feu* (noodle soup).

Tham Piu

ⓘ *The cave is to the west of the Muang Kham-Xam Neua Rd, just after the 183 km post, entry 5000 kip. A rough track leads down to an irrigation dam, built in 1981. To get there from Phonsavanh you can either go the easy way and hire a vehicle US$30-40, or go the hard way, by public transport. For the latter, take the bus to Nong Haet, and request to stop at the Tham Phiu turn-off. From here walk towards the towering limestone cliff and follow the small trails for the last kilometre. It is best to do this with a guide as UXOs still litter the area.*

This cave is more of a memorial than a tourist site but will be of interest to those fascinated by the war. More evidence of the dirty war can be seen here. The intensity of the US bombing campaign under the command of the late General Curtis Le May was such that entire villages were forced to take refuge in caves. If discovered, fighter bombers were called in to destroy them. In Tam Phiu, a cave overlooking the fertile valley near Muang Kham, 374 villagers from nearby Ban Na Meun built a two-storey bomb shelter and concealed its entrance with a high stone wall. They lived there for a year, working in their rice fields at night and taking cover during the day from the relentless bombing raids that killed thousands in the area. On the morning of 24 November 1968 two T-28 fighter-bombers took off from Udon Thani air base in neighbouring Thailand and located the cave mouth that had been exposed on previous sorties. It is likely that the US forces suspected that the cave contained a Pathet Lao hospital complex. Indeed, experts are at odds whether this was a legitimate target or an example of collateral damage. There are a few people still alive whose families died in the cave, and they certainly see it as innocent civilians being targeted. The first rocket destroyed the wall, the second, fired as the planes swept across the valley, carried the full length of the chamber before exploding. There were no survivors and 11 families were completely wiped out; in total 374 people died, many reportedly women and children. Local rescuers claim they were unable to enter the cave for three days, but eventually the dead were buried in a bomb crater on the hillside next to the cave mouth. You will need a torch to explore the cave but there isn't much inside, just eerily black walls. The interior of the cave was completely dug up by the rescue parties and relatives and today there is nothing but rubble inside. It makes for a poignant lesson in military history and locally it is considered a war memorial. Further up the cliff is another cave, **Tham Phiu Song**, which fortunately didn't suffer the same fate. Before the stairway to the caves there is a little memorial centre that displays photographs from the war and is usually attended by a relative of the victims. A poignant sculpture of a soldier carrying a dead child marks the site, free of the victory and glory of most other war monuments. Many bomb craters around the site have been turned into fish ponds now bearing beautiful lotus.

Vieng Xai (Viengsay) → *For listings, see pages 84-86.*

The village of Vieng Xai lies 31 km east of Xam Neua on a road that branches off Route 6 at Km 20. The trip from Xam Neua is possibly one of the country's most picturesque journeys, passing terraces of rice, pagodas, copper- and charcoal-coloured karst formations, dense jungle with misty peaks and friendly villages dotted among the mountains' curves. The area is characterized by lush tropical gardens, a couple of smallish lakes and spectacular limestone karsts, riddled with natural caves that proved crucial in the success of the left-wing insurgency in the 1960s and 1970s.

Getting there

Tourists are often put off visiting Hua Phan Province by the long bus haul to get there but, considering the road passes through gorgeous mountain scenery, the trip is well worth the endeavour. There are three main sealed roads to Xam Neua: Route 6 from the south, linking Xam Neua with Phonsavanh; Route 1 from Vieng Thong and the west, and Road 6A from the Vietnamese border. Due to the upgrading of Route 6, it is now possible to make the journey between Phonsavanh and Xam Neua in a day without an overnight stop in Nam Nouan en route but always check on road conditions before setting off. There is an airport at Xam Neua, 3 km from the centre of town on the road to Vieng Xai and Vietnam. **Houa Phanh Provincial Tourist Office** ⓘ *T064-312567, hp_pto@yahoo.com,* is run by the helpful Kaiphet and his teaam Neua.

Visiting the caves

There eight caves open to visitors. Five were formerly occupied by senior Pathet Lao leaders (Prince Souphanouvong, Kaysone Phomvihan, Nouhak Phounsavanh, Khamtai Siphandon and Phoumi Vongvichit). All the caves are within walking distance of the village. Tickets are sold at the **Viengxay Caves Visitor Centre** ⓘ *T064-314321, www.visit-viengxay.com,* *daily 0800-1200, 1300-1600, guided tours are conducted in English at 0900 and 1300, 30,000 kip with compulsory guide.* If you pitch up out of these hours, tours are 50,000 kip. Tours are usually conducted on bikes which can be rented from the office (20,000-30,000 kip) if you don't have your own transport. Tours last three to four hours. A new set of excellent 90-minute audio tours with personal memories of local people has launched (US$6.50). A taster can be heard on: www.visit-viengxay.com. If you plan on coming across from Xam Neua it is advisable to stay overnight.

From 1964 onwards, Pathet Lao operations were directed from the cave systems at Vieng Xai, which provided an effective refuge from furious bombing attacks. The village of Vieng Xai grew from four small villages consisting of less than 10 families into a thriving hidden city concealing over 20,000 people in in the 100 plus caves in the area. The Pathet Lao leadership renamed the area Vieng Xai, meaning 'City of Victory' and it became the administrative and military hub of the revolutionary struggle.

The caves have a secretive atmosphere, with fruit trees and frangipani decorating the exteriors. Each one burrows deep into the mountainside and features 60-cm-thick concrete walls, encompassing living quarters, meeting rooms, offices, dining and storage areas. The caves are lit but you may find a torch useful.

Plain of Jars and the northeast listings

For hotel and restaurant price codes and other relevant information, see pages 8-9.

⬤ Where to stay

Phonsavanh *p80, map p81*
$$$ Auberge de la Plaine des Jarres (aka Phu Pha Daeng Hotel), 1 km from the centre, T030-517 0282, www.plainedesjarres.com. In a spectacular position on a hill overlooking the town are 15 stone and wood chalets. Cosy and comfortable and the restaurant serves good food. Highly recommended.
$$$ Vansana, on a hill about 1 km out of town, T061-213170, www.vansanahotel-group.com. Big, modern rooms with telephone, TV, minibar, and tea/coffee-making facilities. The best room is the smart suite with polished wooden floors and textile decoration. Phenomenal views of the countryside. Opt for the rooms upstairs, with free-form bathtub and picturesque balcony views. Restaurant offers Lao and foreign cuisine.
$$$-$$ The Hillside Residence, T061-213300, www.thehillresidence.com. New, family-run guesthouse on the track to the

Vansana Resort. Rooms are decorated with textiles and come with luggage racks and floral-tiled bathrooms; twins are larger and a couple of the doubles are tiny. The 1st-floor balcony is a great place to kick back.
$$-$ White Orchid, just off the main road in the centre of town, T061-312403. You can't miss this big green building. Guesthouse, not quite at hotel standard but close enough to be good value. Rooms with TV, hot water, comfy beds and bath. Nicely decorated; twins are spacious and have bathtubs. Free breakfast and airport pick-up (if you ring in advance).
$ Kong Keo, just off the main road, T061-211354, www.kongkeojar.com. This popular hangout is run by the friendly Kong. 13 rooms; the modern rooms are small and basic with tiny bathrooms; the wooden bungalows are darker but larger and more atmospheric but the bathrooms are even smaller. The bonfire inside the cluster bomb case is a nightly draw in the restaurant.

Vieng Xai and Xam Neua *p83*
$ Kheamxam Guesthouse, on the corner by the river, Xam Neua, T064-312111. Wide range of fairly well-appointed large

rooms, with attached spacious hot-water bathroom, some with a/c and TV. These are some of the best rooms (soft pillows) in town by a long way.

$ Naxay Guesthouse 2, opposite Vieng Xai Cave Visitor Centre, T064-314336. The best option with 11 clean, beautiful bungalows with tepid water, comfortable beds and Western toilet set in a leafy compound. Recommended.

🍴 Restaurants

Phonsavanh *p80, map p81*
$$-$ Auberge de la Plaine des Jarres, see Where to stay. Reasonable menu of Lao dishes and some delicious French food; overpriced given the competition but the Asian menu is much better value. The dining room with roaring fire is a welcome retreat.
$$-$ Craters, main street, T020-7780 5775. Modern, Western restaurant offering average burgers, pizza and sandwiches. Good music, attentive service. Delectable but pricey cocktails.
$ Nisha Indian, on the main road. Good north and south Indian food. The sweet Indian chai is very moreish.
$ Sangah, main street. Thai, Lao, Vietnamese and Western dishes. Huge portions.
$ Simmaly, main street, T061-211013. Fantastic *feu* soup. Great service and immensely popular. Recommended.

Vieng Xai and Xam Neua *p83*
$ Dannaomuangxam, 1 block back from the river, near the bridge, Xam Neua, T064-314126. A good option. The fried fish is excellent as is the *feu*, *laap* and French fries. Good service. Menu in English.

The **Xailomyen**, Vieng Xai, does a range of fish, pork, noodle and egg dishes and has a lovely view over the lake.

✦ Festivals

Phonsavanh *p80, map p81*
Dec National Day on the 2 Dec is celebrated with horse-drawn drag-cart racing. Also in Dec is **Hmong New Year** (movable), which is celebrated in a big way in this area.

⚙ What to do

Phonsavanh *p80, map p81*
There is no shortage of tour operators in Phonsavanh and most guesthouses can now arrange tours and transport. A full-day tour for 4 people should cost up to US$50-60, although you may have to bargain for it. Most travel agencies are located within a block of each other on the main road.
Indochina Travel, on the main road, T061-312409, www.indochinatravelco.com. Expensive but well-regarded minivan tours.
Inter-Lao Travel, on the main road, T061-211729. Offers a range of minivan tours to the jars and outlying villages as well as motorbike and bicycle rent and transport to Vientiane.
Lao Youth Travel, on Route 7, T020-5576 1233, www.laoyouthtravel.com. Offers a wide range of tours to the jars and post-conflict sites.

⊖ Transport

Phonsavanh *p80, map p81*
Air
Lao Airlines runs flights to **Vientiane**, 30 mins, and to **Luang Prabang**.

Bus
Full up-to-date bus timetables are available at the tourist office.

From the main bus station outside of town (T030-517 0148): To **Luang Prabang**, 0830 daily (VIP bus), 265 km on a sealed road, 8 hrs, 75,000 kip. To **Vientiane**, 6 daily, 9-10 hrs, 95,000 kip, also a VIP bus (with a/c and TV) daily, 120,000 kip. Also north to **Vang Vieng**, 6 VIP buses daily, 80,000-120,000 kip. To **Xam Neua**, for Vieng Xai, daily 0800, 1900, 2200, 60,000 kip, a 10-hr haul through some of the country's most beautiful scenery and very windy roads towards the end (you may want to take travel sickness medicine).

Also north to **Nam Nouan**, 0900, 4 hrs, 35,000 kip (change here for transport west to **Nong Khiaw**).

Buses also travel to **Vinh**, Vietnam, Tue, Thu, Fri and Sat 0630, 10 hrs, 138,000 kip. A VIP bus heads for **Hanoi** on Mon at 0630, 185,000 kip. If you want to cross the Nam Khan border here you will need to organize a visa in advance as there is no consulate in Phonsavanh or agencies that will send your passport to Vientiane.

Car/songthaew/minivan
A full car with driver to the **Plain of Jars** will cost US$20 (US$5 each) to Site one, or US$30-40 to all 3 sites. To hire a *songthaew* to go to **Tham Phiu** is US$30-40 for the day, a minivan costs US$60.

Vieng Xai and Xam Neua *p83*
Air
Phongsavanh Airlines (T021-513 0000) flies the route to **Vientiane**.

Bus/truck/songthaew
From the Nathong Bus station (T030-312238), regular *songthaew* from Xam Neua to **Vieng Xai**, 50 mins, 10,000 kip, from 0620-1640 every 50 mins. To **Na Maew** (the Vietnam border), 0710, 3 hrs, 20,000

kip. To **Xam Tai**, 0900, 5 hrs, 34,000 kip. To **Thanh Hoa** (Vietnam), 0800 daily, 180,000 kip, 11 hrs. From Phoutanou bus station up the hill (T030-516 0974) to **Vieng Thong**, 0710, 6 hrs, 43,000 kip. To **Phonsavanh**, 0800, 0830, 0900, 1230, 60,000-70,000 kip, 1400 (VIP bus) 165,000 kip (8 hrs). To **Luang Prabang**, 0730, 0800, 14 hrs, 120,000 kip (the Luang Prabang bus goes via **Nong Khiaw**, 12 hrs, 80,000 kip). To **Vientiane**, 0800, 0900, and 1230, 24 hrs, 150,000 kip, VIP bus at 1400, 18 hrs, 165,000 kip.

ⓘ Directory

Phonsavanh *p80, map p81*
Banks   Lao Development Bank, Mon-Fri 0800-1530, near Lao Airlines Office, 2 blocks back from the dry market. Changes cash and TCs and advances on Visa and MC. There are 2 BCEL ATMs on the main road. **Indochine Travel** has an exchange booth with Visa advance,but they charge 6.9% commission. **Internet**   A couple of places. **Medical services** Lao-Mongolian Hospital, T061-312166. Sufficient for minor ailments. Pharmacies are ubiquitous in town. **Post office and telephone**   The post office is opposite the dry market and has IDD telephone boxes outside.

Vieng Xai and Xam Neua *p83*
Banks The Lao Development Bank, Xam Neua, will change Thai baht, US$ and Chinese ¥ into kip but will only accept TCs in US$. **Internet** Available from Tami.com, just ask the **Sam Neua** hotel, over the 1st crossroads.

Central provinces

The central provinces of Laos, sandwiched between the Mekong (and Thailand) to the west and the Annamite Mountains (and Vietnam) to the east, are the least visited in the country, which is a shame as the scenery here is stunning, with dramatic limestone karsts, enormous caves, beautiful rivers and forests. In particular, the upland areas to the east, off Route 8 and Route 12, in Khammouane and Bolikhamxai Province, are a veritable treasure trove of attractions, mottled with scores of caves, lagoons, rivers and rock formations. Visitors will require some determination in these parts, as the infrastructure is still being developed. The Mekong towns of Thakhek and Savannakhet are elegant and relaxed and are the main transport and tourist hubs in the region. Pakse is the optimum place to base yourself to explore the southern provinces.

Thakhek and around → *For listings, see pages 93-96.*

Located on the Mekong, at the junction of Routes 13 and 12, Thakhek is a quiet town, surrounded by beautiful countryside. This will inevitably change, though, with the opening of the third Friendship Bridge to Thailand in 2011. It is the capital of Khammouane Province and was founded in 1911-1912, under the French. Apart from Luang Prabang, Thakhek is probably the most outwardly French-looking town in Laos, with fading pastel villas clustered around a simple fountain area. It has a fine collection of colonial-era shophouses, a breezy riverside position and a relaxed ambience. One of Laos' holiest sites, That Sikhot, the stunning caves of the region and beautiful Mahaxai can all be visited from here. This town is the most popular stopover point in the central provinces, attracting a range of tourists with its vast array of caves, rivers, lakes and other attractions. Despite encompassing some of the most beautiful scenery in Laos: imposing jagged mountains, bottle green rivers, lakes and caves, the region is still not considered a primary tourist destination. Tourism infrastructure is still quite limited but is improving and a trip to this area will prove the highlight of most visitors' holidays to Laos.

Arriving in Thakhek
Getting there There are two bus terminals: the main terminal is about 4 km from town and offers inter-provincial and international buses, and the small *songthaew* station, near Soksombook market, which services local regions.

Getting around Thakhek is small enough to negotiate on foot or by bicycle. A number of places organize motorbike hire, such as the Thakhek Travel Lodge and the Tourism Information Centre, which acts as an agent for motorcycle dealers. ▸▸ *See Transport, page 95.*

Tourist information Tourism Information Centre ① *Vientiane Rd, in a chalet-like building T052-212512, Mon-Fri 0800-1130 and 1330-1630 and Sat-Sun 0800-1130 and 1400-1700.* Mr Somkiad, the head of the centre, is extremely helpful and speaks good English, T020-5575 1791, somkiad@yahoo.com. Motorbike hire for the loop, 100,000 kip per day; for town 70,000 kip per day. The trip to the Blue Lagoon has been recommended.

That Sikhot

① *6 km south of Thakhek, daily 0800-1800; 5000 kip. Tuk-tuk 30,000 kip.*

That Sikhot or **Sikhotaboun** is one of Laos' holiest sites. It overlooks the Mekong and the journey downstream from Thakhek, along a quiet road, reveals bucolic Laos at its best. The *that* is thought to have been built by Chao Anou at the beginning of the 15th century and houses the relics of Chao Sikhot, a local hero, who founded the old town of Thakhek.

According to local legend, Sikhot was bestowed with Herculean strength after eating some rice he had stirred with dirty – but as it turned out, magic – sticks. At that time, the King of Vientiane was having a problem with elephants killing villagers and taking over the country (hard to believe now but Laos was once called Land of a Million Elephants). The King offered anyone who could save the region half his Kingdom and his daughter's hand in marriage. Due to his new-found strength, Sikhot was able to take on the pachyderms and secure most of the surrounding area as well as Vientiane, whereupon he married the King of Vientiane's daughter. The King was unhappy about handing over his kingdom and daughter to this man, and plotted with his daughter to regain control. Sikhot foolishly revealed to his new wife that he could only be killed through his anus, so the King of Vientiane placed an archer at the bottom of Sikhot's pit latrine and when the unfortunate Oriental Hercules came to relieve himself, he was killed by an arrow.

That Sikhot consists of a large gold stupa raised 29 m on a plinth, with a viharn upstream built in 1970 by the last King of Laos. A major annual festival is held here in July and during February.

Kong Leng Lake

① *33 km northeast of Thakhek.*

This site is usually incorporated into hikes as there isn't direct road access to the lake. Steeped in legend, locals believe an underground Kingdom lies beneath the surface of the 100-m-deep lake. As a result, you must request permission to swim here from the local village authority and you can only swim in the designated swimming zone. Fishing is not permitted. The beautiful green waters of the lake morph into different shades season to season due to the dissolved calcium from the surrounding limestone crops. It is very difficult to get to on your own and the track is sometimes completely inaccessible except on foot. The tourism information centre organizes excellent treks to the lake.

Tham Pha (Buddha Cave)

① *Ban Na Khangxang, off Route 12, 18 km from Thakhek, 2000 kip. A tuk-tuk will cost 100,000 kip, use of boat 5000 kip. Women will need to hire a sinh (sarong) at the entrance, 3000 kip.*

A farmer hunting for bats accidentally stumbled across the Buddha Cave (also known Tham Pa Fa, or Turtle Cave) in April 2004. On climbing up to the cave's mouth, he found 229 bronze Buddha statues, believed to be more than 450 years old, and ancient palm leaf scripts. These Buddhas were part of the royal collection believed to have been hidden here when the Thais ransacked Vientiane. Since its discovery, the cave has become widely celebrated, attracting pilgrims from as far away as Thailand, particularly around Pi Mai

(Lao New Year). A wooden ladder and eyesore concrete steps have now been built to access the cave, but it is quite difficult to get to as the dirt road from Thakhek is in poor condition. It is recommended that you organize a guide through the **Thakhek Tourism Information Centre**, page 88, to escort you. In the wet season, it is necessary to catch a boat. The journey itself is half the fun as the cave is surrounded by some truly stunning karst formations sprawling across the landscape like giant dinosaur teeth.

Tham Kong Lor (Kong Lor cave)

ⓘ *Entrance fee at cave 5000 kip; US$12 for boat from Sala Kong Lor and US$17 from Sala Hin Boun; 100,000 kip to go through the cave (maximum 3 people per boat).*

Tham Kong Lor cave can only be described as sensational. The Nam Hinboun River has tunnelled through the mountain, creating a giant rocky cavern, 6 km long, 90 m wide and 100 m high, which opens out into the blinding bright light at Ban Natan on the other side. The cave is apparently named after the drum makers who were believed to make their instruments here. Although very rare, it is also home to the largest living cave-dwelling spiders in the world, though it is unlikely you will have a run in with the massive arachnid. Fisherman will often come into the cave to try their luck as it is believed that 20-kg fish lurk below the surface.

At the start of the cave, you will have to scramble over some boulders while the boatmen carry the canoe over the rapids, so wear comfortable shoes with a good grip. A torch or, better, a head-lamp, is also recommended. It is eerie travelling through the dark, cool cave, with water splashing and bats circulating. The cave can also be visited as part of the 400-km 'loop' from Thakhek, see below.

The best way to get there is by road and boat. There is a small transport terminus at the Route 13/Route 8 intersection in **Ban Lao** (also known as Tham Beng or Vieng Kham) for north-south buses between Vientiane and Pakse. *Songthaew* generally pass through here from early in the morning to well into the afternoon to **Ban Na Hin**, US$1-2. This trip along Route 8 is about 60 km. The drive between Ban Lao and Ban Na Hin is magical and passes through some truly amazing Gothic scenery; keep an eye out for the lookout at Km 54 from Route 13. Generally, a pick-up waits in Ban Na Hin to take passengers to Ban Kong Lor, where you can pick up a boat trip into the cave. There is also one public *songthaew* a day.

Alternatively, if the new road is flooded you can get a *songthaew*, as far as **Ban Napur**, or Na Phouak, and then catch a boat to Ban Phonyang, two to three hours, or **Ban Kong Lor** (closer to the cave), and onto the cave, a further one hour.

If you are staying at **Sala Hin Boun**, see Where to stay, they will send you a boat to Ban Napur to collect you, US$25.

Route 12 and the 'Loop'

ⓘ *Contact Thakhek Travel Lodge (see Where to stay, page 93) for details of the 'Loop' route and for motorbike hire. Mr Ku who rents the motorbikes is based at the lodge from 0700-1100, 1500-1930 daily, T020-2220 5070. Motorbikes (100cc) cost 100,000 kip per day and come with a helmet and a good map. Mr Ku has contacts around the Loop. He recommends riders take 4 days. He will help out in an emergency and advises on no-go times; for example, in Sep and Oct during the rains.*

The impressive karst landscape of the Mahaxai area is visible to the northeast of town and can be explored on a popular motorbike tour from Thakhek, known as the **Loop**, which runs from Thakhek along Route 12 to Mahaxai, then north to Lak Sao, west along Route 8 to Ban Na Hin and then south back to Thakhek on Route 13, taking in caves and other beautiful scenery along the way. The circuit should take approximately three days but allow four to five, particularly if you want to sidetrack to Tham Kong Lor and the other caves.

The 'Loop' is mostly for motorcyclists, who pick up a bike in Thakhek and travel by road. The whole loop covers an area over 400 km (without the side-trips). This includes 50 km from Thakhek to the petrol station before the turn-off to Mahaxai; 45 km between the petrol station and Nakai; 75 km between Nakai and Lak Xao; 58 km between Lak Xao and Ban Na Hin; 41 km between Ban Na Hin and Ban Lao and then 105 km between Ban Lao and Thakhek. The trip between Ban Lao and Ban Na Hin offers some spectacular views.

If on a motorbike pack light: include a waterproof jacket, a torch, a few snacks, a long-sleeved shirt, sunglasses, sun block, closed-toe shoes, a sinh or sarong (to use as a towel, to stop dust and – for women – to bathe along the way), a phrase book and a good map. It is a bumpy, exhausting but enjoyable ride. All of the sites are now well signposted in English. Most sites charge a parking fee for motorbikes.

Note that this whole region is susceptible to change due to the operation of the Nam Theun II dam, a US$1.5 billion hydropower project, and other developments in the area. It is imperative that you check for up-to-date information before travelling. Check on the status of the roads at the Tourism Information Centre and with Mr Ku, see page 88, and check the logbook at the **Thakhek Lodge**. This trip is difficult in the wet season and will probably only be possible for skilled riders on larger dirt bikes. In the dry season it's very dusty.

The caves along Route 12 can also be visited on day trips from Thakhek, although some are difficult to find without a guide and access may be limited in the wet season. Many of the sights have no English signposts but locals will be more than obliging to confirm you are going in the right direction if you ask. Turn south off Route 12 at Km 7 to reach **Tham Xang** (Tham Pha Ban Tham), an important Buddhist shrine that contains some statues and a box of religious scripts. It is considered auspicious due to the 'elephant head' that has formed from calcium deposits and in the Lao New Year the locals sprinkle water on it. At Km 13, turn north on a track for 2 km to **Tha Falang** (Vang Santiphap – Peace Pool), a lovely emerald billabong on the Nam Don River, surrounded by pristine wilderness and breathtaking cliffs. It's a nice place to spend the afternoon or break your journey. In the wet season it may be necessary to catch a boat from the Xieng Liab Bridge to get here. Turn south off Route 12 at Km 14 and follow the track south to reach **Tham Xiang Liab**, a reasonably large cave at the foot of a 300-m-high limestone cliff, with a small swimming hole (in the dry season) at the far end. It is not easy to access the interior of the cavern on your own and, in the wet season, it can only be navigated by boat, as it usually floods. This cave, called 'sneaking around cave' derived its name from a legend of an old hermit who used to meditate in the cave with his beautiful daughter. A novice monk fell in love with the hermit's daughter and the two lovebirds planned their trysts sneakily around this cave and Tham Nan Aen. When the hermit found out he flew into a rage and did away with the novice monk; the daughter was banished to the cave for the rest of her life.

At Km 17, beyond the narrow pass, turn to the north and follow the path for 400 m to reach **Tham Sa Pha In**, a cave with a small lake and a couple of interesting Buddhist shrines. Swimming in the lake is strictly prohibited as the auspicious waters are believed to have magical powers. South of Route 12, at Km 18, a path leads 700 m to the entrance of **Tham Nan Aen** ① *7000 kip*. This is the giant of the local caverns at 1.5 km long and over 100 m high. It has multiple chambers and the entrances are illuminated by fluorescent lighting; it also contains a small underground freshwater pool.

Savannakhet → *For listings, see pages 93-96.*

Situated on the banks of the Mekong at the start of Route 9 to Danang in Vietnam, Savannakhet – or Savan as it is usually known – is an important river port and gateway to the south. The city has a sizeable Chinese population and attracts merchants from both Vietnam and Thailand, while the ubiquitous colonial houses and fading shopfronts are an ever-present reminder of earlier French influence. In 2010 authorities recognised the value of its historic core and 30 billion kip was allocated to be spent on preserving the colonial-era architecture. Savannakhet Province has several natural attractions, although the majority are a fair hike from the provincial capital. For those short on time in Laos, Pakse makes a better stopover than Savannakhet.

Arriving in Savannakhet

Getting there and around Flights on **Lao Airlines** run from Vientiane, Pakse and Bangkok to Savannakhet. It is possible to cross into Vietnam by taking Route 9 east over the Annamite Mountains via Xepon. The border is at Dansavanh (Laos) and Lao Bao (Vietnam) 236 km east of Savannakhet, with bus connections direct from Savannakhet to Danang, Dong Ha and Hué. It is possible to cross the border into Thailand near Mukdahan via the new Friendship Bridge. The government bus terminal is near the Savan Xai market has connections with Vientiane, Thakhek, Pakse and Lao Bao; a tuk-tuk to the centre should cost about 10,000 kip. Just west of the bus station is the *songthaew* terminal, where vehicles depart to provincial destinations. Tuk-tuks, locally known as *Sakaylab*, criss-cross town. ➡ *See Transport, page 95.*

Tourist information The **Provincial Tourism Office** ① *Chaleun Meuang Rd, T041-212755*, is one of the least helpful in the country with staff slumped on desks; 'too busy to help' apparently. Much better, much more helpful, more professional and much friendlier is the nearby **Eco Guide Unit** ① *Rasphanit Rd, T041-214203, www.savannakhet-trekking.com*, which runs excellent ecotours and treks to Dong Natad and Dong Phu Vieng National Protected Areas, which should be organized in advance. Can also arrange guides and drivers for other trips.

Places in Savannakhet

Savan's colonial heritage can be seen throughout the town centre. Perhaps the most attractive area is the square and church east of the former immigration office between Khanthabouli and Phetsalath roads. **Wat Sounantha** has a three-dimensional raised relief on the front of the *sim*, showing the Buddha in the *mudra* of bestowing peace, separating two warring armies. **Wat Sayaphum** on the Mekong is rather more attractive and has several early 20th-century monastery buildings. It is both the largest and oldest monastery in town, although it was only built at the end of the 19th century. Evidence of Savan's diverse population is reflected in the **Chua Dieu Giac**, a Mahayana Buddhist pagoda that serves the town's Vietnamese population. The **Dinosaur Museum** ① *Khanthabouli Rd, daily 0800-1200, 1300-1600, 5000 kip*, houses a collection of four different dinosaur and early mammalian remains, and even some fragments of a meteorite that fell to earth over 100 million years ago.

The **Provincial Museum** ① *Khanthabouli Rd, Mon-Sat 0800-1200 and 1330-1600, 5000 kip*, offers plenty of propaganda-style displays but little that is terribly enlightening unless you are interested in the former revolutionary leader Kaysone Phomvihane.

That Inheng

ⓘ *Any of the regular tuk-tuks will make the trip for 100,000 kip return, or take a shared songthaew to Xeno and ask to hop off at That Inheng. They will usually take you all the way there but if they drop you at the turning it is only a 3-km walk. Alternatively hire a bicycle in town and cycle.*

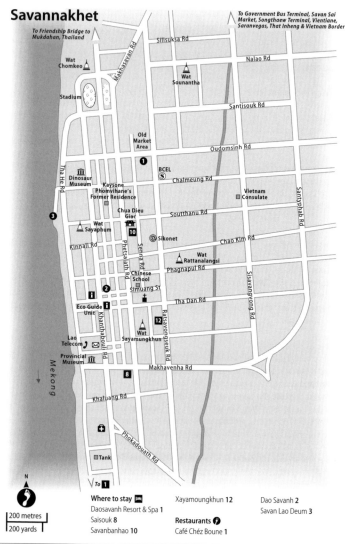

Savannakhet

To Government Bus Terminal, Savan Sai
Market, Songthaew Terminal, Vientiane,
Saranvegas, That Inheng & Vietnam Border

To Friendship Bridge to
Mukdahan, Thailand

Silisuksa Rd
Nalao Rd
Makhavisan Rd
Wat Chomkeo
Stadium
Wat Sounantha
Santisouk Rd
Old Market Area
Oudomsinh Rd
BCEL $
Chalmeung Rd
Dinosaur Museum
Kaysone Phomvihane's Former Residence
Vietnam Consulate
Chua Dieu Giac
Soutthanu Rd
Wat Sayaphum
@Sikonet
Chao Kim Rd
Kinnali Rd
Wat Rattanalangsi
Phagnapul Rd
Phetsalath Rd
Senna Rd
Chinese School
Simuang St
Tha Dan Rd
Eco Guide Unit
Wat Sayamungkhun
Lao Telecom
Khanthaboul Rd
Ratsavongseuk Rd
Sisavangvong Rd
Santyphab Rd
Provincial Museum
Makhavenha Rd
Khatuang Rd
Phokadouath Rd
Tank

Mekong
Tha He Rd

N
200 metres
200 yards

To 1

Where to stay 🛏
Daosavanh Resort & Spa 1
Saisouk 8
Savanbanhao 10

Xayamoungkhun 12

Restaurants 🍴
Café Chéz Boune 1

Dao Savanh 2
Savan Lao Deum 3

This holy 16th-century *that* or stupa is 12 km northeast of Savannakhet and is the second-holiest site in Southern Laos after Wat Phou. It was built during the reign of King Sikhottabong at the same time as That Luang in Vientiane, although local guides may try to convince you it was founded by the Indian emperor Asoka over 2000 years ago. Needless to say, there is no historical evidence to substantiate this claim. The wat is the site of an annual festival at the end of November akin to the one celebrated at Wat Phou, Champasak (see page 115).

Dong Phou Vieng National Protected Area

The **Savannakhet Eco Guide Unit** (see page 91), runs excellent treks through the Dong Phou Vieng National Protected Area, home to wildlife such as Siamese crocodiles, Asian elephants, the endangered Eld's deer, langurs and wild bison (most of which you would be incredibly lucky to see). Located within the NPA is a **Song Sa Kae** (Sacred Forest and Cemetery), revered by the local Katang ethnic group, who are known for their buffalo sacrifices. The well-trained local guides show how traditional natural produce is gathered for medicinal, fuel or other purposes. The tours are exceptionally good value and homestay is included. Most only run during the dry season.

Central provinces listings

For hotel and restaurant price codes and other relevant information, see pages 8-9.

● Where to stay

Thakhek *p87*

$$ Inthira Sikhotabong Hotel, Chao Anou Rd, close to the fountain, T051-251237, www.inthirahotels.com. In a Lao nautical-style building, this small hotel offers attractive rooms that are warmly decorated but twins are cramped, with a tiny toilet closet; doubles are better. Restaurant and Wi-Fi available.

$ Southida Guesthouse, Chao Anou Rd (1 block back from the river), T051-212568. Very popular guesthouse in the centre of town. Clean comfortable rooms with a/c, TV, and hot water; cheaper with fan. Very helpful staff; often booked up.

$ Thakhek Travel Lodge, 2 km from the centre of town, T030-530 0145, www.ede. ch/laos/thakhektravellodge.html. Popular guesthouse set in a beautifully restored and decorated house. Fantastic outdoor seating area and with nightly open fire. The cheaper rooms are very basic but the 9-bed dorm (not bunk beds) is extremely

nice (25,000 kip per person). The a/c rooms are huge with large bathrooms and very comfortable. The restaurant food is not all good but recommended is the Hawaii curry, and barbecue (which needs to be ordered in advance); the service is ridiculously and unacceptably slow and haphazard. The Danish/Lao owners can provide travel advice, when they're around, and there's an excellent log-book for those intending to travel independently around the 'Loop'. Motorcycle hire.

Recommended for those planning adventure travel around the area; tours arranged. Ring them in advance if you're coming in on one of the midnight buses.

Tham Kong Lor

There are 2 guesthouses on Route 13 in **Ban Lao**, just past the Route 8 intersection, which are passable. Homestays are available in **Ban Kong Lor** and **BaNatan**.

$$-$ Sala Hin Boun, Ban Phonyang, 10 km from Kong Lor cave, T020-7775 5220, www.salalao.com. The best option. It enjoys a scenic location on the riverbank amongst karst rock formations and has 10 well-equipped and very pleasant rooms in

2 bungalows. The manager will arrange for a boat to pick you up in Napua for US$25, with advance notice. A tour to Kong Lor for 2-3 people is US$30 with picnic lunch. Discounts in low season.

$$-$ Sala Kong Lor Lodge, 1.5 km from Kong Lor cave, near Ban Tiou, T020-7776 1846. Lodge with 4 small huts with twin beds and several superior rooms.

Savannakhet *p91, map p92*
$$$$-$$$ Daosavanh Resort & Spa Hotel, 1 km south of the historic centre, T041-252188, www.daosavanom. A new resort with attractive rooms (Mekong views cost more), super mattresses, rain shower in bathrooms, great pool and Wi-Fi; bathrooms need much better ventilation though. It's a little stuck out of the centre but great for the spa and pool. Let's hope they preserve the lovely French colonial building in the grounds that used to be the provincial museum.

$ Saisouk, Makhavenha Rd, T041-212207. A real gem. This breezy new guesthouse has good-sized twin and double rooms, immaculately furnished and spotlessly clean, some a/c, communal bathrooms and cold water. Beautifully decorated with interesting *objets d'art* and what look like dinosaur bones. Plenty of chairs and tables on the large verandas. Very friendly staff, reasonable English. Very friendly and homely.

$ Savanbanhao, Senna Rd, T041-212202, sbtour@laotel.com. Centrally located hotel composed of 4 colonial-styles houses set around a quiet but large concrete courtyard, with a range of rooms. Cheaper rooms in '4th class' which are not musty, contrary to appearances. Most expensive have en suite showers and hot water.Some a/c. Large balcony. **Savanbanhao Tourism Co** is attached. Good for those who want to be in and out of Savannakhet, quickly, with relative ease.

$ Xayamoungkhun, 85 Rasavongseuk Rd, T041-212426. An excellent little guesthouse with 16 rooms in an airy colonial-era villa. Centrally positioned with a largish compound. Range of very clean rooms available, more expensive have hot water, a/c and fridge. Very friendly owners. Second-hand books available. Recommended.

❶ Restaurants

Thakhek *p87*
There is the usual array of noodle stalls – try the one in the town 'square' with good fruit shakes. Warmed baguettes are also sold in the square in the morning. The best place to eat is at one of the riverside restaurants on either side of fountain square, where you can watch the sunset, knock back a Beer Lao and tuck into tasty barbecue foods. Otherwise, most restaurants are attached to hotels.

$ Kaysone Restaurant, in the centre of town, T051-212563. Looks like someone's backyard, but once inside you discover a sprawling restaurant. Very popular with the locals. *Sindat*, Korean barbecue and an à la carte menu. The ice cream is fantastic. There's karaoke on site.

$ Sabaidee Thakhek, T051-251245, is a refreshing addition to the restaurant scene serving up great backpacker fare (burgers, salads, sandwiches) plus Laos dishes on its cheery red-checked table cloths. Book exchange and CNN on TV. Closed between 1500-1700.

Savannakhet *p91, map p92*
Several restaurants on the riverside serve good food and beer. The market also sells good, fresh food, including Mekong river fish.

$$$-$ Dao Savanh, Simuang Rd, T041-260888. A new restaurant in a restored French colonial building with good but pricey food. It's worth splashing out for a set menu (65,000 kip-95,000 kip) for the charm and central location. Tables outside afford views of the central square.

$$-$ Savan Lao Deum, T041-252125. This lovely restaurant has taken over the old ferry pier area. The attractive wooden restaurant juts out onto the river on a

floating verandah. It's great for a sunset drink. The food is delicious too – especially steamed fish and herbs. You could also try fried tree ant eggs, grilled buffalo skin and roasted cicadas. Service is exceptional.
$ Café Chéz Boune, T041-215190. Open 0700-2300. Opposite the old market, this place provides good travellers' fare in attractive surrounds.

⊖ Transport

Thakhek *p87*
Bus/truck
Thakhek's **main bus station** is 4 km northeast of town, T051-251519. Frequent connections from 0400-1200 to **Vientiane**, 346 km, 6 hrs, 50,000 kip; the VIP bus also dashes through town at 0915 daily, 70,000 kip. Get off at **Ban Lao**, 15,000 kip, for connections along Route 12. To **Savannakhet**, from 1030, every 30 mins daily, 139 km, 2½-3 hrs, 25,000 kip; to **Pakse**, every hour from 1030 until 2400 daily, 6-7 hrs, 50,000 kip; Pakse VIP bus leaves at 2400, 70,000 kip.

Buses to Vietnam. To Vinh, 0800 daily, 90,000 kip. To **Dong Hoi**, 0700 Mon, Wed, Sat and Sun, 85,000-130,000 kip; to **Hué**, 2000 Wed, Thu, Sat and Sun 90,000 kip. To Hanoi 0800 Sat and Sun, 160,000 kip.

The **local bus station** is at Talaat Lak Sarm. From here *songthaew* to **Na Phao** (Vietnam border) 142 km, 6-7 hrs, 40,000 kip; **Na Hin**, 45,000 kip. There is also a *songthaew* to **Kong Lor** village at 0830, 65,000 kip.

Motorbike
Can be rented from **Thakhek Travel Lodge**, 70,000 kip per day; and from Provincial Tourism Office 70,000 kip in town; 100,000kip per day for The Loop.

Savannakhet *p91, map p92*
Bus/truck
From the bus station (T041-213920) on the northern edge of town, daily to **Vientiane** (0600-1130), 9 hrs, 80,000 kip. Most of the Vientiane-bound buses also stop at **Thakhek**, 125 km, 2½-3 hrs, 25,000 kip. To **Pakse** daily at 0700, 0900, 1030, 1230, 1730, 6-7 hrs, 35,000 kip; buses in transit from Vientiane to Pakse will also usually pick up passengers here. A VIP bus leaves at 2130, 8 hrs, 95,000 kip. To **Lao Bao** (Vietnam border), 0630, 0900 and 1200 daily, 6 hrs, 40,000 kip. A bus also departs at 2200 daily for destinations within Vietnam, including **Hué**, 13 hrs, 90,000 kip; **Danang**, 508 km, 13 hrs, 110,000 kip; and **Hanoi**, 24 hrs, 200,000 kip on Tue and Sat; there are additional services at 1000 (VIP bus to Hué). Luxury Vietnam-bound buses can also be arranged through the **Savanbanhao Hotel** (see Where to stay), 90,000 kip. Although all of these buses claim to be direct, a bus change is required at the border. Buses leave even days at 0800 and arrive in Hué at 1600.

Car/bicycle/motorbike
Car and driver can be hired from the **Savanbanhao Hotel**. Some of the guesthouses rent bicycles for 10,000 kip and motorbikes for 50,000-80,000 kip.

Tuk-tuk and saamlor
10,000 kip per person for a local journey.

⊙ Directory

Thakhek *p87*
Banks Banque pour le Commerce Extérieur Lao (BCEL), Vientiane Rd, T051-212686, will change cash and TCs and does cash advances on Visa and MasterCard. It now also has a 24-hr Visa and MC ATM and there is one close to the fountain in the town centre too. Lao Development Bank, Kouvoravong Rd (eastern end), exchanges cash but doesn't do cash advances.
Internet Thakhek Travel Lodge and (expensive), Inthira Hotel, Mekong Hotel and Mukda internet café. Wi-Fi in the lobby of the Riveria and Inthira hotels. **Post office** Kouvoravong Rd (at crossroads with Nongbuakham Rd); international calls.

Savannakhet *p91, map p92*

Banks Lao Development Bank, Oudomsinh Rd, will change most major currencies. Banque pour le Commerce Exterieur Lao (BCEL), Ratsavongseuk Rd, will exchange currency and has an ATM.

Embassies and consulates Thai Consulate, Thahae Rd, T041-212373, Mon-Fri 0800-1200, 1300-1600. Visas are issued on the same day if dropped off in the morning. Vietnam Consulate, Sisavangvong Rd, T041-212182, Mon-Fri 0730-1100, 1330-1600. Provides Vietnamese visas in 3 days on presentation of 2 photos and US$45.

Internet Sikonet, Chaluanmeung Rd, and others on this road. The Hoongthip hotel offers Wi-Fi in its lobby. **Medical services** Savannakhet Hospital, Khanthabuli Rd, T041-212051. **Police** A block back from the river, near the Tourist Office, T041-212069. **Post office** Makhasavanh Rd, Next to the new provincial museum, T020-22601993. **Telephone** Lao Telecom Office, next door to the post office, for domestic and international calls.

Far south

The far south is studded with wonderful attractions: from pristine jungle scenery to the cooler Bolaven Plateau and the rambling ruins of Wat Phou, once an important regional powerbase. The true gems of the south, however, are the Siphandon (4000 islands), lush green islets that offer the perfect setting for those wanting to kick back for a few days. This region, near the border with Cambodia, is an idyllic picture-perfect ending to any trip in Laos. The three main islands offer something for all tourists: the larger Don Khong is great for exploring and taking in the stunning vista and traditional Lao rural life; Don Deth is a backpacker haven and is good for those who want to while away the days in a hammock with a good book; and Don Khone is better for tourist sites such as the Li Phi falls or old colonial ruins. There are roaring waterfalls nearby and pakha, or freshwater dolphins, can sometimes be spotted here between December and May.

Pakse (Pakxe) → *For listings, see pages 109-121.*

Pakse is the largest town in the south and is strategically located at the junction of the Mekong and Xe Don rivers. It is a busy commercial town, built by the French early in the 20th century as an administrative centre for the south. The town has seen better days but the tatty colonial buildings lend an air of old-world charm. Pakse is a major staging post for destinations further afield such as the old royal capital of Champasak, famed for its pre-Angkor, seventh-century Khmer ruins of Wat Phou. Close to Pakse are ecotourism projects where elephant treks, bird watching and homestays are possible.

Arriving in Pakse (Pakxe)

Getting there Pakse is Southern Laos' transport hub. The upgraded airport is 2 km northwest of town; tuk-tuks will make the journey for around 20,000 kip. International flights from Bangkok, Phnom Penh, Siem Reap, and Ho Chi Minh City as well as domestic flights to/from Vientiane, Savannakhet and Luang Prabang run several times a week. There are three official bus terminals in Pakse: the **Northern terminal** (Km 7 on Route 13 north, T031-251508) is for buses to and from the north; the **Southern terminal** (Km 8 south on Route 13, T031-212981) is for buses to and from the south; and the **VIP Khiang Kai and international bus terminal** (with neighbouring **Seangchaolearn terminal**) is for northbound VIP buses. VIP buses to Ubon in Thailand are available from the evening market; Laos visas are available on arrival at the Chongmek border crossing if you're coming in from Thailand, though, don't expect the bus to wait for you. Tuk-tuks wait to transport passengers from terminals to the town centre; you shouldn't have to pay more than 7000 kip if there are multiple passengers but they will wait until the vehicle is full. ►► *See Transport, page 117.*

Getting around Tuk-tuks and *saamlors* are the main means of local transport and can be chartered for half a day for about US$5. The main tuk-tuk 'terminal' is at the Daoheung market. Cars, motorbikes and bicycles are available for hire from some hotels and tour companies. The town's roads are numbered as if they were highways: No 1 road through to No 46 road.

Tourist information Champasak Provincial Department of Tourism ⓘ *No 11 Rd, T031-212021, www.xepian.org, daily 0800-1130 and 1330-1630.* They have some fantastic ecotours on offer to unique destinations. Some are offered in conjunction with local travel agents, such as **Green Discovery**, see What to do, page 116.

Champasak and around → *For listings, see pages 109-121.*

The small, attractive agricultural town of Champasak, which stretches along the right bank of the Mekong for 4 km, is the nearest town to Wat Phou and with enough comfortable

Pakse

Where to stay ■	Sabaidy 2 Guesthouse **7**	Restaurants ❷
Champasak Palace **1**	Salachampa **8**	Delta Coffee **1**
Pakse **5**		Jasmine **3**

accommodation, is a good base from which to explore the site and the surrounding area. It is about 40 km south of Pakse. The sleepy town is quaint and charming and a fantastic place to spend the night, though the trip can be done in a day. The town itself is dotted with simply stunning colonial buildings. Of these, the former residence of Champasak hereditary Prince Boun Oun and former leader of the right wing opposition, who fled the country in 1975 after the Communist takeover, is quite possibly the most magnificent colonial building in Laos. His daughter-in-law now resides there and although it is not open to tourists it is certainly worth a look from the outside. Champasak is known for its wood handicrafts, and vases, and other carved ornaments are available for sale near the jetty.

Arriving in Champasak

Getting there Most *songthaews* run from Pakse's Southern bus terminal on Route 13 to **Ban Lak Sarm Sip** (which translates as 'village 30 km'), where they take a right turn to **Ban Muang** (2-3 km). Here, people sell tickets for the ferry to Champasak (3000 kip; person and motorbike 10000 kip). The ferry runs from 0630-2000. Public boats from Pakse make the journey to Champasak in two hours (60,000 kip). A tuk-tuk from the ferry port into town costs 5000 kip. Public ferries run from Pakse to Champasak at 0800 daily. It is also possible to charter a boat, at quite a cost. A new road, due for construction, direct from Pakse, will make the little ferry crossing redundant.

Tourist information Champasak District Visitor Information Centre ① *Mon-Fri 0800-1230, 1400-1630 but daily in high season.* Can arrange boats to Don Daeng, guides to Wat Phou and tours to surrounding sites.

Wat Phou

① *The site is officially open 0800-1630 but the staff are happy to let you in if you get there for sunrise, even as early as 0530, and you won't get thrown out until 1800. The admission fee of 30,000 kip goes towards restoration (entry to the Exhibition Centre is included). There is also the Wat Phu Exhibition Centre at the entrance; a surprisingly good museum with an array of artefacts such as the garuda and nandi bull.* From the Champasak dock, you can catch a tuk-tuk to Wat Phou, 8-9 km, around 80,000 kip return. Most people prefer to hire a bicycle from one of the guesthouses in Champasak town and cycle to the ruins. Guides need to be arranged at the Champasak Tourist Information Centre with prices starting at US$15. There are several restaurants within the vicinity of the site. A new full moon event has been launched at Wat Phou, an atmospheric exploration of the site with lights from 1800-2100, 30,000 kip.

Champasak Historic Museum
VIP & Khiang Kai Terminal
VIP Terminal
Afternoon Market
Tuk-tuks & Seang Chaolearn Terminal
No 13 Rd
Stadium
ATM
ATM
ATM
Daoheung (Morning Market)
Taxis & Tuk-tuks
Songthaew & Tuk-tuk to Ban Saphay & Thai Border
Lao Nippon Bridge
To Southern Bus Terminal (8km)

Nazim's **6**
Xuan Mai **12**

The archaeological site of Wat Phou is at the foot of the Phou Pasak, 8 km southwest of Champasak. With its teetering, weathered masonry, it conforms exactly to the Western ideal of the lost city. The mountain behind Wat Phou is called **Linga Parvata**, as the Hindu Khmers thought it resembled a linga – albeit a strangely proportioned one. Although the original Hindu temple complex was built in the fifth and sixth centuries, most of what remains today is believed to have been built in the 10th to 11th centuries.

Wat Phou was a work in progress and was constructed and renovated over a period spanning several hundred years. Most of the ruins date back to the fifth and sixth centuries, making them at least 200 years older than Angkor Wat. At that time, the Champasak area was the centre of power on the lower Mekong. The Hindu temple only became a Buddhist shrine in later centuries.

Archaeologists and historians believe most of the building at Wat Phou was the work of the Khmer king, Suryavarman II (1131-1150), who was also responsible for starting work on Angkor Wat in Cambodia. The temple remained important for Khmer kings even after they had moved their capital to Angkor. They continued to appoint priests to serve at Wat Phou and sent money to maintain the temple until the last days of the Angkor Empire.

Exploring the site The king and dignitaries would originally have sat on a platform above the 'tanks' or *baray* and presided over official ceremonies or watched aquatic games. In 1959 a palace was built on the platform so the king had somewhere to stay during the annual Wat Phou Festival (see page 115). A long avenue leads from the platform to the pavilions. This **processional causeway** was probably built by Khmer King Jayavarman VI (1080-1107) and may have been the inspiration for a similar causeway at Angkor Wat.

Wat Phou

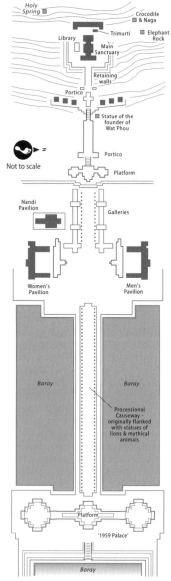

The sandstone **pavilions**, on either side of the processional causeway, were added after the main temple and are thought to date from the 12th century. Although crumbling, with great slabs of laterite and collapsed lintels lying around, both pavilions are remarkably intact. The pavilions were probably used for segregated worship by pilgrims, one for women (left) and the other for men (right). The porticoes of the two huge buildings face each other. The roofs were thought originally to have been poorly constructed with thin stone slabs on a wooden beam-frame and later replaced by Khmer tiles. Only the outer walls now remain but there is enough still standing to fire the imagination: the detailed carving around the window frames and porticoes is well-preserved. The laterite used to build the complex was brought from **Ou Mong**, also called Tomo Temple, another smaller Khmer temple complex a few kilometres downriver, but the carving is in sandstone. The interiors were without permanent partitions, although it is thought that rush matting was used instead, and furniture was limited – reliefs only depict low stools and couches. At the rear of the women's pavilion are the remains of a brick construction, believed to have been the queen's quarters.

Above the pavilions is a small temple, the **Nandi Pavilion**, with entrances on two sides. It is dedicated to Nandi, the bull (Siva's vehicle), and is a common feature in Hindu temple complexes. There are three chambers, each of which would originally have contained statues – these have been stolen. As the hill begins to rise above the Nandi temple, the remains of six brick temples follow the contours, with three on each side of the pathway. All six are completely ruined and their function is unclear. At the bottom of the steps is a portico and statue of the founder of Wat Phou, Pranga Khommatha.

The **main sanctuary**, 90 m up the hillside and orientated east-west, was originally dedicated to Siva. The rear section (behind the Buddha statue) is part of the original sixth-century brick building. Sacred spring water was channelled through the hole in the back wall of this section and used to wash the sacred linga. The water was then thrown out, down a chute in the right wall, where it was collected in a receptacle. Pilgrims would then wash in the holy water. The front of the temple was constructed later, probably in the eighth to ninth century, and has some fantastic carvings: apsaras, dancing Vishnu, Indra on a three-headed elephant and, above the portico of the left entrance, a carving of Siva, the destroyer, tearing a woman in two.

The Hindu temple was converted into a Buddhist shrine, either in the 13th century during the reign of the Khmer king Jayavarman VII or when the Lao conquered the area in the 14th century. A large Buddha statue now presides over its interior.

Don Daeng Island

ⓘ *An ecotour is the way to get here; contact the Provincial Tourism Office in Pakse or the Tourism Office in Champasak. A trip by boat from Champasak will cost around US$1.*

This idyllic river island sits right across from Champasak. It stretches for 8 km and is the perfect place for those wishing to see quintessential village life, with basket weaving, fishing and rice farming, and without the cars and hustle and bustle. There is a path around the island that can be traversed on foot or by bicycle. A crumbling ancient brick stupa, built in the same century as Wat Phu, is in the centre of the island and there are a few ancient remnants in **Sisak Village** from the construction. The local inhabitants of **Pouylao Village** are known for their knife-making prowess. There is a lovely sandy beach on the Champasak side of the island, perfect for a dip. The island has only recently opened up to tourism, so it is important to tread lightly. There is one upmarket hotel and homestay on the island, see Where to stay, page 111.

Tahoy festival

There are several Tahoy settlements around the Bolaven Plateau although the Tahoy population in Laos is only about 30,000. The village of Ban Paleng, not far from Tha Teng on Route 16, is a fascinating place to visit, especially in March (in accordance with the full-moon), when the animist Tahoy celebrate their annual three-day sacrificial festival. The village is built in a circle around the *kuan* (the house of sacrifice). A water buffalo is donated by each family in the village. The buffalo has its throat cut and the blood is collected and drunk. The raw meat is divided among the families and surrounding villages are invited to come and feast on it. The head of each family throws a slab of meat into the *lak khai* – a basket hanging from a pole in front of the *kuan* – so that the spirits can partake too. The sacrifice is performed by the village shaman, then dancers throw spears at the buffalo until it dies. The villagers moved from the Vietnam border area to escape the war, but Ban Paleng was bombed repeatedly: the village is still littered with shells and unexploded bombs.

Xe Pian National Protected Area

① *The provincial authorities are trying to promote ecotourism in this area: www.xepian.org. To organize an elephant trek go to the the Eco-Guide Unit at the tourism office in Pakse (T031-212021), the Kiet Ngong Visitor Centre or the Kingfisher Ecolodge, if you are staying there (see Where to stay, page 111).*

The Xe Pian National Protected Area (NPA) is home to large water birds, great hornbills, sun bears, Asiatic black bears and the yellow-cheeked crested gibbon. The area is rich in bird-life and is one of the most threatened land-types in Laos. **Ban Kiet Ngong Village**, 1½ hours from Pakse, has a community-based project offering elephant trekking and homestay accommodation on the edge of the Xe Pian NPA. The village itself is at the **Kiet Ngong Wetland**, the largest wetland in Southern Laos. The villagers have traditionally been dependent on elephants for agricultural work and their treks can be organized to either the Xe Pian National Protected Area or the amazing fortress of **Phu Asa.** This ancient fortress is located 2 km from Kiet Ngong, at the summit of a small jungle-clad hill. It is an enigmatic site that has left archaeologists puzzled; it consists of 20 stone columns, 2m high, arranged in a semi-circle – they look a bit like a scaled-down version of Stonehenge. To reach the village from Pakse, follow Route 13 until you get to the Km48 junction with Route 18 at Thang Beng Village (the Xe Pian National Protected Area office is here). Follow route 18 east for 7 km, turn right at the signpost for the last 1.5 km to Ban Kiet Ngong (a 30,000 kip per person fee is now levied on entrance to the park).

There are several other two- to three-day trekking/homestay ecotours offered in the area, contact the **Provincial Tourism Information Office** in Pakse or the **Kingfisher Ecolodge**.

Bolaven Plateau → *For listings, see pages 109-121.*

The French identified the Bolaven Plateau, in the northeast of Champasak Province, as a prime location for settlement by hardy French farming stock. It is named after the Laven minority group that reside in the area. The soils are rich and the upland position affords some relief from the summer heat of the lowlands. However, their grand colonial plans came to nought and, although some French families came to live here, they were few in number and all left between the 1950s and 1970s as conditions in the area deteriorated.

Today the plateau is inhabited by a mix of ethnic groups, such as the Laven, Alak, Tahoy and Suay, many of whom were displaced during the war. The premier attraction in the area is the number of roaring falls plunging off the plateau; Tad Lo and Tad Fan are particularly popular tourist destinations, while the grand Tad Yeung makes a perfect picnic destination. The plateau also affords excellent rafting and kayaking trips.

Visiting the Bolaven Plateau
Tourist infrastructure is limited. Trips to **Tad Fan** and other attractions can be organized in Pakse through **Sabaidy 2 Guesthouse** (see page 109), and **Green Discovery** (see page 116). Alternatively, the best base on the plateau is **Tad Lo** (see page 104), which can be reached by a bus or *songthaew* from Pakse, alighting at Ban Houa Set (2½ hours from Pakse). There is a sign here indicating the way to Tad Lo – a 1.5-km walk. You can usually get a tuk-tuk from Ban Houa Set to Tad Lo for around 10,000 kip.
▶ See What to do, page 116, and Transport, page 117.

Paksong (Pakxong) and around
The main town on the Bolaven Plateau is Paksong, a small town 50 km east of Pakse renowned for its large produce market. It was originally a French agricultural centre, popular during the colonial era for its cooler temperatures. The town occupies a very scenic spot, however, the harsh weather in the rainy season changes rapidly making it difficult to plan trips around the area.

On the way to Paksong, just past Km 38, is **Tad Fan**, a dramatic 120-m-high waterfall, which is believed to be one of the tallest cascades in the country. The fall splits into two powerful streams roaring over the edge of the cliff and plummeting into the pool below, with mist and vapour shrouding views from above.

Tad Yeung and around
Around 2 km from Tad Fan and 40 km from Pakse is Tad Yeung. The falls are about 1km from the main road. Set among beautiful coffee plantations and sprinkled with wooden picnic huts, these falls are possibly the best on offer on the plateau as they offer both height and accessibility. Packing a picnic in Pakse and bringing it along for an afternoon trip is recommended. The cascades plummet 50 m to a pool at the bottom, where it's possible to swim in the dry season. During the wet season the waterways create numerous little channels and islands around the cascades. Behind the main falls sits a cave, however it's best to get someone to guide you here. There is a slippery walkway from the top of the falls to the bottom, where you can swim. The falls can be reached by taking a local bus from the Southern Bus station in Pakse to a village at Km 40 (ask to go to **Lak See Sip**). The turn-off is on the right from Pakse (and on the left from Paksong). There is a sign on the main road which indicates **Sihom Sabaidy Guesthouse**, follow this road about 700 m to the falls. These falls are a great option if you are trying to avoid the backpacker hordes.

Just 17 km from Paksong are the twin falls of **Tad Mone** and **Tad Meelook**. Once a popular picnic spot for locals, the area is now almost deserted and the swimming holes at the base of the falls are an idyllic place for a dip.

Some 35 km northwest of Pakse is **Pasuam Waterfall** and **Utayan Bajiang Champasak** ⓘ *T031-251294, 5000 kip*, a strange ethnic theme park popular with Thai tourists. The large compound features small cascades, a model ethnic village, gardens and trails. There are bungalows, a tree house and rooms available. To get here from Pakse follow Route 13 towards Paksong and follow the left fork at 21 km and turn off at 30 km.

Tad Lo and around → *For listings, see pages 109-121.*

Tad Lo is a popular 'resort' on the edge of the Bolaven Plateau, nestled alongside three rolling cascades. There are several places to stay in this idyllic retreat, good hiking, a river to frolic in (especially in the wet season) and elephant trekking. In the vicinity of Tad Lo there are also several villages, which can be visited in the company of a local villager. The guesthouses in Tad Lo can arrange guided treks to Ban Khian and Tad Soung.

The **Xe Xet** (or Houai Set) flows past Tad Lo, crashing over two sets of cascades nearby: **Tad Hang**, the lower series, is overlooked by the Tad Lo Lodge and Saise Guesthouse, while **Tad Lo**, the upper, is a short hike away.

A new Community Guides office has been established with a number of trained guides offering treks around the Tad Lo area and to nearby Ngai villages. Elephant treks can also be arranged from the Tad Lo Lodge for 85,000 kip per person for a 90-minute trek through the jungle and river.

There are two Alak villages, **Ban Khian** and **Tad Soung**, close to Tad Lo. Tad Soung is approximately 10 km away from the main resort area and are the most panoramic falls in the vicinity. The Alak are an Austro-Indonesian ethno-linguistic group. Most fascinating is the Alak's seeming obsession with death. The head of each household carves coffins out of hollowed logs for himself and his whole family (even babies), then stacks them, ready for use, under their rice storage huts. This tradition serves as a reminder that life expectancy in these remote rural areas is around 40 and infant mortality of around 100 per 1000 live births; the number-one killer is malaria.

Katou villages such as **Ban Houei Houne** (on the Salavan–Pakse road) are famous for their weaving of a bright cloth used locally as a *pha sinh* (sarong).

Don Khong → *For listings, see pages 109-121.*

Don Khong is the largest of the Mekong islands at 16 km long and 8 km wide. It's the place to relax or explore by bicycle. Visitors might be surprised by the smooth asphalt roads, electricity and general standard of amenities that exist on the island but two words explain it all – Khamtay Siphandone – Laos' former president, who has a residence on the island.

Visiting Don Khong

Getting there and around The easiest way to get to all three major Siphandon islands from Pakse is by private minivan, 60,000 kip arranged by operators in Pakse. The luxurious way is aboard the **Vat Phou**, www.vatphou.com, a boutique riverborne hotel that does a three-day/two-night cruise from Pakse to Champasak and Wat Phou to Don Khong and then back to Pakse. *Songthaews* depart Pakse's Southern bus terminal hourly between 0800 and 1200. The occasional bus will also ply through but *songthaews* are the most common transport option. The journey to Ban Hat Xai Khoune (to catch a boat to Don Khong) should take between four and five hours and cost US$3; in most cases the bus/truck will board the car ferry at Ban Hat (1 km south of Ban Hat Xai Khoune) and take you right across to Ban Naa on Don Khong (1 km south of Muang Khong). Motorbikes on the car ferry from Ban Hat are charged 5,000 kip. There are also motorboats from Ban Hat Xai Khoune to Muang Khong (20,000 kip, depending on the number of passengers). Passenger boats run 24 hours but after 1800 the crossing costs 15,000 kip.

If there is not a bus directly to Don Khong, catch a bus bound for Ban Nakasang (the stop-off for Don Deth and Don Khone) and jump off at Ban Hat Xai Khoune. All local guesthouses are able to arrange bicycle hire. ▸▸ *See Transport, page 117.*

Around the island
Don Khong's 'capital' is **Muang Khong**, a small former French settlement. Pigs and chickens scrabble for food under the houses and just 50 m inland the houses give way

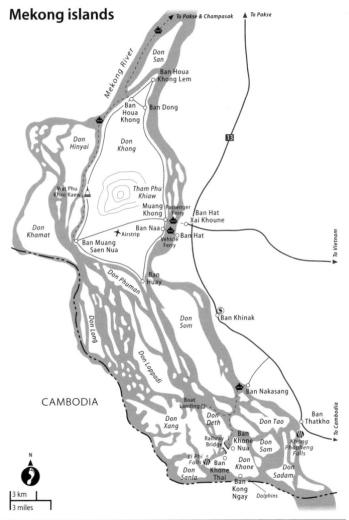

Mekong islands

to paddy fields. There are two wats in the town. **Wat Kan Khong**, also known as Wat Phuang Kaew, is visible from the jetty: a large gold Buddha in the *mudra* of subduing Mara garishly overlooks the Mekong. Much more attractive is **Wat Chom Thong** at the upstream extremity of the village, which may date from the early 19th century but which was much extended during the colonial period. The unusual Khmer-influenced sim may be gently decaying but it is doing so with style. The wat compound, with its carefully tended plants and elegant buildings, is very peaceful. The naga heads on the roof of the main sim are craftily designed to channel water, which issues from their mouths.

Most people come to Muang Khong as a base for visiting the **Li Phi** and **Khong Phapheng Falls** (see page 109) in the far south. However, these trips, alongside the dolphin-watching trips, are much easier to arrange from Don Deth or Don Khone. This island is a destination in itself and offers a great insight into Lao rural life without all the hustle and bustle found in more built-up areas. To a certain extent, except for electricity, a sprinkling of cars and a couple of internet terminals, time stands still in Dong Khong.

The island itself is worth exploring by bicycle and deserves more time than most visitors give it. It is flat – except in the interior where there are approximately 99 hills – the roads are quiet, so there is less risk of being mown down by a timber truck, and the villages and countryside offer a glimpse of traditional Laos. Most people take the southern 'loop' around the island, via **Ban Muang Saen Nua**, a distance of about 25 km (two to three hours by bike). The villages along the section of road south of **Ban Muang Saen Nua** are picturesque with buffalos grazing and farmers tending to their rice crops. Unlike other parts of Laos the residents here are fiercely protective of their forests and logging incurs very severe penalties.

About 6 km north of Ban Muang Saen Nua is a hilltop wat, which is arguably Don Khong's main claim to national fame. **Wat Phou Khao Kaew** (Glass Hill Monastery) is built on the spot where an entrance leads down to the underground lair of the nagas, known as **Muang Nak**. This underground town lies beneath the waters of the Mekong, with several tunnels leading to the surface – another is at That Luang in Vientiane. Lao legend has it that the nagas will come to the surface to protect the Lao whenever the country is in danger.

Tham Phou Khiaw is tucked away among the forests of the **Green Mountain** in the centre of the island. It's a small cave, containing earthenware pots. Buddha images and other relics and offerings litter the site. Every Lao New Year (April) townsfolk climb up to the cave to bathe the images. Although it's only 15 minutes' walk from the road, finding the cave is not particularly straightforward except during Lao New Year when it is possible to follow the crowds. Head 1.5 m north from Muang Khong on the road until you come to a banana plantation, with a couple of wooden houses. Take the pathway just before the houses through the banana plantation and at the top, just to the left, is a small gateway through the fence and a fairly well-defined path. Head up and along this path and, after 300 m or so, there is a rocky clearing. The path continues from the top right corner of the clearing for a further 200 m to a rocky mound that rolls up and to the left. Walk across the mound for about 20 m, until it levels out, and then head back to the forest. Keeping the rock immediately to your right, continue round and after 40 m there are two upturned tree trunks marking the entrance to the cave.

On the northern tip of the island is a sandy beach. Note that swimming is generally not advised due to parasites in the water and potentially strong currents. There is a rumour that Laos' former president, Khamtay Siphandone, is building a resort here. In nearby **Wat Houa Khong**, approximately 13 km north of Muang Khong, is the former President's modest abode set in traditional Lao style.

Don Deth, Don Khone and around → *For listings, see pages 109-121.*

The islands of Don Khone and Don Deth are the pot of gold at the end of the rainbow for most travellers who head to the southern tip of Laos, and it's not hard to see why. The bamboo huts that stretch along the banks of these two staggeringly beautiful islands are filled with contented travellers in no rush to move on. Don Deth is more of a backpacker haven, not dissimilar to the Koh Phangans and Vang Viengs of the region, meanwhile Don Khone has been able to retain a more authentically Lao charm. Travelling by boat in this area is very picturesque: the islands are covered in coconut palms, flame trees, stands of bamboo, kapok trees and hardwoods; the river is riddled with eddies and rapids. In the distance, a few kilometres to the south, are the Khong Hai Mountains, which dominate the skyline and delineate the border between Laos and Cambodia.

In the area are the **Li Phi** (or Somphamit) **Falls** and **Khong Phapheng Falls** – the latter are the largest in Southeast Asia and reputedly the widest in the world.

The French envisaged Don Deth and Don Khone as strategic transit points in their grandiose masterplan to create a major Mekong highway from China. In the late 19th century, ports were built at the southern end of Don Khone and at the northern end of Don Deth and a narrow-gauge railway line was constructed across Don Khone in 1897 as an important bypass around the rapids for French cargo boats sailing upriver from Phnom Penh. In 1920, the French built a bridge across to Don Deth and extended the railway line to Don Deth port. This 5-km stretch of railway has the unique distinction of being the only line the French ever built in Laos. On the southern side of the island lie the rusted corpses of the old locomotive and boiler car. Before pulling into Ban Khone Nua, the main settlement on Don Khone, Don Deth's original 'port' is on the right, with what remains of its steel rail jetty.

Visiting Don Deth and Don Khone

A number of companies run tours to this area, especially from Pakse. To get to Don Deth or Don Khone independently from Pakse the bus/*songthaew* will need to drop you off at **Ban Nakasang**. This is not the most pleasant of Lao towns and several travellers have complained about being ripped off here. However, it has a thriving market, where most of the islanders stock up on goods, so it's worth having a look around before you head off, particularly if you need to pick up necessities like torches and batteries. It's a 500-m walk from the bus stop down to the dock. The 'ticket office' is located in a little restaurant to the right-hand side of the dock. However, you can ask anyone that's jumping across to the islands for a lift, at a dramatically reduced rate. The boats take about 15 to 20 minutes to make the easy trip to the islands and cost around 20,000 kip per person. Prices will be higher if you are travelling solo. A boat between Don Deth and Don Khone costs 30,000 kip; alternatively you can walk between the two islands, paying the 10,000 kip charge to cross the bridge (also used as ticket to see Li Phi Falls). Both islands can easily be navigated on foot or bicycles can be rented from guesthouses for 10,000 kip per day.
➡ *See What to do, page 116, and Transport, page 117.*

Don Deth

The riverbank here is peppered with cheap-as-chips bamboo huts and restaurants geared to accommodate the growing wave of backpackers that flood south to stop and recoup in this idyllic setting. A good book, hammock and icy beverage is the order of the day here, but those with a bit more energy should explore the truly stunning surroundings.

It's a great location for watching the sunrises and sunsets, for walking through shady palms and frangipani trees and for swimming off the beaches, which attract the hordes in the dry season. Away from the picturesque waterfront, the centre of the island comprises rice paddies and farms; you should take care not to harm crops when exploring the island.

The national tourism authorities have been coordinating with locals to ensure that the beautiful island doesn't become 'Vang Vieng-ified', so you'll find no *Friends* DVDs here, although 'happy' shakes have started appearing. The islands got 24-hour electricity in November 2009 although not everyone has signed up to the 24-hour connection, there are no cars (except for the odd truck and tourist open-sided buses) and few other modern conveniences. Internet has amazingly made its way to the island, however, and it's possible to get mobile phone coverage. Most guesthouses run tours to the falls/dolphins. A few entrepreneurial types are starting to promote adventure tourism here. Kayaking and rafting trips can be organized through **Xplore-asia** ① *T031-212893, www.xplore-asia.com*. Several guesthouses also have tubes for rent. It is definitely inadvisable to go tubing in the wet season and probably not a good idea all year round. It is also inadvisable to go alone; there are a huge set of falls at the bottom of Laos. Swimming, visiting the falls and other activities all need to be undertaken with the utmost caution here. The river's current is probably the strongest in all of Laos and several tourists have drowned here.

Don Khone

From the railway bridge, follow the southwest path through **Ban Khone Thai** and then wind through the paddy fields for 1.7 km (20 minutes' walk) to **Li Phi Falls** ① *10000 kip paid at the bridge.* Also known as Somphamit or Khone Yai Falls, these are a succession of rapids, crashing through

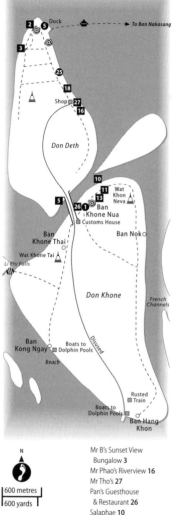

Don Deth & Don Khone

N

| 600 metres |
| 600 yards |

Where to stay 🛏
Auberge Sala Don Khone 11
Boun Guesthouse 13
Deng Guesthouse 18
Little Eden 2
Mr B's Sunset View Bungalow 3
Mr Phao's Riverview 16
Mr Tho's 27
Pan's Guesthouse & Restaurant 26
Salaphae 10
Santiphab Guesthouse 5

Restaurants 🍴
Anny's 1
Lamphone 25
Pool Bar & Restaurant 5

a narrow gorge. In the wet season, when the rice is green, the area is beautiful; in the dry season, it is scorching. From the main vantage point on a jagged, rocky outcrop, the falls aren't that impressive, as a large stretch of them are obscured. 'Phi' means ghost, a reference, it is believed, to the bodies that floated down the river from the north during the war. It's best to visit Li Phi around June or July, when all the fishermen are putting out their bamboo fish traps. These are dangerous waterfalls, do not swim here.

The Mekong, south of Don Khone, is one of the few places in the world where it is possible to see very rare freshwater dolphins. They can be spottedfrom December to May, from the French pier at the end of the island, not far from the village of **Ban Hang Khon**. The walk across Don Khone from the railway bridge is some 4 km and bicycles can be hired. (A much better bicycle route is to head round round the tip and down to Hang Khon, 45 minutes; the disused railway bridge is not a comfortable ride for bikes as it's rocky.) It is more likely, however, to catch a glimpse of the dolphins if you're in a boat (from **Ban Kong Ngay** or **Ban Hang Khon**), as they reside in deep-water pools. There are thought to be 80-120 dolphins. The Laos–Cambodia border transects the dolphin pool and the Lao boatmen have to pay US$1 to the Cambodian authorities in order to access the waters in which the dolphins live. Cambodia gets a bit tetchy about these 'border incursions' and may, on the odd occasion, deny access. ▸▸ *See What to do, page 116.*

Khong Phapheng Falls
ⓘ *Near Ban Thatkho, 10,000 kip. Guesthouses organize trips for around 60,000 kip per person (minimum 4 passengers), usually booked in conjunction with a trip to see the dolphins (at extra cost).*
About 36 km south of Ban Hat Xai Khoune at Ban Thatkho, a road branches off Route 13 towards Khong Phapheng Falls, which roar around the eastern shore of the Mekong for 13 km. One fork of the road leads to a vantage point, where a large wooden structure, built up on stilts, overlooks the cascades for a fantastic head-on view of the falls. When you see the huge volume of white water boiling and surging over the jagged rocks below, it is hard to imagine that there is another 10 km width of river running through the other channels. A path leads down from the viewpoint to the edge of the water, be very careful here. Unsurprisingly, the river is impassable at this juncture. Another road leads down to the bank, 200 m away, just above the lip of the falls; at this deceptively tranquil spot, the river is gathering momentum before it plunges over the edge.

Far south listings

For hotel and restaurant price codes and other relevant information, see pages 8-9.

🛏 Where to stay

Pakse *p97, map p98*
$$$-$$ Pakse Hotel, No 5 Rd, T031-212131, www.hotelpakse.com. This is one of the best places to stay in town –and indeed in the country – with 65 rooms. The French owner, Mr Jérôme, has integrated local handicraft decorations, rosewood accents and tasteful furnishings into this slick hotel. The eco-rooms are good value and the deluxe rooms are a luxury in this part of the country. Breakfast included. Wi-Fi. Good rooftop restaurant with a perfect view over the city and river; the dimly lit eatery oozes ambience. The chicken curry soup is a must – as are the lethal mojitos!
$$ Champasak Palace, No 13 Rd, T031-212263, www.champasakpalacehotel.com. This is a massive chocolate box of a hotel with 55 rooms and lit up like a Christmas

tree. It was conceived as a palace for a minor prince. There are some large rooms and 40 more modern, and very plain rooms. It is quite bizarre to see bellhops in traditional uniforms. Recent renovations have resulted in a loss of original character in favour of modernity but some classic touches remain: wooden shutters, some art deco furniture and lovely tiles. The restaurant is one of the most atmospheric place to eat in town, set on a big veranda overlooking lovely frangipani trees. The friendly staff speak a smattering of English, there's a good terrace and the facilities are good, including a massage centre. It's a great position above the Xe Don and the views from higher levels are stunning. Splash out on the King suite for the kitsch factor, jacuzzi and private balcony.

$$-$ Salachampa, No 10 Rd, salachampa hotel.com. The most characterful place in town. Choose a room in the main 1920s building: huge with large en suite bathrooms with warm-water showers; the upstairs rooms with balconies are best. There are quaintly rustic rooms in a 'new' extension. Recommended for those looking for a touch of colonial elegance and friendly service. Exceptional value for money.

$ Sabaidy 2 Guesthouse, No 24 Rd, T031-212992, www.sabaidy2tour.com. A range of rooms on offer, from dorms to rooms with private bathrooms and hot water. Quite basic but the service is exceptional. The proprietor, Mr Vong offers tours (the Bolaven day tour is recommended; each tourist contributes to a school project when buying a tour), information and visa extensions. Very popular, you may need to book in advance. Basic food available. Motorbike rental.

Champaspak p98
$$$ Inthira Champakone Hotel, diagonally opposite **Vong Pasued**, T031-214059, www.inthirahotels.com. This is a lovely hotel with a friendly US manager. The twins in the courtyard outback come with outdoor rain showers and wooden-floored spacious rooms. The double de luxe

is a mini apartment with mezzanine bed area, balcony, shower room and bathroom. The twins are actually more homely.

$ Anouxa Guesthouse, 1 km north of the roundabout, T031-213272. A wide range of accommodation from wooden bungalows through to concrete rooms with hot water and either a/c (pay extra) or fan and dingy bamboo structures with cold water. The concrete villas are the best, with a serene river vista from the balconies. The restaurant is probably one of the best in town, overlooking the river plus a shady cabaña. The only drawback is that it is a little out of town (although next to the new spa) and some of the staff can't be bothered to serve customers. Bikes (10,000 kip) and motorbikes (70,000 kip) for hire.

$ Khamphouy Guesthouse, on the main road southwest of the roundabout, T031-252700. Delightful family-run place. Fine bright but basic rooms in the main house with en suite shower. Newer rooms, built in the garden, will cost more. Clean, comfortable, friendly, relaxed. The room facing the front room has a semi-private patio with tables and chairs out front and a larger bathroom than most. Bikes for hire (10,000 kip); book exchange. Good value for those on a budget.

$ Vong Pasued Guesthouse, 450 m south of the roundabout, T020-2271 2402. The grimy, dingy shop-front facade is deceiving, as out the back, beside the river, are a range of pleasant rooms for all budgets. Strange resident parrot that squawks 'cow' incessantly. The owners are very pleasant. A firm favourite with the backpacker set, this small family-run guesthouse offers pretty reasonable rooms. The rooms by the river are great value, clean with hot water, The more basic rooms do not face the river and are fan only. Good restaurant, perfect for a natter with fellow travellers. Rents bikes for 10,000 kip per day.

Don Daeng Island p101

$$$$-$$$ La Folie Lodge, T030-534 7603, www.lafolie-laos.com. 24 rooms housed in lovely wooden bungalows, each with its own balcony overlooking the river. The lodge has a stunning pool surrounded by landscaped tropical gardens. Restaurant with good wine and cocktail selection. Bicycle hire and swimming pool use is available to non-guests for a fee. It's a luxurious base from where to explore the island. The German manager is efficient and entertaining.

$ Homestays are offered in a community lodge and 17 homestays in Ban Hua Don Daeng. The wooden lodge has 2 common rooms, sleeping 5 people with shared bathrooms and dining area. Meals are 20,000 kip. The **Champasak Tourism office** can arrange the homestay or call direct to English-speaking Mr Khamfong, T020-5599 6609. Boat transfer 30,000 kip. The restaurant serves meals for 20,000 kip. Bicycle hire, 20,000 kip; boat to Tomo temple, 150,000 kip; guide 20,000 kip.

Xe Pian National Protected Area p102

$$$-$$$ Kingfisher Ecolodge, 1 km east of Kiet Ngong, T030-534 5016, www.king fisherecolodge.com. A bonafide eco-lodge set facing wetlands. The set of 6 glass-fronted bungalows are lovely and romantic with 4-poster beds. There are also 4 attractive thatched rooms with nearby shared bathroom. The restaurant, set on the 2nd floor of the lodge, has simply stunning views over the Pha Pho wetlands. Elephant-related activities and massage can be arranged. The owners Massimo and Bangon are so helpful. Highly recommended.

$ Homestay, Ban Kietong, www.xepian. org/accommodation. 36 villagers offer basic homestay. Meals are 20,000 kip per person. You can book at the **Village Information Center** but in Lao only T030-534 6547. If you cannot make yourself understood on arrival, better to ask for Mr Ho who speaks a little bit of English: first house behind the wat.

Paksong and around p103

$$-$ Tad Fan Resort, T020-5553 1400, www.tadfane.com. Perched on the opposite side of the ravine from the falls is a series of wooden bungalows with nicely decorated rooms and en suite bathrooms (hot showers). The 2nd floor of the excellent open-air restaurant offers the best view of the falls and serves a wide variety of Lao, Thai and Western food. Great service. Treks to the top of falls and the Dan-Sin-Xay Plain can be arranged.

Tad Yeung p103

$ Sihom Sabaidy Guesthouse, T020-5667 6186. It is the only operational guesthouse in the vicinity of these falls. There are 8 basic rooms with shared hot-water bathrooms. There is an adjoining restaurant offering basic Lao meals, noodles, eggs and coffee. The guesthouse is set on a coffee plantation and tours are available to the waterfall as well as to nearby orchid areas and tours to see how coffee is made.

Tad Lo and around p104

$$$-$$ Tad Lo, www.tadlolodge.com. Reception on the east side of the falls with chalet-style accommodation (some accommodation is built right on top of the waterfalls on the opposite side; it's a highly inconvenient hike from one to the other for the restaurant). Rates include breakfast and hot water. The location is attractive (during the wet season) and the accommodation is comfortable; cane rocking chairs on the balconies overlook the cascades on the left bank. Good restaurant serving plenty of Lao and Thai food.

$$$-$ Saise Guesthouse & Resort (aka Sayse Guesthouse), T034-211886. This resort is scattered right across the falls area with varying prices for the accommodation. It is inconvenient to stay in the far-flung buildings (eg the Green and Blue Houses) if the restaurant (at the foot of Tad Hang) is of prime importance. The resort belongs to the Minister of Tourism and his son.

It is beneath contempt, therefore, that a government minister houses in his garden 2 caged gibbons, 2 caged macaques, a caged civet and a caged bird.

$ Tim Guesthouse & Restaurant, down the bridge road, T034-211885, www. geocities.com/tadlo_net. 5 bungalows and 7 twin and double rooms with shared hot-water bathrooms, fans and lock boxes. Also internet access (500 kip per min with all proceeds to the local school), international calls, laundry, book exchange, a substantial music collection. He runs a good range of sevices. Motorbike hire 80,000 kip per day.

Don Khong *p104*

$$$-$$ Pon Arena Hotel, 40 m north of the main st, www.ponarenahotel.com. Mr Pon's has opened a new handsome hotel. You'll want one of the rooms with balconies overlooking the river. All tastefully decorated with high ceilings and bathtubs, minibars and TVs; some rooms have tiny 'smoking' balconies. Wi-Fi throughout. Breakfast served on the upstairs veranda.

$$$-$ Senesothxeune Hotel, 100 m to the left of the main ferry point, T030-526 0577, www.ssxhotel.com. Tastefully designed, modern interpretation of colonial Lao architecture. Beautiful fittings, including carved wooden fish above each entrance and brass chandeliers. Rooms are fitted with mod cons like a/c, TV, hot water and minibar. Superior rooms have fantastic bathtubs. Splurge a little for the superior room with private balcony. The hotel has a modern internet café (Wi-Fi also available) and restaurant. The menu is mainly confined to Asian dishes; the chicken and vermicelli soup is good. A little English is spoken by waiters. This is the island's best accommodation by a long shot although Mr Pon's additional **Arena** hotel, will give it a run for its money. The hotel is run by the gentle, softly spoken Mr Senesavath and his wife, both former mathematics professors from Don Dok University in Vientiane. Both speak English and French. Recommended.

$ River Guesthouse, T031-214037. The large, spotless a/c rooms are very good value, with hot showers, mosquito nets and comfortable beds. Mr Pon, who speaks French and English, is perhaps the most helpful of all accommodation proprietors on the island and can offer an endless supply of tourist information and travel arrangements. Motorbike and bike rental and he can also arrange trips to the Cambodian border, to Don Deth and Don Khon and back to Pakse. In fact, Mr Pon should be your first point of contact for any needs. Recommended. The restaurant is the most popular on the island.

$ Souksan Hotel, northern end of town near Wat Chom Thong, T031-212071. The reception is in a homely building at the front, while the main accommodation area is in a block further back. Well-designed a/c rooms with en suite bathrooms and hot water set around a concrete garden. In a separate building, with bizarre river landscape paintings, the rooms are nicely decorated and comfortable with desk, cane chairs, tiled floorboards and hot water. Fan rooms are cheaper and represent good value. They also run one of the most up-market guesthouses on Don Deth. Friendly management.

$ Villa Khang Kong, set back from the main road, near the ferry point, T031-213539. Fantastic traditional Lao wooden building spruced up with some colourful paint with a great veranda and fab communal lounging area. Spacious clean rooms, with or without a/c. No river views.

Don Deth *p107, map p108*

Many people tend to make their choice of accommodation based on word-of-mouth recommendations from other travellers. Accommodation normally consists of spartan, threadbare bungalows with bed, mosquito net, hammock and shared squat toilets (unless otherwise stated). Always opt for a bungalow with a window, as the huts can get very hot. The wooden bungalows don't provide as much ventilation as the rattan equivalents but tend to attract fewer insects. Also note that tin-roofed huts will heat up quicker than thatch-roofed ones.

The accommodation runs across the both sides of the island, known as the **Sunset Side** and the **Sunrise Side**. As a general rule, if you want peace and quiet, head for the bungalows towards the mid-point along each coast; ask the boat drivers to drop you off directly at the bungalows as it can be a difficult hike with bags.

Sunset side

$$-$ Little Eden, Hua Det, T020-7773 9045, www.littleedenguesthouse-dondet.com. Very close to the island tip and a small hike from the main drop-off dock, this place offers the best view of the stunning sunsets. Miss Noy and her husband Mathieu have built the best concrete bungalows on the island: 5 smart and spacious rooms with fan and a/c, mosquito net, hot water and even a bookcase in the rooms. The restaurant serving top-notch Asian and European dishes (and Belgian fries) is in a prime position. Mathieu is very helpful.

$ Mr B's Sunset View Bungalow, near the northern tip, T020-5418 1171. The bungalows and grounds themselves are a bit lacklustre. However, the river views and the helpful staff make this a good option. The best options are the well-located 4 riverside rooms. Of the others the rooms without shower are nicer and bigger than those with shower.

Sunrise side

$ Deng Guesthouse, next to **Mr Oudomsouk's**. Wooden bungalows on stilts. Very popular with those who want to laze in a hammock overlooking the water.

$ Mr Phao's Riverview, on the riverfront, T020-5656 9651. Brand spanking new 7 wooden bungalows with lovely carved wooden furniture; 2 have inside shower. Mr Phao is one of the friendliest folk on the island and super helpful. He has a new toilet block with Western loo and sqaut options.

He will take guests across to opposite Aan island where there is a wat (10,000 kip) and will make an ATM run for 120,000 kip return, see Banks, page 121.

$ Mr Tho's, T020-5656 7502. Wooden stilt bungalows, good hammocks and views of Don Khone. The staff are friendly. Rooms have been given unusual names, such as 'sticky rice bungalow' and 'bamboo bungalow'. Restaurant attached.

$ Santiphab Guesthouse, far end of the island next to the bridge, T020-5461 4231, www.santiphab-don-det.com. 7 basic rattan bungalows right beside the bridge, most have the quintessential hammock. Idyllic setting, flanked by the Mekong on one side and rice paddies on the other. Good for those who want seclusion but also quick access to Don Khone. Very cheap restaurant serves tasty fare with buckets of atmosphere. Very little English spoken. A friendly, timeless place.

Don Khone *p108, map p108*
Although Don Deth attracts the vast majority of tourists, Don Khone has a much friendlier atmosphere.

$$$-$$ Auberge Sala Don Khone, T030-525 6390, www.salalao.com. A former French hospital built in 1927, this is one of the nicest places to stay on the island with 3 rooms, original tiles and 4 poster beds. In addition, traditional Luang Prabang-style houses have been built in the grounds, with 8 twin rooms, all with en suite hot shower and toilet. 2 rooms have unusual paddy-field views. Breakfast is included. The captured gibbon in a cage in the garden is a disgrace.

$$$-$$ Salaphae, T030-525 6390, www.salalao.com. This is the most unusual accommodation in the whole Siphandon area. 3 rafts (and 6 rooms) are managed by ex-lawyer, Luesak. Rooms have been decorated simply, with all the minor touches that can make accommodation outstanding. Hot water bathrooms. A wonderful deck, with seating overlooks the stunning river scenery.

$$-$ Pan's Guesthouse, T030-534 6939, www.pans-guesthouse.com. A relative newcomer to Don Khone, these wooden bungalows are exceptionally good value for money. The 6 riverside bungalows with hot water, fan and comfy mattresses are simple but comfortable and ultra clean. The owner is one of the most helpful hosts in Siphandon. Highly recommended for those on a limited budget. Breakfast included.

$ Boun Guesthouse, next door to Auberge Sala Don Khone, T020-2271 0163. Mr Boun has built a couple of cream-painted wooden bungalows, with en suite bathrooms but a private concrete block in the garden obscures the view from some of his wooden rooms.

Restaurants

Pakse *p97, map p98*
There are a couple of fantastic *sindat* (barbeque) places near the Da Heung market that are extremely popular with the locals.

If the weather is fine, the **Pakse Hotel** has a fantastic rooftop restaurant offering a range of Lao dishes plus pretty good pizza, totally delicious chicken curry soup and some delectable mojitos from 1600. It has an excellent selection of coffees.

$ Delta Coffee, Route 13, opposite the Champasak Palace Hotel, T020-5534 5895. This place is a real find for those craving some Western comfort food. The extensive menu is varied and offers everything from pizza and lasagne to Thai noodles. The coffee is brilliant and the staff are very friendly.

$ Jasmine Restaurant, No 13 Rd, T031-251002. This small place has outdoor seating and is a firm favourite with travellers. Offering the standard Indian fare and a few Malaysian dishes, it's reasonable value.

$ Nazim's Restaurant, in a new location, T031-252912. Serving a very similar selection of Indian/Malaysian dishes, although the service is a little slower.

$ Xuan Mai, near Pakse Hotel, T031-213245. Vietnamese restaurant with outdoor kitchen and eating area. Good shakes and fresh spring rolls. Can be a bit hit and miss.

Champasak *p98*
Most restaurants are located in the guesthouses; all are cheap (**$**).

$ Anouxa Guesthouse, see Where to stay. Has a small but delectable menu and lovely restaurant set over the river; opt for a fish dish. They also have a selection of wines.

$ Inthira Champakone Hotel, see Where to stay. The **Inthira** does Western burgers and pizzas and Asian dishes too in handsome surrounds. The iced coffee is fabulous.

$ Vong Paseud Guesthouse, see Where to stay. Has a cheap and extensive menu ranging from backpacker favourites like pancakes through to *tom yum* soup.

Xe Pian National Protected Area *p102*
Eating in Ban Kiet Ngong is very basic and you will have to rely on the local food. *Feu* and noodle soup can be made on the spot.

$ The Kingfisher Ecolodge, see Where to stay. A fantastic restaurant serving a range of Western and Lao dishes. Also stocks wine.

Paksong and around *p103*
$ Borravan Plateau, Route 23 about 1 km from the market towards Tha Teng. Standard selection of Lao dishes in an indoor setting, safe from the weather. Unfortunately there is no menu and no English spoken – so opt for something easy like *feu* or *laap*. The owner is very friendly.

Tad Lo and around *p104*
$ Tad Lo Lodge, see Where to stay. A variety of Thai, Lao and Western dishes on offer.

$ Tim Guesthouse & Restaurant, see Where to stay. A popular restaurant serving good hearty breakfasts and Western dishes.

Don Khong p104

The majority of restaurants only serve fish and chicken. In the low season most restaurants will only be able to fulfil about half of the menu options. Special dishes such as a roast or *hor mok* will also need to be ordered at least a few hours, if not a day, in advance to ensure the proprietors have the required produce in stock. Although many other towns and areas also make such a claim, Don Khong is renowned for the quality of its *lao-lao* (rice liquor). Local fish with coconut milk cooked in banana leaves, *mok pa*, is truly a divine local speciality and makes a trip to the islands worthwhile in itself.

$$-$ Souksan Chinese Restaurant. Attractive place with a stunning, unobscured view of the river. Funnily enough there is an absence of Chinese food but there are other more generic Asian options including good local fish, tasty honeyed chicken and basil pork with chilli.

$ Pon's Hotel and Restaurant, see Where to stay. Good atmosphere and excellent food, try the fish soup. Also the *mok pa* here is excellent, order 2 hrs in advance. Very popular.

Don Deth p107, map p108

Most people choose to eat at their guesthouses; they all have pretty much the same menu.

$$-$ Lamphone, see Where to stay. The resident Australian baker cooks up a mean focaccia, and chocolate and banana donuts and other delicious freshly baked goodies including carrot cake and lemon sponge. Also burgers in freshly baked buns and other dishes bringing variety to the island's offerings.

$$-$ Little Eden, see Where to stay. A large menu with some good Western dishes: grilled chicken breast and creamy pepper sauce, salads, sandwiches and soup and lots of catfish dishes; for example, grilled catfish in a white wine sauce. It's a change from the rest of the places on the island.

$$-$ Mr B's Sunset View Bungalow, near the northern tip. Italian bruschetta, rice pudding and a selection of burgers including chicken and pumpkin. Good cocktails.

$ The Pool Bar and Restaurant, near the main port. Has a pool table and fantastic Indian and Malay food. Good service. Good book exchange.

Don Khone p108, map p108

$$ Auberge Sala Don Khone, see Where to stay. There's a beautiful view from the restaurant and some fine options on the menu, such as tuna and orange salad or steak salad. Unfortunately, the service has deteriorated significantly and is too slow. Lunch menu is sandwich-based and not all ingredients may be available.

$ Anny's, village centre. A new addition to the eating scene, this popular place is offering dishes on smart plates. The fried garlic fish is recommended.

$ Pan's Restaurant, see Where to stay. Across from the guesthouse, this is a fantastic, cheap option serving up brilliant homemade meals. The fish here is outstanding.

❂ Festivals

Wat Phou p99

Feb (movable) Wat Phou Festival lasts for 3 days around the full moon of the 3rd lunar month. Pilgrims come from far and wide to leave offerings at the temple. In the evening there are competitions – football, boat racing, bullfighting and cockfighting, Thai boxing, singing contests and the like.

Don Khong p104

Dec A 5-day Boat Racing festival on the river opposite Muang Khong. It coincides with National Day on 2 Dec and is accompanied by a great deal of celebration, eating and drinking.

Shopping

Don Deth *p107, map p108*
There isn't much to buy here. A small grocery store just down from the port has a few essential items and snacks but is not well stocked. If you're in desperate need of any items, make a quick trip to Ban Nakasang and pick up things from the market there. Most guesthouses go to Ban Nakasang on an almost daily basis and will usually buy things for you if you pay them 5000 kip or so.

What to do

Pakse *p97, map p98*
Most of the hotels in town arrange day tours to Wat Phou and Tad Lo; of these the best is the **Pakse Hotel**. There are a number of tour agencies in town.
Green Discovery, on the main road, T031-252908, www.greendiscoverylaos.com. Offers a range of adventure tours and eco-tourism treks around Champasak Province including Ban Kiet Ngong, rafting, kayaking and cycling trips. Highly recommended.
Sabaidy 2, see Where to stay, T031-212992. Mr Vong and crew offer a wide range of tours around a variety of top-notch provincial sites, very good value and recommended for visitors who are only around for 1-2 days. The 1-day Bolaven tour costs US$24 per person and is great fun. Mr Vong contributes to a school project charity in the province: www.kokphungtai-primaryschool-fund.com.
Xplore Asia, opposite **Jasmine Restaurant**, Rd 13, T031-212893, www.xplore-laos.com. Offers a variety of tours and useful tour services (including a minivan service to Siphandon). Open-tour trip to Bolaven with stops at Tad Fane, Tad Yuang, Tad Lo, Lao Ngam, 140,000 kip.

Xe Pian National Protected Area
p102
There are several 2- to 3-day trekking/homestay trips offered in the area. These include elephant treks across the **Xe Pian** forests, wetlands and rocky outcrops; treks from Kiet Ngong Village to the top of **Phu Asa** (this one takes about 2 hrs; the elephant baskets can carry 2 people); and birdwatching trips. There is a 2-day canoe/trekking/homestay trip called the **Ban Ta Ong Trail** with guides trained in wildlife and the medicinal uses of plants (from US$95 per person; min 2 people). A challenging 3-day camping Kiet Ngong-Ta Ong Trail is a walking/elephant back/canoeing trip in Xe Pian from US$280 per person. These tours are designed to ensure that local communities reap the rewards of tourism in a sustainable fashion and are highly recommended. The best time for birdwatching is between Dec and Feb.

The **Kingfisher Ecolodge** (see Where to stay), T030-534 5016, can arrange for you to train to be a bona fide elephant rider with a traditional *mahout* (elephant keeper).

Tour operators in Pakse can also organize trips to the area. Contact the **Provincial Tourism Office** in Pakse for complete information, T031-676 4144, www.xepian.org. It can also offer a 1-day elephant safari from US$100 per person, for 2 people.

Bolaven Plateau *p102*
To organize kayaking and rafting trips to the Bolaven Plateau contact **Green Discovery** in Pakse, see above.

Tad Lo and around *p104*
Elephant treks
This is an excellent way to see the area as there are few roads on the plateau and elephants can go where jeeps cannot. The Tad Lo lodge organizes treks at 0800, 1000, 1300 and 1500, 85,000 kip per person (2 people per elephant).

Don Khong p104

All the guesthouses run tours to Don Deth and Don Khone taking in the Phaphaeng Falls and dolphin watching. Mr Pon's charges 150,000 kip per person for a full-day trip.

Don Deth and Don Khone
p107, map p108

Almost every guesthouse on the island can arrange tours, transport and tickets. All tour operators offer trips to Khong Phapheng, 60,000-70,000 kip each, minimum 4 people. From Don Khone, it is possible to hire a boat for the day, to visit the islands including one where the rice pots are made. Ask at **Mr Pan's**; 2-3 hrs, 150,000 kip for 4 people.

Dolphin watching

From **Don Khone**, it is possible to hire a boat from Kong Ngay, 90,000 kip, maximum 3 people to a boat Further south, at Ban Hang Khon, it's 60,000 kip per boat, maximum 3 people. Tours from Don Deth to the dolphins and Phapheng Falls cost 80,000 kip per person, minimum 6 people. **X-plore Asia** runs tours to the Phapheng tours and dolphin watching for 180,000 per person, minimum 2 people. Costs reduce the larger the group of people. Note that if the dolphins are hanging out across the border in Cambodia, you will need to pay an extra US$1 per person to criss-cross the waters. (There are now restaurants at Hang Khon and Kong Ngay.)

Fishing and kayaking

Most tour operators would be able to arrange a day out fishing if you asked. **Happy Island Adventure Tour**, T020-2267 7698, happytour_bs@hotmail.com. Runs fishing trips for 120,000 per person, minimum 5 people. Kayaking is also possible including trips to the falls and dolphins, 200,000 kip per person, minimum 3 people.

For boat trips further afield, see Transport, page 120.

⊖ Transport

Pakse p97, map p98
Air
To **Vientiane**, **Luang Prabang**, **Savannakhet**, **Siem Reap**, **Ho Chi Minh City** and **Bangkok**. Lao Airlines has offices at the airport and by the river in town, T031-212140.

Boat
A boat to **Champasak** leaves at 0830 daily, 80,000 kip, 2 hrs. If you have enough people and money it is possible to charter a boat to **Don Khong** or **Champasak**, contact **Mr Boun My**, T020-5563 1008. A charter to Champasak, US$70; to the **4000 Islands**, US$210.

The **Luang Say** company and **Mekong Islands Tours** run cruises from Pakse to Wat Phou and down to the 4000 Islands. The **Vat Phou** (T031-251446, www.vatphou. com) offers 3-day cruises in 12 cabins from US$448. The **Mekong Islands** has 11 cabins (T031-410155, www.mekongislands.com). Its 4-night cruise costs from US$620.

Bus
You can charter a tuk-tuk to the airport, northern bus station or southern bus station for about 15,000 kip. To get to the VIP bus station, 2 km from the town centre, at *talaat lak song*, costs about 10,000 kip.

Northern terminal 7 km north of town on Route 13. Hourly departures daily 0730-1630 to **Savannakhet**, 250 km, 5 hrs, 40,000 kip; to **Thakhek**, 7-8 hrs, 55,000 kip; to **Vientiane**, 16-18 hrs, 100,000 kip. Local buses can be painfully slow due to the number of stops they make. For those heading to Vientiane it makes more sense to pay a couple of extra dollars and get on the much quicker and more comfortable VIP bus at the VIP station.

Southern terminal 8 km south of town of Route 13. There are regular connections with **Champasak** from 1030-1400, 20,000 kip including the ferry fare; stay on the bus if you are travelling to **Wat Phou** (see page 99). Ask for Ban Lak Sarm Sip (translates as 'village 30 km'), here there is a signpost and you turn right and travel 4 km towards Ban Muang (5 km). In the village there are people selling tickets for the ferry. Local buses coming through from Vientiane provide the main means of transport to other destinations down south, so can be slightly off kilter. *Songthaews* to the **Bolaven Plateau**; **Paksong**, 0930, 1000, 1230, 20,000 kip; **Tad Fan**, 5 morning departures, 1 hr, 20,000 kip. A *songthaew* leaves for **Ban Kiet Ngong** 1200, 2 hrs, 25,000 kip.

Buses/*songthaews* leave for **Siphandon** (Muang Khong) at 0830, 1030, 1130, 1300 and 1430 3-4 hrs, 30,000 kip; for **Ban Nakasang** (the closest port to Don Deth/ Don Khone) several departures at 0700, 0800, 0900, 1130, 1200, 1430 and 1400, 30,000 kip, 3-4 hrs. Several of the buses to Ban Nakasang also stop at **Ban Hat Xai Khoune** (the stop-off for Don Khong). Make sure that you let the bus/*songthaew* driver know that you are going to Ban Nakasang or Ban Hat Xai Khoune rather than saying the name of the islands.

A more comfortable alternative to Siphandon is to take the minivan service to **Don Deth/Don Khong** offered by Pakse operators, 2-2½ hrs, 60,000 kip. This is highly recommended as, once you have paid all the fees involved with local transport, it costs about the same. It is also a shorter trip.

Kiang Kai, VIP and international bus terminal Near the football stadium and Talaat Lak Song, T031-212228, just off Route 13. VIP buses to **Ubon** (Thailand) leave at 0830 and 1530, 55,000 kip, 3 hrs; VIP seat buses leave for **Vientiane** at 2000 arriving at 0600 (stopping in **Thakhek** en route), 150,000 kip. A VIP sleeping bus with comfy beds, duvet, cake and films leaves at 0830 arriving in Vientiane at 0600 (stopping en route to Thakhek), 150,000 kip. The beds are double, so unless you book 2 spaces you might end up sleeping next to a stranger. If you are tall ask for a bed towards the back of the bus. Make sure

you secure your belongings on any of the overnight buses, as some passengers have sticky fingers.

Buses to Vietnam Buses leave for Vietnam via the Bo Y border, see box above. To **Danang**, 1900, 18 hrs, 200,000 kip; to **Hué**, 1830, 15.5 hrs, 190,000 kip; to **Dong Ha**, 1800, 14hrs, 150,000 kip; to **Lao Bao**, 1700, 11 hrs, 120,000 kip.

Buses to Cambodia Leave from the adjacent Seangchaolearn terminal. **Sorya** buses (www.ppsoryatransport.com) leave Pakse for **Stung Treng** at 0730, US$15, 4.5hrs; to **Kratie**, US$15, 6.5 hrs, to **Kampong Cham**, 0730, US$15, 9.5 hrs; to **Phnom Penh** at 0730, US$30, 13.5 hrs. Warning: that it is not possible to get to Siem Reap in 1 day from southern Laos. You will need to stay the night in Kampong Cham. Agents that tell you it's possible appear to be operating a scam in southern Laos where they charge travellers extra to transfer onto a minibus at Kampong Cham to get to the traveller to Siem Reap well into the night. **Sorya** is a bit more expensive than most operators, but reliable and recommended.

Motorbike/bicycle

The **Lankham Hotel**, near the Xplore Asia office, rents out bicycles (US$1 per day) standard small bikes (US$8 per day) and larger dirt bikes (US$20 per day). Guesthouses and travel agencies are starting to withdraw motorbike hire because of the responsibility. Tourists who have never hired motorbikes before and the death of a US citizen in Sekong in 2009 in a motorbike accident are too much to bear. The **Sang Aroun** rents bicycles for 30,000 kip.

Private transport

If you miss public transport, a private *songthaew* from Pakse to Champasak (with ferry and tuk-tuk included) will cost you 300,000 kip. A half day Pakse City tour costs 150,000 kip, full-day 250,000 kip. Ask at **Pakse Hotel** for reliable drivers.

Tuk-tuk/saamlor

A tuk-tuk to the northern bus station should cost 30,000 kip. Shared tuk-tuks to local villages leave from the Daoheung market and from the stop on No 11 Rd near the jetty. Tuk-tuks can also be chartered by the hour.

Champasak *p98*
Bus/songthaew

A shared local *songthaew* to **Ban Thong Kop**, the village opposite Wat Phou costs around 10,000 kip; direct to **Wat Phou** is 60-80,000 kip return (chartered).To **Pakse** direct at 0630, 0730 and 0800, 15,000 kip 2 hrs (with wait for ferry). A private chartered van to **Pakse** costs 500,000 kip; to **Paksong**, 700,000 kip, to **Ban Kiet Ngong**, 400,000 kip.

A tourist minibus leaves from the tourist information centre daily at 0800 for **Siphandon**, 70,000 kip. Most of the guesthouses can organize tickets.

Boat

A tuk-tuk from the ferry port to Champasak town is 5000 kip. The return boat journey to **Ban Muang** depends on passengers but it usually returns at 1430, 70,000 kip. A tuk-tuk from Ban Muang on the other side of the river to Ban Lak Sarm Sip on the main road is 10,000 kip.

A ferry to **Don Daeng** island costs 50,000 kip and can be arranged through the Champasak tourist office. The boat departs from behind the tourist office.

Paksong and around *p103*

Regular connections to **Pakse**, 0830-1530, 1½ hrs, 20,000 kip.

Tad Lo *p104*

There are buses from Ban Houei Set (1.8 km north of Tad Lo) to **Pakse**, hourly 0730-1130 then 1300 and 1400, 20,000 kip. You may be able to catch the daily service to **Vientiane** on its way north, daily 1600 but you will need to book.

Don Khong *p104*
Boat

See also Visiting Don Khong, page 104. **Pon's Hotel** (reliable and recommended) can arrange boats to **Don Deth** or **Don Khone**, 30,000 kip, 1½ hrs. Other guesthouses also offer this price (**Don Khong** guesthouse) while **Villa Muang Khong** and **Senesothxeune** are a bit more expensive. There are also several boatmen on the riverfront who are more than happy to take people for the right price. Fares tend to fluctuate according to international fuel prices but the going rate at the time of publication was 150,000 kip for up to 10 people, one way. Most boats leave at 0830. Private boat charter to Pakse, US$150.

Bus/songthaew

Songthaew and buses head to **Pakse** at 0630, 0700, 0800, 0830, 3-4 hrs, from in front of What Kan Khong, 30,000 kip. Or cross to Ban Hat Xai Khoune and try for transport south.

The minibus service back to Pakse can be organized by Mr Pon, it costs 50,000 kip and includes ferry and drop off directly at your hotel in Pakse (2 hrs). Leaves at 1130; drop off at Ban Muang for Champasak possible, 50,000 kip. **Xplore-Asia** also passes the Don Khong turn-off at 1230 for the return journey, 50,000 kip.

Guesthouses also arrange transport to the Cambodian border and beyond (to **Siem Reap**, US$23; to **Phnom Penh**, US$18, **Kratie**, US$12, **Stung Treng**, US$8; to the **border** US$5. Private transport to anywhere can also be arranged eg transfer to **Pakse Airport**, US$80; to **Kingfisher Ecolodge**, US$60.

Motorbike and bicycle

Many of the gueshouses offer motorbikes (100,000 kip a day at Senesothxeune; 80,000 kip with Mr Pon) and bikes (10,000-20,000 kip).

Don Deth, Don Khone and around
p107, map p108
Ban Nakasang
To **Don Deth** and **Don Khone**, 15-20 mins, 20,000 kip per person. To **Don Khong**, 2 hrs, 180,000 per boat. Between Don Khone and Don Deth, 30,000 kip.

Bus/songthaew
Decent buses depart from Ban Nakasang's market, hourly from 0600-1000 daily, northbound for **Pakse**, 40,000 kip; some continue onwards to **Vientiane**; get off at **Ban Hat Xai Khoune** for the crossing to **Don Khong**. Xplore-Asia tourist buses go to Pakse at 1100, 50,000 kip including ferry crossing. The same minivan will stop at **Ban Muang** for **Champasak**, 50,000 kip. To get to **Don Kralor** (on the Cambodian border) most guesthouses can organize the trip on a minivan. (There is no public transport now; a motorbike taxi costs 40,000 kip). Cambodian visas are available on the border and Lao visas are now available. To **Don Kralor**, the largest town on the other side of th Cambodian border, US$4, 2 hrs. Tickets can also be bought further to **Stung Treng**, US$6, **Kratie**, US$11, **Kampong Cham**, US$12 or **Phnom Penh**, US$13. The Siem Reap bus requires an overnight stop in Kampong Cham, US$18. Note that the **Paramount** company requires a change of bus in Cambodia but the **Sorya** company goes right through to the further destinations. For the Cambodia border; see page 118.

X-plore Asia and other agencies can also arrange bus tickets to further afield: **Attapeu**, 120,000 kip, **Ubon Ratchathani**, 110,000 kip, **Bangkok**, 250,000 kip and **Vientiane**, 220,000 kip.

Don Deth and Don Khone
To **Ban Nakasang**, 20,000 kip per person. The first boat is the market boat at 0630; before that you will need to pay 40,000 kip.

There are 2 ways to get to **Don Khong**, from Ban Nakasang, either by boat,

2 hrs,180,000 kip per boat (bargain hard), or by bus (see above); motorbike taxis also make the trip for US$3. Although it's slower and more expensive, the boat trip is one of the loveliest in Laos. Boats between Don Khong and Don Deth cost 30,000 kip.

❶ Directory

Pakse *p97, map p98*
Banks BCEL Bank, No 11 Rd (beside the river), changes US$ and most currencies, and offers a better commission rate on cash exchange than other banks, also Visa/MasterCard cash advances at 3% commission, Mon-Fri 0830-1530, they have 2 ATMs; Lao Development Bank, No 13 Rd, T031-212168, cash and TCs exchanged.
Embassies and consulates Vietnam, No 24 Rd, T031-212827, www.vietnam consulate-pakse.org, Mon-Fri 0830-1330, 1400-1630, visas for Vietnam cost US$45 and take 4 days to process, so you are better off organizing your Vietnamese visa in Vientiane. **Internet** Expect to pay around 200 kip per min but discounts kick in usually after 1 hr: SK internet, No 13 Rd. **Medical services** There is a huge hospital between No 1 Rd and No 46 Rd, T031-212018, but neither their English skills nor medical service will suffice for complex cases; in case of emergencies go across to Ubon in Thailand; there is a pretty good pharmacy at the hospital that stocks most medications. A new international clinic is under construction. **Police** T031-212641. **Post office** No 8 Rd, overseas telephone calls can also be made from here. **Telephone** Telecommunications office for fax and overseas calls on No 1 Rd, near No 13 Rd; all internet cafés have Skype.

Champasak *p98*
Banks Lao Development Bank, changes cash only Mon-Fri. **Internet** There are 3 internet places including the school and Inthira Hotel.

Don Khong p104
Muang Khong
Banks There is a basic Lao Agriculture Promotion bank in town, hours are erratic and it accepts only US$ or Thai.
Internet Nearly all the accommodation offer internet at between 500-1000 kip per min. **Senesothxeune** also offers Wi-Fi (US$5 a day); **Mr Pon's Arena Hotel** also has Wi-Fi.

Don Deth, Don Khone and around
p107, map p108
Banks There are no banks on the islands; some guesthouses will change money.

Mr Phao of **Phao's Riverview** on Don Deth will take you by boat to Ban Khinak, north of Ban Nakasang where there is a Visa and MasterCard ATM for 120,000 kip return.
Internet There are several internet cafés on Don Deth and Don Khone; minimum 400 kip per min; calls can also be made, minimum 10 mins. **Telephone** The best way to make a call is via the net, although most guesthouses will let you make calls from their mobiles, which can be incredibly expensive, up to US$4 per min.

Background

Scholars of Lao history, before they even begin, need to decide whether they are writing a history of Laos; a history of the Lao ethnic group; or histories of the various kingdoms and principalities that have, through time, been encompassed by the present boundaries of the Lao People's Democratic Republic. Historians have tended to confront this problem in different ways without, often, acknowledging on what basis their 'history' is built. It is common to see 1365, the date of the foundation of the kingdom of Lane Xang, as marking the beginning of Lao history. But, as Martin Stuart-Fox points out, prior to Lane Xang the principality of Muang Swa, occupying the same geographical space, was headed by a Lao. The following account provides a brief overview of the histories of those peoples who have occupied what is now the territory of the Lao PDR.

Archaeological and historical evidence indicates that most Lao originally migrated south from China. This was followed by an influx of ideas and culture from the Indian subcontinent via Myanmar (Burma), Thailand and Cambodia – something which is reflected in the state religion, Theravada Buddhism.

Being surrounded by large, powerful neighbours, Laos has been repeatedly invaded over the centuries by the Thais (or Siamese) and the Vietnamese – who both thought of Laos as their buffer zone and backyard. They too have both left their mark on Lao culture. In recent history, Laos has been influenced by the French during the colonial era, the Japanese during the Second World War, the Americans during the Indochinese wars and, between 1975 and the early 1990s, by Marxism-Leninism.

It is also worth noting, in introduction, that historians and regimes have axes to grind. The French were anxious to justify their annexation of Laos and so used dubious Vietnamese documents to provide a thin legal gloss to their actions. Western historians, lumbered with the baggage of Western historiography, ignored indigenous histories. And the Lao People's Revolutionary Party uses history for its own ends too. The official three volume *History of Laos* is currently being written by Party-approved history hacks. The third volume (chronologically speaking) was published in 1989 and, working back in time, the first and second thereafter. As Martin Stuart-Fox remarks in his *A History of Laos*, "the Communist regime is as anxious as was the previous Royal Lao government [pre-1975] to establish that Laos has a long and glorious past and that a continuity exists between the past and the present Lao state". In other words, Laos has not one history, but many.

First kingdom of Laos

Myth, archaeology and history all point to a number of early feudal Lao kingdoms in what is now South China and North Vietnam. External pressures from the Mongols under Kublai Khan and the Han Chinese forced the Tai tribes to migrate south into what had been part of the Khmer Empire. The mountains to the north and east served as a cultural barrier to Vietnam and China, leaving the Lao exposed to influences from India and the West. There are no documentary records of early Lao history (the first date in the Lao chronicles to which historians attach any real veracity is 1271), although it seems probable that parts of present-day Laos were annexed by Lannathai (Chiang Mai) in the 11th century and by the **Khmer Empire** during the 12th century. But neither of these states held sway over the entire area of Laos. Xieng Khouang, for example, was probably never under Khmer domination. This was followed by strong Siamese influence over the cities of Luang

Prabang and Vientiane under the Siamese Sukhothai Dynasty. Laos (the country) in effect did not exist, although the Laos (the people) certainly did.

The downfall of the kingdom of Sukhothai in 1345 and its submission to the new Siamese Dynasty at Ayutthaya (founded in 1349) was the catalyst for the foundation of what is commonly regarded as the first truly independent Lao Kingdom – although there were smaller semi-independent Lao *muang* (city states) existing prior to that date.

Fa Ngum and Lane Xang

The kingdom of Lane Xang (Lan Chang) emerged in 1353 under Fa Ngum, a Lao prince who had grown up in the Khmer court of Angkor. There is more written about Fa Ngum than about the following two centuries of Lao history. It is also safe to say that his life is more fiction than fact. Fa Ngum was reputedly born with 33 teeth and was banished to Angkor after his father, Prince Yakfah, was convicted of having an incestuous affair with a wife of King Suvarna Kamphong. In 1353 Fa Ngum led an army to Luang Prabang and confronted his grandfather, King Suvarna Kamphong. Unable to defeat his grandson on the battlefield, the aged king is said to have hanged himself and Fa Ngum was invited to take the throne. Three years later, in 1356, Fa Ngum marched on Vientiane – which he took with ease – and then on Vienkam, which proved more of a challenge. He is credited with piecing together Lang Xang – the Land of a Million Elephants – the golden age to which all histories of Laos refer to justify the existence (and greatness) of Laos.

In some accounts Lang Xang is portrayed as stretching from China to Cambodia and from the Khorat Plateau in present-day Northeast Thailand to the Annamite mountains in the east. But it would be entirely wrong to envisage the kingdom controlling all these regions. Lane Xang probably only had total control over a comparatively small area of present-day Laos and parts of Northeast Thailand; the bulk of this grand empire would have been contested with other surrounding kingdoms. In addition, the smaller *muang* and principalities would themselves have played competing powers off, one against another, in an attempt to maximize their own autonomy. It is this 'messiness' that led scholars of Southeast Asian history to suggest that territories as such did not exist, but rather zones of variable control. The historian OW Wolters coined the term *mandala* for "a particular and often unstable political situation in a vaguely defined geographical area without fixed boundaries and where smaller centres tended to look in all directions for security. *Mandalas* would expand and contract in concertina-like fashion. Each one contained several tributary rulers, some of whom would repudiate their vassal status when the opportunity arose and try to build up their own network of vassals".

Legend relates that Fa Ngum was a descendant of Khoum Borom, "a king who came out of the sky from South China". He is said to have succeeded to the throne of Nanchao in 729, aged 31, and died 20 years later, although this historical record is, as they say, exceedingly thin. Khoum Borom is credited with giving birth to the Lao people by slicing open a gourd in Muong Taeng (Dien Bien Phu, Vietnam) and his seven sons established the great Tai kingdoms. He returned to his country with a detachment of Khmer soldiers and united several scattered Lao fiefdoms. In those days, conquered lands were usually razed and the people taken as slaves to build up the population of the conquering group. (This largely explains why today there are far more Lao in northeastern Thailand than in Laos – they were forcibly settled there after King Anou was defeated by King Rama III of Siam in 1827 – see page 125). The kings of Lane Xang were less philistine, demanding only subordination and allegiance as one part of a larger *mandala*.

Luang Prabang became the capital of the kingdom of Lane Xang. The unruly highland tribes of the northeast did not come under the kingdom's control at that time. Fa Ngum made Theravada Buddhism the official religion. He married the Cambodian king's daughter, Princess Keo Kaengkanya, and was given the Pra Bang (a golden statue, the most revered religious symbol of Laos), by the Khmer court.

It is common to read of Lane Xang as the first kingdom of Laos; as encompassing the territory of present-day Laos; and as marking the introduction of Theravada Buddhism to the country. On all counts this portrait is, if not false, then deeply flawed. As noted above, there were Lao states that predated Lane Xang; Lane Xang never controlled Laos as it currently exists; and Buddhism had made an impact on the Lao people before 1365. Fa Ngum did not create a kingdom; rather he brought together various pre-existing *muang* (city states) into a powerful *mandala*. As Martin Stuart-Fox writes, "From this derives [Fa Ngum's] historical claim to hero status as the founder of the Lao Kingdom." But, as Stuart-Fox goes on to explain, there was no central authority and rulers of individual *muang* were permitted considerable autonomy.

After Fa Ngum's wife died in 1368, he became so debauched, it is said, that he was deposed in favour of his son, Samsenthai (1373-1416), who was barely 18 when he acceded the throne. He was named after the 1376 census, which concluded that he ruled over 300,000 Tais living in Laos; *samsen* means, literally, 300,000. He set up a new administrative system based on the existing *muang*, nominating governors to each that lasted until it was abolished by the Communist government in 1975. Samsenthai's death was followed by a period of unrest. Under King Chaiyachakkapat-Phaenphaeo (1441-1478), the kingdom came under increasing threat from the Vietnamese. How the Vietnamese came to be peeved with the Lao is another story which smacks of fable more than fact. King Chaiyachakkapat's eldest son, the Prince of Chienglaw, secured a holy white elephant. The emperor of Vietnam, learning of this momentous discovery, asked to be sent some of the beast's hairs. Disliking the Vietnamese, the Prince dispatched a box of its excrement instead, whereupon the Emperor formed an army of an improbably large 550,000 men. The Prince's army numbered 200,000 and 2000 elephants. The massive Vietnamese army finally prevailed and entered and sacked Luang Prabang. But shortly thereafter they were driven out by Chaiyachakkapat-Phaenphaeo's son, King Suvarna Banlang (1478-1485). Peace was only fully restored under King Visunarat (1500-1520).

Increasing prominence and Burmese incursions

Under King Pothisarath (1520-1548) Vientiane became prominent as a trading and religious centre. He married a Lanna (Chiang Mai) princess, Queen Yotkamtip, and when the Siamese King Ketklao was put to death in 1545, Pothisarath's son claimed the throne at Lanna. He returned to Lane Xang when his father died in 1548. Asserting his right as successor to the throne, he was crowned Setthathirat in 1548 and ruled until 1571 – the last of the great kings of Lane Xang.

At the same time, the Burmese were expanding East and in 1556 Lanna fell into their hands. Setthathirat gave up his claim to that throne, to a Siamese prince, who ruled under Burmese authority. (He also took the **Phra Kaeo** – Thailand's famous 'Emerald' Buddha and its most sacred and revered image – with him to Luang Prabang and then to Vientiane. The Phra Kaeo stayed in Vientiane until 1778 when the Thai general Phya Chakri 'repatriated' it to Thailand.) In 1563 Setthathirat pronounced Vieng Chan (Vientiane) the principal capital of Lane Xang. Seven years later, the Burmese King Bayinnaung launched an unsuccessful attack on Vieng Chan itself.

Setthathirat is revered as one of the great Lao kings, having protected the country from foreign domination. He built Wat Phra Kaeo (see page 23) in Vientiane, in which he placed the famous Emerald Buddha brought from Lanna. Setthathirat mysteriously disappeared during a campaign in the southern province of Attapeu in 1574, which threw the kingdom into crisis. Vientiane fell to invading Burmese the following year and remained under Burmese control for seven years. Finally the anarchic kingdoms of Luang Prabang and Vientiane were reunified under Nokeo Koumane (1591-1596) and Thammikarath (1596-1622).

Disputed territory

From the time of the formation of the kingdom of Lane Xang to the arrival of the French, the history of Laos was dominated by the struggle to retain the lands it had conquered. Following King Setthathirat's death, a series of kings came to the throne in quick succession. King Souligna Vongsa, crowned in 1633, brought long awaited peace to Laos. The 61 years he was on the throne are regarded as Lane Xang's golden age. Under him, the kingdom's influence spread to Yunnan in South China, the Burmese Shan States, Issan in Northeast Thailand and areas of Vietnam and Cambodia.

Souligna Vongsa was even on friendly terms with the Vietnamese: he married Emperor Le Thanh Ton's daughter and he and the Emperor agreed the borders between the two countries. The frontier was settled in a deterministic – but nonetheless amicable – fashion: those living in houses built on stilts with verandas were considered Lao subjects and those living in houses without piles and verandas owed allegiance to Vietnam.

During his reign foreigners first visited the country, but other than a handful of adventurers, Laos remained on the outer periphery of European concerns and influence.

The three kingdoms

After Souligna Vongsa died in 1694, leaving no heir, dynastic quarrels and feudal rivalries once again erupted, undermining the kingdom's cohesion. In 1700 Lane Xang split into three: Luang Prabang under Souligna's grandson, Vientiane under Souligna's nephew and the new kingdom of Champasak was founded in the south 'panhandle'. This weakened the country and allowed the Siamese and Vietnamese to encroach. Muang, which previously owed clear allegiance to Lane Xang, began to look towards Vietnam or Siam. Isan muang in present day Northeast Thailand, for example, paid tribute to Bangkok; while Xieng Khouang did the same to Hanoi and, later, to Hué. The three main kingdoms that emerged with the disintegration of Lane Xang leant in different directions: Luang Prabang had close links with China, Vientiane with Vietnam's Hanoi/Hué and Champassak with Siam.

By the mid-1760s Burmese influence once again held sway in Vientiane and Luang Prabang and before the turn of the decade, they sacked Ayutthaya, the capital of Siam. Somehow the Siamese managed to pull themselves together and only two years later in 1778 successfully rampaged through Vientiane. The two sacred Buddhas, the Phra Bang and the Phra Kaeo (Emerald Buddha), were taken as booty back to Bangkok. The Emerald Buddha was never returned and now sits in Bangkok's Wat Phra Kaeo.

King Anou (an abbreviation of Anurutha), was placed on the Vientiane throne by the Siamese. With the death of King Rama II of Siam, King Anou saw his chance of rebellion, asked Vietnam for assistance, formed an army and marched on Bangkok in 1827. In mounting this brave – some would say foolhardy – assault, Anou was apparently trying to emulate the great Fa Ngum. Unfortunately, he got no further than the Northeast

Thai town of Korat where his forces suffered a defeat and were driven back. Nonetheless, Anou's rebellion is considered one of the most daring and ruthless rebellions in Siamese history and he was lauded as a war hero back home.

King Anou's brief stab at regional power was to result in catastrophe for Laos – and tragedy for King Anou. The first US arms shipment to Siam allowed the Siamese to sack Vientiane, a task to which they had grown accustomed over the years. (This marks America's first intervention in Southeast Asia.) Lao artisans were frogmarched to Bangkok and many of the inhabitants were resettled in Northeast Siam. Rama III had Chao Anou locked in a cage where he was taunted and abused by the population of Bangkok. He died soon afterwards, at the age of 62. One of his supporters is said to have taken pity on the king and brought him poison, other explanations simply say that he wished himself dead or that he choked. Whatever the cause, the disconsolate Anou, before he died, put a curse on Siam's monarchy, promising that the next time a Thai king set foot on Lao soil, he would die. To this day no Thai king has crossed the Mekong River. When the agreement for the supply of hydroelectric power was signed with Thailand in the 1970s, the Thai king opened the Nam Ngum Dam from a sandbank in the middle of the Mekong.

Disintegration of the kingdom

Over the next 50 years, Anou's kingdom was destroyed. By the time the French arrived in the late 19th century, the virtually unoccupied city was subsumed into the Siamese sphere of influence. Luang Prabang also became a Siamese vassal state, while Xieng Khouang province was invaded by Chinese rebels – to the chagrin of the Vietnamese, who had always considered the Hmong mountain kingdom (they called it Tran Ninh), to be their exclusive source of slaves. The Chinese had designs on Luang Prabang too and in order to quash their expansionist instincts, Bangkok dispatched an army there in 1885 to pacify the region and ensure the north remained firmly within the Siamese sphere of influence. This period was one of confusion and rapidly shifting allegiances.

The history of Laos during this period becomes, essentially, the history of only a small part of the current territory of the country: namely, the history of Luang Prabang. And because Luang Prabang was a suzerain state of Bangkok, the history of that kingdom is, in turn, sometimes relegated to a mere footnote in the history of Siam.

The French and independence

Following King Anou's death, Laos became the centre of Southeast Asian rivalry between Britain, expanding east from Burma, and France, pushing west through Vietnam. In 1868, following the French annexation of South Vietnam and the formation of a protectorate in Cambodia, an expedition set out to explore the Mekong trade route to China. Once central and north Vietnam had come under the influence of the Quai d'Orsay in Paris, the French became increasingly curious about Vietnamese claims to chunks of Laos. Unlike the Siamese, the French – like the British – were concerned with demarcating borders and establishing explicit areas of sovereignty. This seemed extraordinary to most Southeast Asians at the time, who could not see the point of mapping space when land was so abundant. However, it did not take long for the Siamese king to realize the importance of maintaining his claim to Siamese territories if the French in the east and the British in the south (Malaya) and west (Burma) were not to squeeze Siam to nothing.

However, King Chulalongkorn was not in a position to confront the French militarily and instead he had to play a clever diplomatic game if his kingdom was to survive. The

French, for their part, were anxious to continue to press westwards from Vietnam into the Lao lands over which Siam held suzerainty. Martin Stuart-Fox argues that there were four main reasons underlying France's desire to expand West: the lingering hope that the Mekong might still offer a 'back door' into China; the consolidation of Vietnam against attack; the 'rounding out' of their Indochina possessions; and a means of further pressuring Bangkok. In 1886, the French received reluctant Siamese permission to post a vice consul to Luang Prabang and a year later he persuaded the Thais to leave. However, even greater humiliation was to come in 1893 when the French, through crude gunboat diplomacy – the so-called Paknam incident – forced King Chulalongkorn to give up all claim to Laos on the flimsiest of historical pretexts. Despite attempts by Prince Devawongse to manufacture a compromise, the French forced Siam to cede Laos to France and, what's more, to pay compensation. It is said that after this humiliation, King Chulalongkorn retired from public life, broken in spirit and health. So the French colonial era in Laos began.

What is notable about this spat between France and Siam is that Laos – the country over which they were fighting – scarcely figures. As was to happen again in Laos' history, the country was caught between two competing powers who used Laos as a stage on which to fight a wider and to them, more important, conflict.

Union of Indochina
In 1893 France occupied the left bank of the Mekong and forced Thailand to recognize the river as the boundary. The French Union of Indochina denied Laos the area that is now Isan, northeast Thailand, and this was the start of 50 years of colonial rule. Laos became a protectorate with a *résident-superieur* in Vientiane and a vice-consul in Luang Prabang. However, Laos could hardly be construed as a 'country' during the colonial period. "Laos existed again", writes Martin Stuart-Fox, "but not yet as a political entity in its own right, for no independent centre of Lao political power existed. Laos was but a territorial entity within French Indochina." The French were not interested in establishing an identifiable Lao state; they saw Laos as a part and a subservient part at that, of Vietnam, serving as a resource-rich appendage. Though they had grand plans for the development of Laos, these were only expressed airily and none of them came to anything. "The French were never sure what to do with Laos", Stuart-Fox writes. Unlike Cambodia to the south, the French did not perceive Laos to have any historical unity or coherence and therefore it could be hacked about and developed or otherwise, according to their whim.

In 1904 the Franco-British convention delimited respective zones of influence. Only a few hundred French civil servants were ever in Vientiane at any one time and their attitude to colonial administration – described as 'benign neglect' – was as relaxed as the people they governed. To the displeasure of the Lao, France brought in Vietnamese to run the civil service (in the way the British used Indian bureaucrats in Burma). But for the most part, the French colonial period was a 50-year siesta for Laos. The king was allowed to stay in Luang Prabang, but had little say in administration. Trade and commerce was left to the omni-present Chinese and the Vietnamese. A small, French-educated Lao élite did grow up and by the 1940s they had become the core of a typically laid-back Lao nationalist movement.

Japanese coup
Towards the end of the Second World War, Japan ousted the French administration in Laos in a coup in March 1945. The eventual surrender of the Japanese in August that year gave impetus to the Lao independence movement. Prince Phetsarath, hereditary viceroy and premier of the Luang Prabang Kingdom, took over the leadership of the Lao Issara,

the Free Laos Movement (originally a resistance movement against the Japanese). They prevented the French from seizing power again and declared Lao independence on 1 September 1945. Two weeks later, the north and south provinces were reunified and in October, Phetsarath formed a Lao Issara government headed by Prince Phaya Khammao.

France refused to recognize the new state and crushed the Lao resistance. King Sisavang Vong, unimpressed by Prince Phetsarath's move, sided with the French, who had their colony handed back by British forces. He was crowned the constitutional monarch of the new protectorate in 1946. The rebel government took refuge in Bangkok. Historians believe the Issara movement was aided in their resistance to the French by the Viet Minh – Hanoi's Communists.

Independence

In response to nationalist pressures, France was obliged to grant Laos ever greater self government and, eventually, formal independence within the framework of the newly reconstructed French Union in July 1949. Meanwhile, in Bangkok, the Issara movement had formed a government-in-exile, headed by Phetsarath and his half-brothers: Prince Souvanna Phouma (see box, page 140) and Prince Souphanouvong. Both were refined, French-educated men. The Issara's military wing was led by Souphanouvong who, even at that stage, was known for his Communist sympathies. This was due to a temporary alliance between the Issara and the Viet Minh, who had the common cause of ridding their respective countries of the French. Within just a few months the so-called Red Prince had been ousted by his half-brothers and joined the Viet Minh where he is said to have been the moving force behind the declaration of the Democratic Republic of Laos by the newly-formed Lao National Assembly. The Lao People's Democratic Republic emerged – albeit in name only – somewhere inside Vietnam, in August 1949. Soon afterwards, the Pathet Lao (the Lao Nation) was born. The Issara movement quickly folded and Souvanna Phouma went back to Vientiane and joined the newly formed Royal Lao Government.

By 1953, Prince Souphanouvong had managed to move his Pathet Lao headquarters inside Laos and with the French losing their grip on the north provinces, the weary colonizers granted the country full independence. France signed a treaty of friendship and association with the new royalist government and made the country a French protectorate.

The rise of Communism

French defeat

While all this was going on, King Sisavang Vong sat tight in Luang Prabang instead of moving to Vientiane. But within a few months of independence, the ancient royal capital was under threat from the Communist Viet Minh and Pathet Lao. Honouring the terms of the new treaty, French commander General Henri Navarre determined in late 1953 to take the pressure off Luang Prabang by confronting the Viet Minh who controlled the strategic approach to the city at Dien Bien Phu. The French suffered a stunning defeat that presaged their withdrawal from Indochina. The subsequent occupation of two north Lao provinces by the Vietnam-backed Pathet Lao forces, meant the kingdom's days as a Western buffer state were numbered. The Vietnamese, not unlike their previous neighbours, did not respect Laos as a state, but as an extension of their own territory to be utilized for their own strategic purposes during the ensuing war.

With the **Geneva Accord** in July 1954, following the fall of Dien Bien Phu in May, Ho Chi Minh's government gained control of all territory north of the 17th parallel in neighbouring Vietnam. The Accord guaranteed Laos' freedom and neutrality, but with the Communists on the threshold, the US was not prepared to be a passive spectator: the demise of the French sparked an increasing US involvement. In an operation that was to mirror the much more famous war with Vietnam to the East, Washington soon found itself supplying and paying the salaries of 50,000 royalist troops and their corrupt officers. Clandestine military assistance grew, undercover special forces were mobilized and the CIA began meddling in Lao politics. In 1960 a consignment of weapons was dispatched by the CIA to a major in the Royal Lao Army called Vang Pao – or VP, as he became known – who was destined to become the leader of the Hmong.

US involvement: the domino effect
Laos had become the dreaded first domino, which, using the scheme of US President Dwight D Eisenhower's famous analogy, would trigger the rapid spread of Communism if ever it fell. The time-trapped little kingdom became the focus of superpower brinkmanship. At a press conference in March 1961, President Kennedy is said to have been too abashed to announce to the American people that US forces might soon become embroiled in conflict in a far-away flashpoint that went by the inglorious name of 'Louse'. For three decades Americans have unwittingly mispronounced the country's name as Kennedy decided, euphemistically, to label it 'Lay-os' throughout his national television broadcast.

Coalitions, coups and counter-coups
The US-backed Royal Lao Government of independent Laos – even though it was headed by the neutralist, Prince Souvanna Phouma – ruled over a divided country from 1951 to 1954. The US played havoc with Laos' domestic politics, running anti-Communist campaigns, backing the royalist army and lending support to political figures on the right (even if they lacked experience or political qualifications). The Communist Pathet Lao, headed by Prince Souphanouvong and overseen and sponsored by North Vietnam's Lao Dong party since 1949, emerged as the only strong opposition. By the mid-1950s, Kaysone Phomvihane, later prime minister of the Lao PDR, began to make a name for himself in the Indochinese Communist Party. Indeed the close association between Laos and Vietnam went deeper than just ideology. Kaysone's father was Vietnamese, while Prince Souphanouvong and Nouhak Phounsavanh both married Vietnamese women.

Government of National Union
Elections were held in Vientiane in July 1955 but were boycotted by the Pathet Lao. Souvanna Phouma became prime minister in March 1956. He aimed to try to negotiate the integration of his half-brother's Pathet Lao provinces into a unified administration and coax the Communists into a coalition government. In 1957 the disputed provinces were returned to royal government control under the first coalition government. This coalition government, much to US discontent, contained two Pathet Lao ministers including Souphanouvong and Phoumi Vongvichit. This was one of Souvanna Phouma's achievements in trying to combine the two sides to ensure neutrality, although it was only short-lived. In May 1958 elections were held. This time the Communists' Lao Patriotic Front (Neo Lao Hak Xat) clinched 13 of the 21 seats in the Government of National Union. The Red Prince, Souphanouvong and one of his aides were included in the cabinet and former Pathet Lao members were elected deputies of the National Assembly.

Almost immediately problems that had been beneath the surface emerged to plague the government. The rightists and their US supporters were shaken by the result and

Prince Souvanna Phouma

Prince Souvanna Phouma was Laos' greatest statesman. He was prime minister on no less than eight occasions for a total of 20 years between 1951 and 1975. He dominated mainstream politics from independence until the victory of the Pathet Lao in 1975. But he was never able to preserve the integrity of Laos in the face of much stronger external forces. "Souvanna stands as a tragic figure in modern Lao history," Martin Stuart-Fox writes, a "stubborn symbol of an alternative, neutral, 'middle way'."

In 1950 Souvanna became a co-founder of the Progressive Party and in the elections of 1951 he headed his first government, which negotiated and secured full independence from France.

Souvanna made two key errors of judgement during these early years. First, he ignored the need for nation building in Laos. Second, he underestimated the threat that the Communists posed to the country. With regard to the first of these misjudgements, he seemed to believe – and it is perhaps no accident that he trained as an engineer and architect – that Laos just needed to be administered efficiently to become a modern state. He appeared either to reject or ignore the idea that the government first had to try and inculcate a sense of Lao nationhood.

The second misjudgement was his long-held belief that the Pathet Lao was a nationalist and not a Communist organization. He let the Pathet Lao grow in strength and this, in turn, brought the US into Lao affairs.

By the time the US began to intervene in the late 1950s, the country already seemed to be heading for catastrophe. But in his struggle to maintain some semblance of independence for his tiny country, he ignored the degree to which Laos was being sucked into the quagmire of Indochina. As Martin Stuart-Fox writes: "He [Souvanna] knew he was being used, and that he had no power to protect his country from the war that increasingly engulfed it. But he was too proud meekly to submit to US demands – even as Laos was subjected to the heaviest bombing in the history of warfare. At least a form of independence had to be maintained."

When the Pathet Lao entered Vientiane in victory in 1975, Souvanna did not flee into exile. He remained to help in the transfer of power. The Pathet Lao, of course, gave him a title and then largely ignored him as they pursued their Communist manifesto.

From Martin Stuart-Fox's *Buddhist Kingdom, Marxist State: the Making of Modern Laos* (White Lotus, 1996).

the much-vaunted coalition lasted just two months. Driven by Cold War prerogatives, the US could not abide by any government that contained Communist members and withdrew their aid, which the country had become much dependent upon. Between 1955 and 1958 the US had given four times more aid to Laos than the French had done in the prior eight years and it had become the backbone of the Lao economy. If Laos was not so dependent on this aid, it is quite plausible that the coalition government may have survived. The National Union fell apart in July 1958 and Souvanna Phouma was forced out of power. Pathet Lao leaders were jailed and the rightwing Phoui Sananikone came to power. With anti-Communists in control, Pathet Lao forces withdrew to the Plain of Jars in Xieng Khouang province. A three-way civil war ensued, between the rightists (backed by the US), the Communists (backed by North Vietnam) and the neutralists (led by Souvanna Phouma, who wanted to maintain independence).

Civil war

CIA-backed strongman General Phoumi Nosavan thought Phoui's politics rather tame and with a nod from Washington he stepped into the breach in January 1959, eventually overthrowing Phoui in a coup in December and placing Prince Boun Oum in power. Pathet Lao leaders were imprisoned without trial.

Within a year, the rightist regime was overthrown by a neutralist *coup d'état* led by General Kong Lae and Prince Souvanna Phouma was recalled from exile in Cambodia to become prime minister of the first National Union. Souvanna Phouma incurred American wrath by inviting a Soviet ambassador to Vientiane in October. With US support, Nosavan staged yet another armed rebellion in December and sparked a new civil war. In the 1960 general elections, provincial authorities were threatened with military action if they did not support the rightwing groups and were rigged to ensure no Pathet Lao cadres could obtain a seat in office. By this stage, the Pathet Lao had consolidated considerable forces in the region surrounding the Plain of Jars and, with support from the Vietnamese, had been able to expand their territorial control in the north. This represented a major crisis to the incoming Kennedy administration that Stuart Martin-Fox describes as "second only to Cuba".

Zurich talks and the Geneva Accord

The new prime minister, the old one and his Marxist half-brother finally sat down to talks in Zurich in June 1961, but any hope of an agreement was overshadowed by escalating tensions between the superpowers. In 1962, an international agreement on Laos was hammered out in Geneva by 14 participating nations and accords were signed, once again guaranteeing Lao neutrality. By implication, the accords denied the Viet Minh access to the **Ho Chi Minh Trail**. But aware of the reality of constant North Vietnamese infiltration through Laos into South Vietnam, the head of the American mission concluded that the agreement was "a good bad deal".

Another coalition government of National Union was formed under the determined neutralist Prince Souvanna Phouma (as prime minister), with Prince Souphanouvong for the Pathet Lao and Prince Boun Oum representing the right. A number of political assassinations derailed the process of reconciliation. Moreover, antagonisms between the left and the right, both backed financially by their respective allies, made it impossible for the unfunded neutralists to balance the two sides into any form of neutrality. It was no surprise when the coalition government collapsed within a few months and fighting resumed. This time the international community just shrugged and watched Laos sink back into civil war. Unbeknown to the outside world, the conflict was rapidly degenerating into a war between the CIA and North Vietnamese jungle guerrillas.

Secret war

The war that wasn't

In the aftermath of the Geneva agreement, the North Vietnamese, rather than reducing their forces in Laos, continued to increase their manpower on the ground. With the Viet Minh denying the existence of the Ho Chi Minh Trail, while at the same time enlarging it, Kennedy dispatched an undercover force of CIA men, green berets and US-trained Thai mercenaries to command 9000 Lao soldiers. By 1963, these American forces had grown to 30,000 men. Historian Roger Warner believes that by 1965 "word spread among a select circle of congressmen and senators about this exotic program run by Lone Star rednecks and Asian hillbillies that was better and cheaper than anything the Pentagon was doing in

South Vietnam." To the north, the US also supplied Vang Pao's force of Hmong guerrillas, dubbed 'Mobile Strike Forces'. With the cooperation of Prince Souvanna Phouma, the CIA's commercial airline, Air America, ferried men and equipment into Laos from Thailand (and opium out, it is believed). Caught between Cold War antagonisms it was impossible to maintain a modicum of neutrality as even the most staunch neutralist, Souvanna Phouma, began to become entangled. As Robbins argues, by the early 1960s, Sovanna Phouma – trying to reinforce the middle way – had given permission "for every clandestine manoeuvre the United States made to match the North Vietnamese. In turn Souvanna demanded that his complicity in such arrangements be kept secret, lest his position in the country become untenable." Owing to the clandestine nature of the military intervention in Laos, the rest of the world – believing that the Geneva settlement had solved the foreign interventionist problem – was oblivious as to what was happening on the ground. Right up until 1970, Washington never admitted to any activity in Laos beyond 'armed reconnaissance' flights over northern provinces.

Meanwhile the North Vietnamese were fulfilling their two major strategic priorities in the country: continued use of the Ho Chi Minh trail (by this stage the majority of North Vietnamese munitions and personnel for the Viet Cong was being shuffled along the trail) and ensuring that the Plain of Jars did not fall under the control of the right, where the US could launch attacks on North Vietnam. This latter goal amounted to supporting the Pathet Lao in their aim to hold on to as much territory as possible in the north. The Pathet Lao, in turn, were dependent on the North Vietnamese for supplies – both material and manpower. With both the US bankrolling the Royalist right and the Vietnamese puppeteering the Pathet Lao, within the country any pretence of maintaining a balance in the face of Cold War hostilities was shattered for neutralists like Souvanna Phouma.

Souvanna Phouma appropriately referred to it as 'the forgotten war' and it is often termed now the 'non-attributable war'. The willingness on the part of the Americans to dump millions of tonnes of ordnance on a country which was ostensibly neutral may have been made easier by the fact that some people in the administration did not believe Laos to be a country at all. Bernard Fall wrote that Laos at the time was "neither a geographical nor an ethnic or social entity, but merely a political convenience", while a Rand Corporation report written in 1970 described Laos as "hardly a country except in the legal sense". More colourfully, Secretary of State Dean Rusk described it as a "wart on the hog of Vietnam". Perhaps those in Washington could feel a touch better about bombing the hell out of a country which, in their view, occupied a sort of political never never land – or which they could liken to an unfortunate skin complaint.

Not everyone agrees with this view that Laos never existed until the French wished it into existence. Scholar of Laos Arthur Dommen, for example, traces a true and coherent Lao identity back to Fa Ngum and his creation of the kingdom of Lane Xang in 1353, writing that it was "a state in the true sense of the term, delineated by borders clearly defined and consecrated by treaty" for 350 years. He goes on:

"Lao historians see a positive proof of the existence of a distinct Lao race (*sua sat Lao*), a Lao nation (*sat Lao*), a Lao country (*muong Lao*) and a Lao state (*pathet Lao*). In view of these facts, we may safely reject the notion, fashionable among apologists for a colonial enterprise of a later day, that Laos was a creation of French colonial policy and administration".

American bombing of the North Vietnamese Army's supply lines through Laos to South Vietnam along the Ho Chi Minh Trail in East Laos started in 1964 and fuelled the conflict between the Royalist Vientiane government and the Pathet Lao. The neutralists had been forced into alliance with the Royalists to avoid defeat in Xieng Kouang province. US bombers crossed Laos on bombing runs to Hanoi from air bases in Thailand and gradually the war in Laos escalated.

America's side of the secret war was conducted from a one-room shack at the US base in Udon Thani, 'across the fence' in Thailand. This was the CIA's Air America operations room and in the same compound was stationed the 4802 Joint Liaison Detachment – or the CIA logistics office. In Vientiane, US pilots supporting Hmong General Vang Pao's rag-tag army, were given a new identity as rangers for the US Agency for International Development; they reported directly to the air attaché at the US embassy. In his book *The Ravens* (1987), Christopher Robbins writes that they "were military men, but flew into battle in civilian clothes – denim cut-offs, T-shirts, cowboy hats and dark glasses. Their job was to fly as the winged artillery of some fearsome warlord, who led an army of stone age mercenaries in the pay of the CIA and they operated out of a secret city hidden in the mountains of a jungle kingdom."

The most notorious of the CIA's unsavoury operatives was Anthony Posepny – known as Tony Poe, on whom the character of Kurtz, the crazy colonel played by Marlon Brando in the film *Apocalypse Now*, was based. Originally, Poe had worked as Vang Pao's case officer; he then moved to North Laos and operated for years, on his own, in Burmese and Chinese border territories, offering his tribal recruits one US dollar for each set of Communist ears they brought back. Many of the spies and pilots of this secret war have re-emerged in recent years in covert and illegal arms-smuggling rackets to Libya, Iran and the Nicaraguan Contras.

By contrast, the Royalist forces were reluctant warriors: despite the fact that civil war was a deeply ingrained tradition in Laos, the Lao themselves would go to great lengths to avoid fighting each other. One foreign journalist, reporting from Luang Prabang in the latter stages of the war, related how Royalist and Pathet Lao troops, encamped on opposite banks of the Nam Ou, agreed an informal ceasefire over Pi Mai (Lao New Year), to jointly celebrate the king's annual visit to the sacred Pak Ou Caves (see page 53). Most Lao did not want to fight. Correspondents who covered the war noted that without the constant goading of their respective US and North Vietnamese masters, many Lao soldiers would have happily gone home. Prior to the war, one military strategist described the Lao forces as one of the worst armies ever seen, adding that they made the (poorly regarded) "South Vietnamese Army look like Storm Troopers". "The troops lack the basic will to fight. They do not take initiative. A typical characteristic of the Laotian Army is to leave an escape route. US technicians attached to the various training institutions have not been able to overcome Lao apathy". (Ratnam, P, *Laos and the Superpowers*, 1980).

Air Force planes were often used to carry passengers for money – or to smuggle opium out of the **Golden Triangle**. In the field, soldiers of the Royal Lao Army regularly fled when faced with a frontal assault by the Vietnam People's Army (NVA). The officer corps was uncommitted, lazy and corrupt; many ran opium-smuggling rackets and saw the war as a ticket to get rich quick. In the south, the Americans considered Royal Lao Air Force pilots unreliable because they were loath to bomb their own people and cultural heritage.

The air war

The clandestine bombing of the Ho Chi Minh Trail caused many civilian casualties and displaced much of the population in Laos' eastern provinces. By 1973, when the bombing stopped, the US had dropped over two million tonnes of bombs on Laos – equivalent to 700 kg of explosives for every man, woman and child in the country. It is reported that up to 70% of all B-52 strikes in Indochina were targeted at Laos. To pulverize the country to this degree 580,994 bombing sorties were flown. The bombing intensified during the

Nixon administration: up to 1969 less than 500,000 tonnes of bombs had been dropped on Laos; from then on nearly that amount was dropped each year. In the 1960s and early 1970s, more bombs rained on Laos than were dropped during the Second World War – the equivalent of a plane load of bombs every eight minutes around the clock for nine years. This campaign cost American taxpayers more than US$2 million a day but the cost to Laos was incalculable. The activist Fred Branfman, quoted by Roger Warner in *Shooting at the Moon*, wrote: "Nine years of bombing, two million tons of bombs, whole rural societies wiped off the map, hundreds of thousands of peasants treated like herds of animals in a Clockwork Orange fantasy of an aerial African Hunting safari."

The war was not restricted to bombing missions – once potential Pathet Lao strong-holds had been identified, fighters, using rockets, were sent to attempt to destroy them. Such was the intensity of the bombing campaign that villagers in Pathet Lao-controlled areas are said to have turned to planting and harvesting their rice at night. Few of those living in Xieng Khouang province, the Bolaven Plateau or along the Ho Chi Minh Trail had any idea of who was bombing them or why. The consequences were often tragic, as in the case of Tham Piu Cave (see page 82).

After the war, the collection and sale of war debris turned into a valuable scrap metal industry for tribes' people in Xieng Khouang province and along the Ho Chi Minh Trail. Bomb casings, aircraft fuel tanks and other bits and pieces that were not sold to Thailand have been put to every conceivable use in rural Laos. They are used as cattle troughs, fence posts, flower pots, stilts for houses, water carriers, temple bells, knives and ploughs.

But the bombing campaign has also left a more deadly legacy of unexploded bombs and anti-personnel mines. Today, over 30 years after the air war, over 500,000 tonnes of deadly **unexploded ordnance** (UXO) is believed to still be scattered throughout nine of Laos' 13 provinces. Most casualties are caused by cluster bombs, or 'bombis' as they have become known. Cluster bombs are carried in large canisters called Cluster Bomb Units (CBUs), which open in mid-air, releasing around 670 tennis ball-sized bomblets. Upon detonation, the bombie propels around 200,000 pieces of shrapnel over an area the size of several football fields. This UXO contamination inhibits long-term development, especially in Xieng Khouang Province, turning Laos' fertile fields, which are critical for agricultural production, into killing zones.

The land war

Within Laos, the war largely focused on the strategic Plain of Jars in Xieng Khouang province and was co-ordinated from the town of Long Tien (the secret city), tucked into the limestone hills to the southwest of the plain. Known as the most secret spot on earth, it was not marked on maps and was populated by the CIA, the Ravens (the air controllers who flew spotter planes and called in air strikes) and the Hmong.

The Pathet Lao were headquartered in caves in Xam Neua province, to the north of the plain. Their base was equipped with a hotel cave (for visiting dignitaries), a hospital cave, embassy caves and even a theatre cave.

The Plain of Jars (colloquially known as the PDJ, after the French Plaine de Jarres), was the scene of some of the heaviest fighting and changed hands countless times, the Royalist and Hmong forces occupying it during the wet season, the Pathet Lao in the dry. During this period in the conflict the town of Long Tien, known as one of the country's 'alternate' bases to keep nosy journalists away (the word 'alternate' was meant to indicate that it was unimportant), grew to such an extent that it became Laos' second city. James Parker in his book *Codename Mule* claims that the air base was so busy that at its peak it was handling more daily flights than Chicago's O'Hare airport. Others claim that it was the busiest airport in the world. There was also fighting around Luang Prabang and the Bolaven Plateau to the south.

The end of the war

Although the origins of the war in Laos were distinct from those that fuelled the conflict in Vietnam, the two wars had effectively merged by the early 1970s and it became inevitable that the fate of the Americans to the east would determine the outcome of the secret war on the other side of the Annamite Range. By 1970 it was no longer possible for the US administration to shroud the war in secrecy: a flood of refugees had arrived in Vientiane in an effort to escape the conflict.

During the dying days of the US-backed regime in Vientiane, CIA agents and Ravens lived in quarters south of the capital, known as KM-6 – because it was 6 km from town. Another compound in downtown Vientiane was known as 'Silver City' and reputedly also sometimes housed CIA agents. On the departure of the Americans and the arrival of the new regime in 1975, the Communists' secret police made Silver City their new home. Today, Lao people still call military intelligence officers 'Silvers' – and from time to time during the early 1990s, as Laos was opening up to tourism, Silvers were assigned as tour guides.

A ceasefire was agreed in February 1973, a month after Washington and Hanoi struck a similar deal in Paris. Power was transferred in April 1974 to yet another coalition government set up in Vientiane under the premiership of the ever-ready Souvanna Phouma. The neutralist prince once again had a Communist deputy and foreign affairs minister. The Red Prince, Souphanouvong, headed the Joint National Political Council. Foreign troops were given two months to leave the country. The North Vietnamese were allowed to remain along the Ho Chi Minh Trail, for although US forces had withdrawn from South Vietnam, the war there was not over.

The Communists' final victories over Saigon (and Phnom Penh) in April 1975 were a catalyst for the Pathet Lao who advanced on the capital. Grant Evans in a *Short History of Laos* says that the most intriguing element of the Communist takeover of Laos was the slow pace in which it was executed. It is widely hailed as the 'bloodless' takeover. Due to the country's mixed loyalties the Pathet Lao government undertook a gradual process of eroding away existing loyalties to the Royalist government. As the end drew near and the Pathet Lao began to advance out of the mountains and towards the more populated areas of the Mekong valley – the heartland of the Royalist government – province after province fell with scarcely a shot being fired. The mere arrival of a small contingent of Pathet Lao soldiers was sufficient to secure victory – even though these soldiers arrived at Wattay Airport on Chinese transport planes to be greeted by representatives of the Royal Lao government. It is possible that they were not even armed.

Administration of Vientiane by the People's Revolutionary Committee was secured on 18 August. The atmosphere was very different from that which accompanied the Communist's occupation of Saigon in Vietnam the same year. In Vientiane peaceful crowds of several hundred thousand turned out to hear speeches by Pathet Lao cadres. The King remained unharmed in his palace and while a coffin representing 'dead American imperialism' was ceremonially burned this was done in a 'carnival' atmosphere. Vientiane was declared 'officially liberated' on 23 August 1975. The coalition government was dismissed and Souvanna Phouma resigned for the last time. All communications with the outside world were cut.

While August 1975 represents a watershed in the history of Laos, scholars are left with something of a problem: explaining why the Pathet Lao prevailed. According to Martin Stuart-Fox, the Lao revolutionary movement "had not mobilized an exploited peasantry with promises of land reform, for most of the country was underpopulated and peasant families generally owned sufficient land for their subsistence needs. The appeal of the Pathet Lao to their lowland Lao compatriots was in terms of nationalism and independence and the preservation of Lao culture from the corrosive American influence; but no urban uprising occurred until the very last minute when effective government had virtually ceased to exist … The small Lao intelligentsia, though critical of the Royal Lao government, did not desert it entirely and their recruitment to the Pathet Lao was minimal. Neither the monarchy, still less Buddhism, lost legitimacy." He concludes that it was external factors, and in particular the intervention of outside powers, which led to the victory of the Pathet Lao. Without the Vietnamese and Americans, the Pathet Lao would not have won. For the great mass of Laos' population before 1975, Communism meant nothing. This was not a mass uprising but a victory secured by a small ideologically committed elite and forged in the furnace of the war in Indochina.

As the Pathet Lao seized power, rightist ministers, ranking civil servants, doctors, much of the intelligentsia and around 30,000 Hmong escaped into Thailand, fearing they would face persecution from the Pathet Lao. Although the initial exodus was large, the majority of refugees fled in the next few years up until 1980 as the Lao government introduced new reforms aimed at wiping out decadence and reforming the economic system.

The refugee camps

By the late 1980s, a total of 340,000 people – 10% of the population and mostly middle class – had fled the country. At least half of the refugees were Hmong, the US's key allies during the war, who feared reprisals and persecution. From 1988, refugees who had made it across the border began to head back across the Mekong from camps in Thailand and to asylum in the US and France. More than 2000 refugees were also repatriated from Yunnan Province in China. For those prepared to return from exile overseas, the government offered to give them back confiscated property so long as they stayed for at least six months and become Lao citizens once again.

Nonetheless, many lived for years in squalid refugee camps, although the better connected and those with skills to sell secured US, Australian and French passports. For Laos, a large proportion of its human capital drained westwards, creating a vacuum of skilled personnel that would hamper – and still does – efforts at reconstruction and development. But while many people fled across the Mekong, a significant number who had aligned themselves with the Royalists decided to stay and help build a new Laos.

Laos under communism

The People's Democratic Republic of Laos was proclaimed in December 1975 with Prince Souphanouvong as president and Kaysone Phomvihane as secretary-general of the Lao People's Revolutionary Party (a post he had held since its formation in 1955). The king's abdication was accepted and the ancient Lao monarchy was abolished, together with King Samsenthai's 600-year-old system of village autonomy. But instead of executing their vanquished foes, the LPRP installed Souvanna and the ex-king, Savang Vatthana, as 'special advisers' to the politburo. On Souvanna's death in 1984, he was accorded a full state funeral. The king did not fare so well: he later died ignominiously while in detention after his alleged involvement in a counter-revolutionary plot (see below).

Surprisingly, the first actions of the new revolutionary government was not to build a new revolutionary economy and society, but to stamp out unsavoury behaviour. Dress and hairstyles, dancing and singing, even the food that was served at family celebrations, was all subject to rigorous official scrutiny by so-called 'Investigation Cadres'. If the person(s) concerned were found not to match up to the Party's scrupulous standards of good taste they were bundled off to re-education camps.

Relations with Thailand, which in the immediate wake of the revolution remained cordial, deteriorated in late 1976. A military coup in Bangkok led to rumours that the Thai military, backed by the CIA, was supporting Hmong and other right-wing Lao rebels. The regime feared that Thailand would be used as a spring-board for a royalist coup attempt by exiled reactionaries. This prompted the arrest of King Savang Vatthana, together with his family and Crown Prince Vongsavang, who were all dispatched to a Seminar re-education camp in Sam Neua province. They were never heard of again. In December 1989 Kaysone Phomvihane admitted in Paris, for the first time, that the king had died of malaria in 1984 and that the queen had also died "of natural causes" – no mention was made of Vongsavang. The Lao people have still to be officially informed of his demise.

Re-education camps

Between 30,000 and 40,000 reactionaries who had been unable to flee the country were interned in remote, disease-ridden camps for 're-education'. These camps, referred to as *Samanaya*, took their name from the Western word, seminar. The reluctant scholars were forced into slave labour in squalid jungle conditions and subjected to incessant political propaganda for anything from a few months up to 15 years. Historian Grant Evans suggests that many internees were duped into believing that the government wanted complete reconciliation and so went away for re-education willingly. Evans says the purpose of the camps was to "break the will of members of the old regime and instil in them fear of the new regime." Old men, released back into society after more than 15 years of re-education were cowed and subdued, although some were prepared to talk in paranoid whispers about their grim experiences in Xam Neua.

By 1978, the re-education policy was starting to wind down, although, in 1986, Amnesty International released a report on the forgotten inhabitants of the re-education camps, claiming that 6000-7000 were still being held. By that time incarceration behind barbed wire had ended and the internees were 'arbitrarily restricted' rather than imprisoned. They were assigned to road construction teams and other public works projects. Nonetheless, conditions for these victims of the war in Indochina suffered from malnutrition, disease and many died prematurely in captivity. It is unclear how many died, but at least 15,000 have been freed. Officials of the old regime, ex-government ministers and former Royalist air force and army officers, together with thousands of others unlucky enough to have been on the wrong side, were released from the camps, largely during the mid to late 1980s. Most of the surviving political prisoners have now been re-integrated into society. Some work in the tourism industry and one, a former colonel in the Royal Lao Army, jointly owns the Asian Pavilion Hotel (formerly the Vieng Vilai) on Samsenthai Road in downtown Vientiane. After years of being force-fed Communist propaganda he now enjoys full government support as an ardent capitalist entrepreneur.

The Lao are a gentle people and it is hard not to leave the country without that view being reinforced. Even the Lao People's Revolutionary Party seems quaintly inept and it is hard to equate it with its more brutal sister parties in Vietnam, Cambodia, China or the former Soviet Union. Yet five students who meekly called for greater political freedom in 1999 were whisked off by police and have not been heard of since.

The troublesome Hmong

The Hmong are probably the best-known ethnic group in Laos. In the 19th century, Chinese opium farmers drove many thousands of Hmong off their poppy fields and forced them south into the mountains of Laos. They now mainly inhabit the mountain areas of Luang Prabang, Xieng Khouang and Xam Neua and have an inherent mistrust of the lowland Lao, exacerbated by years of war.

The Hmong are fiercely independent and this trait, in addition to their former association with poppy cultivation and their siding with the US and French during the Indochina War, has meant that they have been persecuted. They have, in recent history, been perceived as a threat to the security of the state; a group that needs to be controlled and watched.

When the war ended in 1975 there was a mass exodus of Hmong from Laos. Hmong refugees poured into Thailand, the exodus reaching a peak in 1979 when 3000 a month were fleeing across the Mekong. Many ended up in Thai refugee camps, where they lived in terrible conditions for many years, sometimes decades.

Thousands of Hmong also ended up in the US and France, fresh from the mountains of Laos: unsurprisingly they did not adapt easily. Today more than 100,000 Hmong live in the US – mostly on the west coast and in Minnesota – where they regularly lobby politicians. They are a very powerful pressure group but they are increasingly out of touch with the situation in Laos. Where the US-based Hmong remain important, however, is in the money they remit to their relatives in Laos.

A small group of Hmong, led from the USA by the exiled CIA-trained general, Vang Pao, remained in Laos and continued to fight the Lao government. A spate of bombings in Vientiane in 2000 was probably linked to the Hmong resistance and in 2004-2005 at least 15 civilians were killed by Hmong insurgents

Reflecting on 10 years of 'reconstruction'

It is worth ending this short account of the country's history by noting the brevity of Laos' experiment with full-blown Communism. Just 10 years after the Pathet Lao took control of Vientiane, the leadership were on the brink of far-reaching economic reforms. By the mid-1980s it was widely acknowledged that Marxism-Leninism had failed the country and its people. The population were still dreadfully poor; the ideology of Communism had failed to entice more than a handful into serious and enthusiastic support for the party and its ways; and graft and nepotism were on the rise.

Modern Laos

Politics

President Kaysone Phomvihane died in November 1992, aged 71. (His right-hand man, Prince Souphanouvong died just over two years later, on 9 January 1995.) As one obituary put it, Kaysone was older than he seemed, both historically and ideologically. He had been chairman of the LPRP since the mid-1950s and had been a protégé and comrade of Ho Chi Minh, who led the Vietnamese struggle for independence from the French. After leading the Lao Resistance Government – or Pathet Lao – from caves in Xam Neua province in the north, Kaysone assumed the premiership on the abolition of the monarchy in 1975. But under his leadership – and following the example of his mentors in Hanoi – Kaysone in the north of the country. The Hmong claim to be fighting for democracy and freedom but most are living in terrible conditions and starving, so robbery seems a more likely motivation behind their attacks.

The Lao government tends publicly to sidestep the issue, saying there is no official policy towards the Hmong. However, the eradication of opium and related resettlement programme has had a negative impact on the Hmong and there is indisputable evidence of human rights violations against the Hmong by the Lao government.

Between 2004 and 2006 several groups of hundreds of Hmong insurgents surrendered. In December 2006 alone more than 400 members of the Hmong ethnic insurgents and their families came out of the jungle and surrendered to the authorities. With his power draining away things came to head for Vang Pao when in 2007 American officials in the US arrested him on a charge of conspiring to stage a coup in Vientiane. The criminal complaint said Vang Pao and the other Hmong defendants formed a committee "to evaluate the feasibility of conducting a military expedition or enterprise to engage in the overthrow of the existing government of Laos by violent means, including murder, assaults on both military and civilian officials of Laos and destruction of buildings and property." This included charges of inspecting shipments of military equipment that were to be purchased and shipped to Thailand. That equipment included machine guns, ammunition, rocket-propelled grenade launchers, anti-tank rockets, stinger missiles, mines and C-4 explosives. By July 2007, after a lot of pressure on the USA government and a huge bond being paid, Vang Pao was released on bail; charges were later dropped in 2009. General Vang Pao died in exile in the US, aged 81, in January 2011.

became the driving force behind the market-orientated reforms. The year before he died, he gave up the post of prime minister for that of president.

His death didn't change much, as other members of the old guard stepped into the breach. Nouhak Phounsavanh – a 78-year-old former truck driver and hardline Communist – succeeded him as president. Nouhak didn't last long in the position and in February 1998 he was replaced by 75-year-old General Khamtai Siphandon – the outgoing prime minister and head of the LPRP. Khamtai represents the last of the revolutionary Pathet Lao leaders who fought the Royalists and the Americans. In April 2006, Siphandon, the last of the old guard from the caves in Vieng Xai, was replaced as president by Choummaly Sayasone.

Recent years

With the introduction of the New Economic Mechanism in 1986 there were hopes, in some quarters at least, that economic liberalization would be matched by political *glasnost*. So far, however, the monolithic Party shows few signs of equating capitalism with democracy. While the Lao brand of Communism has always been seen as relatively tame, it remains a far cry from political plurm.

The politburo still largely controls the country and, for now, sweeping changes are unlikely. Most of the country's leaders are well into their 60s and were educated in Communist countries like Russia and Vietnam. However, the younger Lao (particularly those

Nam Theun II and the lure of hydro-gold

One of Laos' greatest economic resources is hydropower, leading to it being dubbed the 'battery' or 'Kuwait' of Southeast Asia with only 1% of the country's hydropower potential of some 18,000 MW so far exploited and myriad schemes being discussed. By far the largest of these is Nam Theun II, which became operational in 2010. The huge dam is expected to generate up to US$150 million revenue a year for Laos or approximately US$2 billion over a 25-year period.

Funded by the World Bank, Nam Theun II was delayed by the discoveries of rare bats and birds. The World Bank, all too conscious that its environmental credentials have been tarnished by dam developments in India and elsewhere, went out of its way to ensure that all the required studies were undertaken.

But Nam Theun II dam is not quite the open-and-shut case it might appear, with the international environmental lobby on the side of local people and animals and the dastardly World Bank supporting businessmen and the interests of international capital. Yet when local people were asked their views of the dam, many apparently welcomed it. Even some environmentalists argued that having the dam might be preferable to having the forests logged (for without the money to be gained from selling electricity to Thailand, one of the few alternatives is selling wood).

The results are yet to be fully determined. The majority of villagers seem happy with relocation efforts, while conservationists argue that the environmental damage is yet to be properly evaluated. Plans are underway to further exploit the potential of the Mekong and its tributaries, with over 60 projects slated for development over the next decade.

who have studied in Japan, Australia, the UK or the US) are starting to embrace new political and economic ideas. The government takes inspiration from Vietnam's success and is more likely to follow its neighbour's lead than adopt any Western model of government.

As Laos moved towards the end of the first decade of the 21st century progress was being maintained. The troublesome Hmong, whose US-based leadership's attempts to undermine the Laos government's authority came to nothing. The nation's first railway line opened in early 2009 and huge Chinese investment poured into the country. With the ASEAN Free Trade Agreement set to open up trade throughout the region (Laos will be subject to this in 2015), the inauguration of the Nam Theun II dam (see box, above) and Laos still working on joining the World Trade Organisation, the challenges facing Laos are some of the greatest in its history.

In 2010 the country opened its own stock market in Vientiane in conjunction with Korea Exchange to invigorate the economy in the downturn and former prime minster Bouasone Bouphavanh told the World Economic Forum on East Asia in June 2010 that Laos is aiming for 'no less than' eight percent annual economic growth until 2015. It also wants to elevate its status out of that of underdevelopment by 2020, Bouphavanh told the conference. Bouphavanh was replaced as prime minister by Thongsing Thammavong in late 2010. Choummaly Sayasone was re-elected by the National Assembly as President of the Lao People's Revolutionary Party (LPRP) in June 2011.

Contents

Footnotes

Index

Titles available in the Footprint *Focus* range

Latin America	UK RRP	US RRP
Bahia & Salvador	£7.99	$11.95
Brazilian Amazon	£7.99	$11.95
Brazilian Pantanal	£6.99	$9.95
Buenos Aires & Pampas	£7.99	$11.95
Cartagena & Caribbean Coast	£7.99	$11.95
Costa Rica	£8.99	$12.95
Cuzco, La Paz & Lake Titicaca	£8.99	$12.95
El Salvador	£5.99	$8.95
Guadalajara & Pacific Coast	£6.99	$9.95
Guatemala	£8.99	$12.95
Guyana, Guyane & Suriname	£5.99	$8.95
Havana	£6.99	$9.95
Honduras	£7.99	$11.95
Nicaragua	£7.99	$11.95
Northeast Argentina & Uruguay	£8.99	$12.95
Paraguay	£5.99	$8.95
Quito & Galápagos Islands	£7.99	$11.95
Recife & Northeast Brazil	£7.99	$11.95
Rio de Janeiro	£8.99	$12.95
São Paulo	£5.99	$8.95
Uruguay	£6.99	$9.95
Venezuela	£8.99	$12.95
Yucatán Peninsula	£6.99	$9.95

Asia	UK RRP	US RRP
Angkor Wat	£5.99	$8.95
Bali & Lombok	£8.99	$12.95
Chennai & Tamil Nadu	£8.99	$12.95
Chiang Mai & Northern Thailand	£7.99	$11.95
Goa	£6.99	$9.95
Gulf of Thailand	£8.99	$12.95
Hanoi & Northern Vietnam	£8.99	$12.95
Ho Chi Minh City & Mekong Delta	£7.99	$11.95
Java	£7.99	$11.95
Kerala	£7.99	$11.95
Kolkata & West Bengal	£5.99	$8.95
Mumbai & Gujarat	£8.99	$12.95

Africa & Middle East	UK RRP	US RRP
Beirut	£6.99	$9.95
Cairo & Nile Delta	£8.99	$12.95
Damascus	£5.99	$8.95
Durban & KwaZulu Natal	£8.99	$12.95
Fès & Northern Morocco	£8.99	$12.95
Jerusalem	£8.99	$12.95
Johannesburg & Kruger National Park	£7.99	$11.95
Kenya's Beaches	£8.99	$12.95
Kilimanjaro & Northern Tanzania	£8.99	$12.95
Luxor to Aswan	£8.99	$12.95
Nairobi & Rift Valley	£7.99	$11.95
Red Sea & Sinai	£7.99	$11.95
Zanzibar & Pemba	£7.99	$11.95

Europe	UK RRP	US RRP
Bilbao & Basque Region	£6.99	$9.95
Brittany West Coast	£7.99	$11.95
Cádiz & Costa de la Luz	£6.99	$9.95
Granada & Sierra Nevada	£6.99	$9.95
Languedoc: Carcassonne to Montpellier	£7.99	$11.95
Málaga	£5.99	$8.95
Marseille & Western Provence	£7.99	$11.95
Orkney & Shetland Islands	£5.99	$8.95
Santander & Picos de Europa	£7.99	$11.95
Sardinia: Alghero & the North	£7.99	$11.95
Sardinia: Cagliari & the South	£7.99	$11.95
Seville	£5.99	$8.95
Sicily: Palermo & the Northwest	£7.99	$11.95
Sicily: Catania & the Southeast	£7.99	$11.95
Siena & Southern Tuscany	£7.99	$11.95
Sorrento, Capri & Amalfi Coast	£6.99	$9.95
Skye & Outer Hebrides	£6.99	$9.95
Verona & Lake Garda	£7.99	$11.95

North America	UK RRP	US RRP
Vancouver & Rockies	£8.99	$12.95

Australasia	UK RRP	US RRP
Brisbane & Queensland	£8.99	$12.95
Perth	£7.99	$11.95

For the latest books, e-books and a wealth of travel information, visit us at:
www.footprinttravelguides.com.

footprinttravelguides.com

Join us on facebook for the latest travel news, product releases, offers and amazing competitions:
www.facebook.com/footprintbooks.